Uncommon Wisdom

BANTAM NEW AGE BOOKS

This important imprint includes books in a variety of fields and disciplines and deals with the search for meaning, growth and change. They are books that circumscribe our times and our future.

Ask your bookseller for the books you have missed.

Fritjof Capra

Uncommon

Conversations with

Wisdom

Remarkable People

BANTAM BOOKS
TORONTO · NEW YORK · LONDON · SYDNEY · AUCKLAND

UNCOMMON WISDOM
*A Bantam Book / published by arrangement with
Simon & Schuster Inc.*

PRINTING HISTORY
Simon & Schuster edition published January 1988

Bantam New Age *and the accompanying figure design as well as the statement
"the search for meaning, growth and change" are trademarks of Bantam Books,
a division of Bantam Doubleday Dell Publishing Group, Inc.*

Bantam edition / February 1989

Library of Congress Cataloging-in-Publication Data

Capra, Fritjof.
 Uncommon wisdom.

 Bibliography: p.
 Includes index.
  1. New Age movement. 2. Capra, Fritjof. I. Title.
[BP605.N48C37 1989]   191   88-16656
ISBN 0-553-34610-5 (pbk.)

Published simultaneously in the United States and Canada

PRINTED IN THE UNITED STATES OF AMERICA

S   0 9 8 7 6 5 4 3 2 1

Acknowledgments

More than with any other book it is obvious that this one could not have been written without the inspiration and support of the many remarkable men and women mentioned in its pages, and of the many more not mentioned. To all of them I would like to express my deep gratitude. I am also grateful to my family and friends for their critical reading of various portions of the manuscript; especially to my mother, Ingeborg Teuffenbach, for valuable editorial suggestions, and to my wife, Elizabeth Hawk, for helping me to refine my text throughout the entire writing. Finally, I would like to thank my editors at Simon and Schuster, Alice Mayhew, John Cox, and Debra Makay, for their superb and sensitive editing of the text.

Contents

Preface

In April 1970 I received my last paycheck for research in theoretical particle physics. Since then I have continued this research at various American and European universities, but none of them could be persuaded to give me financial support. The reason for this lack of support is that since 1970 my research in physics, even though it has been an essential part of my work, has taken only a relatively small portion of my working time. The far larger part is spent doing research of a much broader scope, research that transcends the narrow confines of current academic disciplines, research in which I often explore uncharted territory, sometimes going beyond the limits of science as they are currently understood or, rather, trying to push those limits outward into new areas. Although I have pursued this research as tenaciously, systematically, and carefully as my colleagues in the physics community are pursuing theirs, and although I have published my results in a series of papers and two books, it was and still is far too novel and controversial to be supported by any academic institution.

It is characteristic of any research at the frontiers of knowledge that one never quite knows where it will lead, but, in the end, if everything goes well, one can often discern a consistent pattern of evolution in one's ideas and understanding. This has certainly been the case with my work. Over the past fifteen years I spent many hours in intense discussions with some of the leading scientists of our time; I explored various altered states of consciousness, with and without teachers and guides; I spent time with philosophers and artists; I discussed and experienced a whole range of therapies, physical as well as psychological; and I participated in many meetings of social activists in which the theory and practice of social change were debated from different perspectives against a variety of cultural backgrounds. It often seemed that each new understanding opened up more new avenues to be pursued, more questions to be asked. However, looking back on this time from the vantage point of the mid-eighties, I can see that throughout the past fifteen years I have consistently pursued a single theme—the fundamental change of world view that is occurring in science and in society, the unfolding of a new vision of reality, and the social implications of this cultural transformation. I have published the results of my research in two books, *The Tao of Physics* and *The Turning Point*, and have discussed the concrete political implications of the cultural transformation in a third book, *Green Politics*, which I co-authored with Charlene Spretnak.

The purpose of the book you are reading is not to present any new ideas, or to elaborate or modify the ideas presented in my previous books, but rather to tell the personal story behind the evolution of these ideas. It is the story of my encounters with many remarkable men and women who inspired me, helped me, and supported my search—Werner Heisenberg, who described to me most vividly his personal experience of the change of concepts and ideas in physics; Geoffrey Chew, who taught me not to accept anything as fundamental; J. Krishnamurti and Alan Watts, who helped me to transcend thinking without losing my commitment to science; Gregory Bateson, who broadened my world view by placing life in its center;

Stanislav Grof and R. D. Laing, who challenged me to explore the full range of human consciousness; Margaret Lock and Carl Simonton, who showed me new avenues to health and healing; E. F. Schumacher and Hazel Henderson, who shared with me their ecological visions of the future; and Indira Gandhi, who enriched my awareness of global interdependence. From these women and men, and from the many more I met and interacted with over the past decade and a half, I learned the main elements of what I have come to call the new vision of reality. My own contribution has been to establish the links between their ideas and between the scientific and philosophical traditions they represent.

The conversations recorded here took place between 1969, the year I first experienced the dance of subatomic particles as the Dance of Shiva, and 1982, the year *The Turning Point* was published. I have reconstructed these conversations partly from tapes, partly from my extensive notes, and partly from memory. They culminated in the "Big Sur Dialogues," three days of exciting and enlightening discussions among an extraordinary group of people, which will remain among the high moments in my life.

My search was accompanied by a deep personal transformation, which began under the impact of a magical era, the 1960s. The decades of the forties, fifties, and sixties correspond roughly to the first three decades of my life. The forties were my childhood, the fifties my adolescence, the sixties my youth and young adulthood. Looking back on my experience of these decades, I can best characterize the fifties by the title of the famous James Dean movie *Rebel Without a Cause*. There was friction between generations, but the James Dean generation and the older generation really shared the same world view: the same belief in technology, in progress, in the educational system. None of that was questioned in the fifties. It was only in the sixties that the rebels began to see a cause, which resulted in a fundamental challenge to the existing social order.

In the sixties we questioned society. We lived according to different values, we had different rituals and different lifestyles. But we could not really formulate our critique in a succinct way. Of course, we did have concrete criticism on single issues, such as the Vietnam War, but we did not develop any comprehensive alternative system of values and ideas. Our critique was based on intuitive feeling; we lived and embodied our protest rather than verbalizing and systematizing it.

The seventies brought consolidation of our views. The magic of the sixties faded; the initial excitement gave way to a period of focusing, digesting, integrating. Two new political movements, the ecology movement and the feminist movement, emerged during the seventies and together provided the much-needed broad framework for our critique and alternative ideas.

The eighties, finally, are again a period of social activity. In the sixties, we sensed the cultural transformation with great enthusiasm and wonder; in the seventies, we outlined the theoretical framework; in the eighties, we are fleshing it out. The worldwide Green movement, which emerged from a coalescence of the ecology, peace, and feminist movements, is the most impressive sign of the political activity of the eighties, which may well be remembered as the decade of Green politics.

The era of the sixties, which had the most decisive impact on my view of the world, was dominated by an expansion of consciousness in two directions. One was toward a new kind of spirituality akin to the mystical traditions of the East, an expansion of consciousness toward experiences that psychologists began to call transpersonal. The other was an expansion of social consciousness, triggered by a radical questioning of authority. This happened independently in several areas. The American civil rights movement demanded that black citizens be included in the political process; the free speech movement at Berkeley and the student movements at other universities throughout the United States and Europe demanded the same for students; Czech citizens, during the "Prague Spring," questioned the authority of the Soviet regime; the women's movement began to question patriarchal authority; and humanistic psychologists undermined the authority of doctors and therapists. The two dominant trends of the sixties—the expansion of consciousness toward the transpersonal and that toward the social—had a strong influence on my life and my work. My first two books clearly have their roots in that magical decade.

The end of the sixties coincided for me with the end of my employment, but not of my work, as a theoretical physicist. In the fall of 1970 I moved from California, where I had been on the faculty of the University of California at Santa Cruz, to London, where I would spend the next four years exploring the parallels between modern physics and Eastern mysticism. This work in London was my first step toward a long, systematic effort of formulating, synthesizing, and communicating a new vision of reality. The stages of this intellectual journey and the meetings and conversations with the many remarkable men and women who shared with me their uncommon wisdom comprise the story of this book.

FRITJOF CAPRA
Berkeley
October 1986

1

Howling with the Wolves

WERNER HEISENBERG

My interest in the change of world view in science and society was stimulated when as a young physics student of nineteen I read Werner Heisenberg's *Physics and Philosophy*, his classic account of the history and philosophy of quantum physics. This book exerted an enormous influence on me and still does. It is a scholarly work, quite technical at times, but also full of personal and even highly emotional passages. Heisenberg, one of the founders of quantum theory and, along with Albert Einstein and Niels Bohr, one of the giants of modern physics, describes and analyzes in it the unique dilemma encountered by physicists during the first three decades of the century, when they explored the structure of atoms and the nature of subatomic phenomena. This exploration brought them in contact with a strange and unexpected reality that shattered the foundations of their world view and forced them to think in entirely new ways. The material world they observed no longer appeared as a machine, made up of a multitude of separate objects, but rather as an indivisible whole; a network of relationships that included the human observer in an essential way. In their struggle to grasp the nature of atomic phenomena, scientists became painfully aware that their basic concepts, their language, and their whole way of thinking were inadequate to describe this new reality.

In *Physics and Philosophy*, Heisenberg provides not only a brilliant analysis of the conceptual problems but also a vivid account of the tremendous personal difficulties these physicists faced when their research forced them to expand their consciousness. Their atomic experiments impelled them to think in new categories about the nature of reality, and it was Heisenberg's great achievement to recognize this clearly. The story of his struggle and triumph is also the story of the meeting and symbiosis of two exceptional personalities, Werner Heisenberg and Niels Bohr.

Heisenberg became involved in atomic physics at the age of twenty when he attended a series of lectures given by Bohr at Göttingen. The topic of the lectures was Bohr's new atomic theory, which had been hailed as an enormous achievement and was being studied by physicists throughout Europe. In the discussion following one of these lectures Heisenberg disagreed with Bohr on a particular technical point, and Bohr was so impressed by the clear arguments of this young student that he invited him to come for a walk so that they could carry on their discussion. This walk, which lasted for several hours, was the first meeting of two outstanding minds whose further interaction was to become the major force in the development of atomic physics.

Niels Bohr, sixteen years older than Heisenberg, was a man with supreme intuition and a deep appreciation for the mysteries of the world; a man influenced by the religious philosophy of Kierkegaard and the mystical writings of William James. He was never fond of axiomatic systems and declared repeatedly: "Everything I say must be understood not as an affirmation but as a question." Werner Heisenberg, on the other hand, had a clear, analytic, and mathematical mind and was rooted philosophically in Greek thought, with which he had been familiar since his early youth. Bohr and Heisenberg represented complementary poles of the human mind, whose dynamic and often dramatic interplay was a unique process in the history of modern science and led to one of its greatest triumphs.

When I read Heisenberg's book as a young student I was fascinated by his account of the paradoxes and apparent contradictions that plagued the investigation of atomic phenomena in the early 1920s. Many of these paradoxes were connected with the dual nature of subatomic matter, which appears sometimes as particles, sometimes as waves. "Electrons," physicists used to say in those days, "are particles on Mondays and Wednesdays and waves on Tuesdays and Thursdays." And the strange thing was that the more physicists tried to clarify the situation, the sharper the paradoxes became. It was only very gradually that physicists would develop a certain intuition for when an electron would appear as a particle and when as a wave. They would, as Heisenberg put it, "get into the spirit of the quantum theory" before developing its exact mathematical formulation. Heisenberg himself played a decisive role in this development. He saw that the paradoxes in atomic physics appeared whenever one tried to describe atomic phenomena in classical terms, and he was bold enough to throw away the classical conceptual framework. In 1925 he published a paper in which he abandoned the conventional description of electrons within an atom in terms of their positions and velocities, which was used by Bohr and everybody else, and replaced it with a much more abstract framework, in which physical quantities were represented by mathematical structures called matrices. Heisenberg's "matrix mechanics" was the first logically consistent formulation of quantum theory. It was supplemented one year later by a different formalism, worked out by Erwin Schrödinger and known as "wave mechanics." Both formalisms are logically consistent and are mathematically equivalent— the same atomic phenomenon can be described in two mathematically different languages.

At the end of 1926, physicists had a complete and logically consistent mathematical formalism, but they did not always know how to interpret it to describe a given experimental situation. During the following months Heisenberg, Bohr, Schrödinger, and others gradually clarified the situation in intensive, exhaustive, and often highly emotional discussions. In *Physics and Philosophy* Heisenberg described this crucial period in the history of quantum theory most vividly:

> An intensive study of all questions concerning the inter-
> pretation of quantum theory in Copenhagen finally led to a
> complete . . . clarification of the situation. But it was not
> a solution which one could easily accept. I remember dis-
> cussions with Bohr which went through many hours till
> very late at night and ended almost in despair; and when at
> the end of the discussion I went alone for a walk in the
> neighboring park I repeated to myself again and again the
> question: Can nature possibly be so absurd as it seemed to
> us in these atomic experiments?

Heisenberg recognized that the formalism of quantum theory cannot be interpreted in terms of our intuitive notions of space and time or of cause and effect; at the same time he realized that all our concepts are linked to these intuitive notions. He concluded that there was no other way out than to retain the classical intuitive concepts but to restrict their applicability. Heisenberg's great achievement was to express these limitations of classical concepts in a precise mathematical form which now bears his name and is known as the Heisenberg uncertainty principle. It consists of a set of mathematical relations that de-termine the extent to which classical concepts can be applied to atomic phenomena and thus stake out the limits of human imagination in the subatomic world.

The uncertainty principle measures the extent to which the scientist influences the properties of the observed objects through the process of measurement. In atomic physics scien-tists can no longer play the role of detached, objective ob-servers; they are involved in the world they observe, and Heisenberg's principle measures this involvement. At the most fundamental level the uncertainty principle is a measure of the unity and interrelatedness of the universe. In the 1920s physi-cists, led by Heisenberg and Bohr, came to realize that the world is not a collection of separate objects but rather appears as a web of relations between the various parts of a unified whole. Our classical notions, derived from our ordinary experi-ence, are not fully adequate to describe this world. Werner Heisenberg, like no one else, has explored the limits of human imagination, the limits to which our conventional concepts can be stretched, and the extent to which we must become involved in the world we observe. His greatness was that he not only recognized these limitations and their profound philosophical implications but was able to specify them with mathematical clarity and precision.

At the age of nineteen, I did not by any means understand all of Heisenberg's book. In fact, most of it remained a mystery to me at this first reading, but it sparked a fascination with that epochal period of science that has never left me since. For the time being, however, a more thorough study of the paradoxes of quantum physics and their resolution had to wait while, for several years, I received a thorough education in physics; first in classical physics, and then in quantum mechanics, relativity theory, and quantum field theory. Heisenberg's *Physics and Philosophy* remained my companion during these studies and, looking back on this time, I now can see that it was Heisenberg who planted the seed that would mature, more than a decade later, in my systematic investigation of the limitations of the Cartesian world view. "The Cartesian partition," wrote Heisenberg, "has penetrated deeply into the human mind during the three centuries following Descartes, and it will take a long time for it to be replaced by a really different attitude toward the problem of reality."

The sixties

Between my student years in Vienna and the writing of my first book lies the period of my life during which I experienced the most profound and most radical personal transformation—the period of the sixties. For those of us who identify with the movements of the sixties this period represents not so much a decade as a state of consciousness, characterized by the transpersonal expansion, the questioning of authority, a sense of empowerment, and the experience of sensuous beauty and community. This state of consciousness reached well into the seventies. In fact, one could say that the sixties came to an end only in December 1980 with the shot that killed John Lennon. The immense sense of loss felt by so many of us was to a great extent the loss of an era. For a few days after the fatal shooting we relived the magic of the sixties. We did so in sadness and in tears, but the same feeling of magic and of community was once again alive. Wherever you went during those few days—in every neighborhood, in every city, in every country around the world—you heard John Lennon's music, and that intense feeling, which had carried us through the sixties, manifested itself again one last time:

> *You may say I'm a dreamer,*
> *but I'm not the only one.*
> *I hope some day you'll join us*
> *and the world will live as one.*

After graduating from the University of Vienna in 1966 I spent my first two years of postdoctoral research in theoretical physics at the University of Paris. In September 1968, my wife Jacqueline and I moved to California, where I had a teaching and research appointment at the University of California at Santa Cruz. I remember reading Thomas Kuhn's *The Structure of Scientific Revolutions* on the transatlantic flight and being slightly disappointed by this much-talked-about book when I discovered that its principal ideas were already familiar to me from my repeated readings of Heisenberg. However, Kuhn's book did introduce me to the notion of a scientific paradigm, which would become central to my work many years later. The term "paradigm," from the Greek *paradeigma* ("pattern"), was used by Kuhn to denote a conceptual framework shared by a community of scientists and providing them with model problems and solutions. Over the next twenty years it would become very popular to speak of paradigms and paradigm shifts outside of science as well, and in *The Turning Point* I would use these terms in a very broad sense. A paradigm, for me, would mean the totality of thoughts, perceptions, and values that forms a particular vision of reality, a vision that is the basis of the way a society organizes itself.

In California, Jacqueline and I encountered two very different cultures: the dominant "straight" culture of the American mainstream and the "counterculture" of the hippies. We were enchanted by the physical beauty of California but also amazed by the general lack of taste and esthetic values in the straight culture. The contrast between the stunning beauty of nature and the dismal ugliness of civilization was strongest out here on the American West Coast, where it seemed to us that all European heritage had long been left behind. We could easily understand why the protest of the counterculture against the American way of life had originated here, and we were naturally drawn to this movement.

The hippies opposed many cultural traits that we, too, found highly unattractive. To distinguish themselves from the crew cuts and polyester suits of the straight business executives they wore long hair, colorful and individualistic clothes, flowers, beads, and other jewelry. They lived naturally without disinfectants or deodorants, many of them vegetarians, many practicing yoga or some other form of meditation. They would often bake their own bread or practice some craft. They were called "dirty hippies" by the straight society but referred to themselves as "the beautiful people." Dissatisfied with a system of education that was designed to prepare young people for a society they rejected, many hippies dropped out of the educational system even though they were often highly talented. This subculture was immediately identifiable and tightly bound together. It had its own rituals, its music, poetry, and literature, a common fascination with spirituality and the occult, and the shared vision of a peaceful and beautiful society. Rock music and psychedelic drugs were powerful bonds that strongly influenced the art and life-style of the hippie culture.

While I continued my research at UC Santa Cruz, I became involved in the counterculture as much as my academic duties would allow, leading a somewhat schizophrenic life—part-time postdoctoral research fellow and part-time hippie. Very few people who picked me up when I was hitchhiking with my sleeping bag suspected that I had a Ph.D., and even fewer that I had just turned thirty and hence could not be trusted, according to the celebrated hippie adage. During the years 1969 and 1970 I experienced all facets of the counterculture—the rock festivals, the psychedelics, the new sexual freedom, the communal living, the many days on the road. Traveling was easy in those days. All you had to do was stick out your thumb and you would get a ride without any problem. Once a car picked you up, you would be asked your astrological sign, invited to share a "joint," and serenaded by the Grateful Dead, or you would get involved in a conversation about Hermann Hesse, the *I Ching*, or some other esoteric subject.

The sixties brought me without doubt the deepest and most radical personal experiences of my life: the rejection of conventional, "straight" values; the closeness, peacefulness, and trust of the hippie community; the freedom of communal nudity; the expansion of consciousness through psychedelics and meditation; the playfulness and attention to the "here and now"—all of which resulted in a continual sense of magic, awe, and wonder that, for me, will forever be associated with the sixties.

The sixties were also the time when my political consciousness was raised. This happened first in Paris, where many graduate students and young research fellows were also active in the student movement that culminated in the memorable revolt that is still known simply as "May '68." I remember long discussions at the Science Faculty at Orsay, during which the students not only analyzed the Vietnam War and the Arab-Israeli war of 1967, but also questioned the power structure within the university and discussed alternative, nonhierarchical structures.

In May 1968, finally, all research and teaching activities came to a complete halt when the students, led by Daniel Cohn-Bendit, extended their critique to society as a whole and sought the solidarity of the labor movement to change the entire social organization. For about a week the city administration, public transport, and businesses of every kind were completely paralyzed by a general strike; people spent most of the time discussing politics in the streets, and the students, who had occupied the Odéon, the spacious theater of the Comédie Française, transformed it into a twenty-four-hour "people's parliament."

I shall never forget the excitement of those days, which was tempered only by my fear of violence. Jacqueline and I would spend the day participating in huge rallies and demonstrations, carefully avoiding the clashes between demonstrators and riot squads, meeting people in the streets, in restaurants and in cafés, and carrying on a never-ending political discussion. In the evening we would go to the Odéon or the Sorbonne to hear Cohn-Bendit and others air their highly idealistic but extremely stimulating visions of a future social order.

The European student movement, which was largely Marxist oriented, was not able to turn its visions into realities during

the sixties. But it kept its social concerns alive during the subsequent decade, during which many of its members went
through profound personal transformations. Influenced by the
two major concerns of the seventies, the feminism movement
and ecology, these members of the new left broadened their
horizons without losing their social consciousness, and at the
end of the decade began to join the newly formed European
Green parties.

When I moved to California in the fall of 1968, the evidence of racism, the oppression of blacks, and the resulting
Black Power movement became another important part of my
experience of the sixties. Not only would I participate in anti-
war rallies and marches, but I would also attend political events
organized by the Black Panthers and hear lectures by speakers
like Angela Davis. My political consciousness, which had become very acute in Paris, was further expanded by these events,
as well as by reading Eldridge Cleaver's *Soul on Ice*, and other
books by black authors.

I remember that my sympathy with the Black Power
movement was aroused by a dramatic and unforgettable event
shortly after we moved to Santa Cruz. We read in the newspaper that an unarmed black teenager had been brutally shot
to death by a white policeman in a small record store in San
Francisco. Outraged, my wife and I drove to San Francisco and
went to the boy's funeral, expecting to find a large crowd of
like-minded white people. Indeed, there was a large crowd, but
to our great shock we found that, together with another two or
three, we were the only whites. The congregation hall was
lined with fierce-looking Black Panthers clad in black leather,
arms crossed. The atmosphere was tense and we felt insecure
and frightened. But when I approached one of the guards and
asked whether it would be all right for us to attend the funeral,
he looked straight into my eyes and said simply, "You're welcome, brother, you're welcome!"

The way of Alan Watts

My first contact with Eastern mysticism occurred while I was
in Paris. At that time I knew several people who were inter-

ested in Indian and Japanese culture, but the one who really introduced me to Eastern thought was my brother Bernt. Since our childhood we have remained very close, and Bernt shares my interest in philosophy and spirituality. In 1966 he was a student of architecture in Austria and, as a student, maybe had more time to be open to the new influences of Eastern thought on the European and American youth culture than I, being as busy as I was establishing myself as a theoretical physicist. Bernt gave me an anthology of the Beat poets and writers, which introduced me to the works of Jack Kerouac, Lawrence Ferlinghetti, Allen Ginsberg, Gary Snyder, and Alan Watts. Through Alan Watts I learned about Zen Buddhism, and shortly after that Bernt suggested that I read the Bhagavad Gita, one of the most beautiful and profound spiritual texts of India.

After moving to California, I soon found out that Alan Watts was one of the heroes of the counterculture, whose books were on the shelves of most hippie communes, along with those of Carlos Castaneda, J. Krishnamurti, and Hermann Hesse. Although I had read books about Eastern philosophy and religion before reading Watts, it was he who helped me most to understand its essence. His books would take me as far as one could go with books and would stimulate me to go further through direct, nonverbal experience. Although Alan Watts was not as great a scholar as D. T. Suzuki, or some of the other well-known Eastern authors, he had the unique gift of being able to describe the Eastern teachings in Western language, and in a way that was light and witty, elegant, and full of playfulness. Thus, while he transformed the form of the teachings, he adapted them to our cultural context without distorting their meaning.

Although I was very attracted to the exotic aspects of Eastern mysticism, like most of my friends at that time I also sensed that those spiritual traditions would be most meaningful for us if we could adapt them to our own cultural context. Alan Watts could do that superbly, and I have felt a strong kinship with him ever since I read *The Book* and *The Way of Zen*. In fact, I got to know his writing so well that I subconsciously absorbed his technique of reformulating the Eastern teachings and used it in my own writing many years later. Part of the reason *The Tao of Physics* has been so successful may well be that it is a book written in the tradition of Alan Watts.

I met Watts before I had formulated any of my ideas about the relationship between science and mysticism. He gave a lecture at UC Santa Cruz in 1969, and I was chosen to sit next to him during the preceding faculty dinner, probably because I was considered the most "hip" among the professors. Watts was highly entertaining throughout the dinner, telling us many tales from Japan and keeping up an animated conversation that touched on philosophy, art, religion, French cuisine, and many other subjects dear to his heart. The following day we continued the conversation over a beer at the Catalyst, the local hippie hangout where I usually spent time with my friends and where I met many interesting and colorful people. (It was at the Catalyst that I also heard Carlos Castaneda give an informal talk on his adventures with Don Juan, the mythical Yaqui sage, shortly after he had written his first book.)

After I left California for London in 1970, I stayed in touch with Watts, and when I wrote "The Dance of Shiva," my first article about the parallels between modern physics and Eastern mysticism, he was one of the first to receive a copy. He sent me a very encouraging letter, saying that he considered this to be a most important field of investigation. He also suggested some Buddhist literature and asked me to keep him informed about my progress. Unfortunately, that was our last contact. Throughout my work in London I looked forward to seeing Alan Watts again—I thought about the time when I'd move back to California and about discussing my book with him—but he died one year before *The Tao of Physics* was finished.

J. KRISHNAMURTI

One of my first direct contacts with Eastern spirituality was my meeting with J. Krishnamurti in late 1968. At the time Krishnamurti came to UC Santa Cruz to give a series of lectures he was seventy-three and had an absolutely stunning appearance. His sharp Indian features, the contrast between his dark skin and his white, perfectly combed hair, his elegant European clothes, his dignified countenance, his measured, flawless English, and—above all—the intensity of his concentration and entire presence left me absolutely spellbound. At that time, Castaneda's *Teachings of Don Juan* had just come out, and when I saw Krishnamurti I could not help comparing his appearance to the mythical figure of that Yaqui sage.

The impact of Krishnamurti's physical appearance and charisma was enhanced and deepened by what he said. Krishnamurti was a very original thinker who rejected all spiritual authority and traditions. His teachings were quite close to those of Buddhism, but he never used any terms from Buddhism or from any other branch of traditional Eastern thought. The task he set himself was extremely difficult—to use language and reasoning in order to lead his audience beyond language and reasoning—and the way in which he went about it was highly impressive.

Krishnamurti would select a well-known existential problem—fear, desire, death, time—as the topic of a particular lecture, and he would begin his talk with something like the following words: "Let us go into this together. I am not going to tell you anything; I have no authority; we are going to explore this question together." He would then show the futility of all conventional ways of eliminating (for example) fear, whereupon he would ask slowly, with great intensity, and with an acute sense of drama: "Is it possible for you, at this very moment, right here, to get rid of fear? Not to suppress it, or deny it, or resist it, but to get rid of it once and for all? This is our task tonight—to get rid of fear completely, totally, once and for all. If we cannot do that, my lecture will be useless."

Now the stage was set; the audience was rapt and utterly attentive. "So let us examine this question," Krishnamurti would continue, "without judging, without condemning, without justifying. What is fear? Let us go into this together, you and the speaker. Let us see whether we can really communicate, being at the same level, at the same intensity, at the same time. Using the speaker as a mirror, can you find the answer to this extraordinarily important question: What is fear?" And then he would begin to weave an immaculate web of concepts. He would show that in order to understand fear you have to understand desire; to understand desire you have to understand thought; and therefore time, and knowledge, and the self, and so on and so forth. Krishnamurti would present a brilliant analysis of how these basic existential problems are interrelated—not theoretically

but experientially. He would not merely confront you with the
results of his analysis but urge and persuade you to get involved
in the analyzing process yourself. At the end you would come
away with the strong and clear feeling that the only way to
solve any of your existential problems was to go beyond thought,
beyond language, beyond time—to achieve, as he put it in the
title of one of his best books, *Freedom from the Known.*

I remember that I was fascinated as well as deeply disturbed by Krishnamurti's lectures. After each evening talk Jacqueline and I stayed up for several hours more, sitting at our
fireplace and discussing what Krishnamurti had said. This was
my first direct encounter with a radical spiritual teacher, and I
was immediately faced with a serious problem. I had just embarked on a promising scientific career, in which I had considerable emotional involvement, and now Krishnamurti told me
with all his charisma and persuasion to stop thinking, to liberate myself from all knowledge, to leave reasoning behind. What
did this mean for me? Should I give up my scientific career at
this early stage, or should I remain a scientist and abandon all
hope of attaining spiritual self-realization?

I longed to ask Krishnamurti for advice, but he did not allow any questions at his lectures, nor would he see anybody
afterward. We made several attempts to see him but were told
firmly that Krishnamurti did not wish to be disturbed. It was a
lucky coincidence—or was it?—that finally brought us an audience. It turned out that Krishnamurti had a French secretary,
and after the last lecture Jacqueline, who is a native of Paris,
managed to strike up a conversation with this man. They hit it
off well, and as a result we ended up seeing Krishnamurti in his
apartment the following morning.

I was rather intimidated when I finally sat face to face
with the Master, but I did not lose any time. I knew what I had
come for. "How can I be a scientist," I asked, "and still follow
your advice of stopping thought and attaining freedom from
the known?" Krishnamurti did not hesitate for a moment. He
answered my question in ten seconds, in a way that completely
solved my problem. "*First* you are a human being," he said;
"*then* you are a scientist. First you have to become free, and
this freedom cannot be achieved through thought. It is achieved
through meditation—the understanding of the totality of life in
which every form of fragmentation has ceased." Once I had

reached this understanding of life as a whole, he told me, I would be able to specialize and work as a scientist without any problems. And, of course, there was no question of abolishing science. Switching to French Krishnamurti added, *"J'adore la science. C'est merveilleux!"*

After this brief but decisive meeting I did not see Krishnamurti again until six years later, when I was invited along with several other scientists to spend a week in discussion with him at his educational center at Brockwood Park, south of London. His appearance was still very striking, even though he had lost some of his intensity. During that week I came to know Krishnamurti much better, including some of his shortcomings. When he spoke he was again very powerful and charismatic, but I was disappointed by the fact that we could never really draw Krishnamurti into a discussion. He would speak, but he would not listen. On the other hand, I had many exciting discussions with my fellow scientists—David Bohm, Karl Pribram, and George Sudarshan, among others.

Thereafter I all but lost touch with Krishnamurti. I always acknowledged his decisive influence on me, and I would often hear about him from various people, but I did not attend another lecture nor did I read any of his other books. Then, in January 1983, I found myself in Madras in southern India at a conference of the Theosophical Society opposite Krishnamurti's estate, and since Krishnamurti happened to be there and gave an evening lecture I went to pay my respects. The beautiful park with its huge old trees was packed with people, mostly Indian, who sat quietly on the ground and waited for the beginning of a ritual that most of them had participated in many times before. At eight o'clock Krishnamurti appeared, dressed in Indian clothes, and walked slowly but with great assurance toward the prepared platform. It was wonderful to see him, at eighty-eight, making his entrance the way he had done for more than half a century, climbing the stairs to the platform without any help, sitting down on a cushion, and folding his hands in the traditional Indian salute to begin his talk.

Krishnamurti spoke for seventy-five minutes without any hesitation and with almost the same intensity I had witnessed fifteen years before. The topic of the evening was desire and he laid out his web as clearly and skillfully as he had always done. This was a unique opportunity for me to gauge the evolution of my own understanding from the time I had first met him, and

I felt for the first time that I clearly understood his method and his personality. His analysis of desire was clear and beautiful. Perception causes a sensory response, he said; then thought intervenes—"I want . . . ," "I don't want . . . ," "I wish . . ."—and thus desire is generated. It is not caused by the object of desire and will persist with varying objects as long as thought intervenes. Therefore, to free oneself from desire cannot be achieved by suppressing or avoiding sensory experience (the way of the ascetic). The only way to be free from desire is to be free from thought.

What Krishnamurti did not say is *how* freedom from thought can be achieved. Like the Buddha, he offered a brilliant analysis of the problem, but unlike the Buddha he did not show a clear path toward liberation. Perhaps, I wondered, Krishnamurti himself had not gone far enough on this path? Perhaps he had not sufficiently freed himself from all conditioning to lead his disciples to full self-realization?

After the lecture I was invited to join Krishnamurti and several other people for dinner. Understandably, he was quite exhausted from his lecture and not in the mood for any discussion. Nor was I. I had come simply to show my gratitude, and had been richly rewarded. I told Krishnamurti the story of our first meeting and thanked him once more for his decisive influence and help, being well aware that this would probably be our last encounter, as indeed it turned out to be.

The problem that Krishnamurti had solved for me, Zen-like with one stroke, is the problem most physicists face when confronted with the ideas of mystical traditions—how can one transcend thinking without losing one's commitment to science? It is the reason, I believe, that so many of my colleagues feel threatened by my comparisons between physics and mysticism. Perhaps it will help them to know that I, too, felt the same threat. I felt it with my whole being, but it appeared at an early stage of my career and I had the great fortune that the person who made me realize the threat also helped me to transcend it.

Parallels between physics and mysticism

When I first learned about the Eastern traditions I discovered parallels between modern physics and Eastern mysticism al-

most immediately. I remember reading a French book about
Zen Buddhism in Paris from which I first learned about the
important role of paradox in mystical traditions. I learned that
spiritual teachers in the East would often use paradoxical riddles in a very skillful way to make their students realize the
limitations of logic and reasoning. The Zen tradition, in particular, developed a system of nonverbal instruction through
seemingly nonsensical riddles, called koans, which cannot be
solved by thinking. They are designed precisely to stop the
thought process and thus to make the student ready for the nonverbal experience of reality. All koans, I read, have more or
less unique solutions which a competent master recognizes immediately. Once the solution is found, the koan ceases to be paradoxical and becomes a profoundly meaningful statement made
from the state of consciousness that it has helped to awaken.

When I first read about the koan method in Zen training,
it had a strangely familiar ring to me. I had spent many years
studying another kind of paradox that seemed to play a similar
role in the training of physicists. There were differences, of
course. My own training as a physicist certainly had not had
the intensity of Zen training. But then I thought about Heisenberg's account of the way in which physicists in the 1920s experienced the quantum paradoxes, struggling for understanding in a situation where nature alone was the teacher. The
parallel was obvious and fascinating and, later on, when I
learned more about Zen Buddhism, I found that it was indeed
very significant. As in Zen, the solutions to the physicists' problems were hidden in paradoxes that could not be solved by logical reasoning but had to be understood in terms of a new awareness, the awareness of the atomic reality. Nature was their
teacher and, like the Zen masters, she did not provide any
statements; she just provided the riddles.

The similarity of the experiences of quantum physicists
and of Zen Buddhists was very striking to me. The descriptions
of the koan method all emphasized that the solving of such a
riddle demands a supreme effort of concentration and involvement from the student. The koan, it is said, grips the student's
heart and mind and creates a true mental impasse, a state of
sustained tension in which the whole world becomes an enormous mass of doubt and questioning. When I compared this description to the passage from Heisenberg's book that I remem-

bered so well, I felt very strongly that the founders of quantum theory experienced exactly the same situation:

> I remember discussions with Bohr which went through many hours till very late at night and ended almost in despair; and when at the end of the discussion I went alone for a walk in the neighboring park I repeated to myself again and again the question: Can nature possibly be so absurd as it seemed to us in these atomic experiments?

Later on, I also came to understand why quantum physicists and Eastern mystics were faced with similar problems and went through similar experiences. Whenever the essential nature of things is analyzed by the intellect, it will seem absurd or paradoxical. This has always been recognized by mystics but has become a problem in science only very recently. For centuries, the phenomena studied in science belonged to the scientists' everyday environment and thus to the realm of their sensory experience. Since the images and concepts of their language were abstracted from this very experience, they were sufficient and adequate to describe the natural phenomena.

In the twentieth century, however, physicists penetrated deep into the submicroscopic world, into realms of nature far removed from our macroscopic environment. Our knowledge of matter at this level is no longer derived from direct sensory experience, and therefore our ordinary language is no longer adequate to describe the observed phenomena. Atomic physics provided the scientists with the first glimpses of the essential nature of things. Like the mystics, physicists were now dealing with a nonsensory experience of reality and, like the mystics, they had to face the paradoxical aspects of this experience. From then on, the models and images of modern physics became akin to those of Eastern philosophy.

The discovery of the parallel between the Zen koans and the paradoxes of quantum physics, which I would later call "quantum koans," greatly stimulated my interest in Eastern mysticism and sharpened my attention. In subsequent years, as I became more involved in Eastern spirituality, I would again and again encounter concepts that would be somewhat familiar to me from my training in atomic and subatomic physics. The discovery of these similarities was at first not much more than an intellectual exercise, albeit a very exciting one, but then, one late afternoon in the summer of 1969, I had a powerful experience that made me take the parallels between physics and mysticism much more seriously. The description of this experience that I gave on the opening page of *The Tao of Physics* is still the best I can find:

> I was sitting by the ocean one late summer afternoon, watching the waves rolling in and feeling the rhythm of my breathing, when I suddenly became aware of my whole environment as being engaged in a gigantic cosmic dance. Being a physicist, I knew that the sand, rocks, water, and air around me were made of vibrating molecules and atoms, and that these consisted of particles which interacted with one another by creating and destroying other particles. I knew also that the earth's atmosphere was continually bombarded by showers of "cosmic rays," particles of high energy undergoing multiple collisions as they penetrated the air. All this was familiar to me from my research in high-energy physics, but until that moment I had only experienced it through graphs, diagrams, and mathematical theories. As I sat on that beach my former experiences came to life; I "saw" cascades of energy coming down from outer space, in which particles were created and destroyed in rhythmic pulses; I "saw" the atoms of the elements and those of my body participating in this cosmic dance of energy; I felt its rhythm and I "heard" its sound, and at that moment I *knew* that this was the Dance of Shiva, the Lord of Dancers worshiped by the Hindus.

At the end of 1970, my American visa expired and I had to return to Europe. I was not sure where I wanted to continue my research, so I planned to visit the best research institutes in my field, in each case making contact with people I knew, with a view to obtaining a fellowship or some other position. My first stop was London, where I arrived in October, still a hippie at heart. When I entered the office of P. T. Matthews, a particle physicist I had met in California and who was then the head of the theory division at Imperial College, the first thing I saw was a giant poster of Bob Dylan. I took this as a good omen and decided on the spot that I would stay in London, and Matthews told me that he would be very happy to offer me hospitality at Imperial College. I have never regretted this decision, which resulted in my staying in London for four years, even though the first few months after my arrival were, perhaps, the hardest in my life.

The end of 1970 was a difficult time of transition for me. I was at the beginning of a long series of painful separations from my wife that would eventually end in divorce. I had no friends in London, and I soon found out that it was impossible for me to get a research grant or academic position because I had already begun my search for the new paradigm and was not willing to give it up and accept the narrow confines of a full-time academic job. It was during these first weeks in London, when my spirits were at the lowest they had ever been, that I made the decision that gave my life a new direction.

Shortly before leaving California I had designed a photomontage—a dancing Shiva superimposed on tracks of colliding particles in a bubble chamber—to illustrate my experience of the cosmic dance on the beach. One day I sat in my tiny room near Imperial College and looked at this beautiful picture, and suddenly I had a very clear realization. I knew with absolute certainty that the parallels between physics and mysticism, which I had just begun to discover, would someday be common knowledge; I also knew that I was best placed to explore these parallels thoroughly and to write a book about them. I resolved there and then to write that book, but I also decided that I was not yet ready to do so. I would first study my subject further and write a few articles about it before attempting the book.

Encouraged by this resolution I took my photomontage, which for me contained a profound and powerful statement, to Imperial College to show it to an Indian colleague of mine with whom I happened to share an office. When I showed him the photomontage, without any comment, he was deeply moved and spontaneously began reciting sacred verses in Sanskrit which he remembered from his childhood. He told me that he had grown up as a Hindu but had forgotten everything about his spiritual heritage when he became "brainwashed," as he put it, by Western science. He himself would never have thought of the parallels between particle physics and Hinduism, he said, but upon seeing my photomontage they immediately became evident to him.

Over the next two and a half years I undertook a systematic study of Hinduism, Buddhism, and Taoism, and of the parallels I saw between the basic ideas of those mystical traditions and the basic concepts and theories of modern physics. During the sixties I had tried various techniques of meditation and read a number of books on Eastern mysticism without really engaging myself to follow any of their paths. But now, as I studied the Eastern traditions more carefully, I was most attracted to Taoism.

Among the great spiritual traditions, Taoism offers, in my view, the most profound and most beautiful expressions of ecological wisdom, emphasizing both the fundamental oneness of all phenomena and the embeddedness of individuals and societies in the cyclical processes of nature. Thus Chuang Tzu:

> In the transformation and growth of all things, every bud and feature has its proper form. In this we have their gradual maturing and decay, the constant flow of transformation and change.

And Huai Nan Tzu:

> Those who follow the natural order flow in the current of the Tao.

The Taoist sages concentrated their attention fully on the observation of nature in order to discern the "characteristics of the Tao." In doing so they developed an attitude that was essentially scientific; only their deep mistrust of the analytic method of reasoning prevented them from constructing proper scientific theories. Nevertheless, their careful observation of nature, combined with a strong mystical intuition, led them to profound insights which are confirmed by modern scientific theories. The deep ecological wisdom, the empirical approach, and the special flavor of Taoism, which I can best describe as "quiet ecstasy," were enormously attractive to me, and so Taoism quite naturally became the way for me to follow.

Castaneda, too, exerted a strong influence on me in those years, and his books showed me yet another approach to the spiritual teachings of the East. I found the teachings of the American Indian traditions, expressed by the legendary Yaqui sage Don Juan, very close to those of the Taoist tradition, transmitted by the legendary sages Lao Tzu and Chuang Tzu. The awareness of being embedded in the natural flow of things and the skill to act accordingly are central to both traditions. As the

Taoist sage flows in the current of the Tao, the Yaqui "man of knowledge" needs to be light and fluid to "see" the essential nature of things.

Taoism and Buddhism are both traditions that deal with the very essence of spirituality, which is not bound to any particular culture. Buddhism, in particular, has shown throughout its history that it is adaptable to various cultural situations. It originated with the Buddha in India, then spread to China and Southeast Asia, ending up in Japan and, many centuries later, jumping across the Pacific to California. The strongest influence of the Buddhist tradition on my own thinking has been the emphasis on the central role of compassion in the attainment of knowledge. According to the Buddhist view, there can be no wisdom without compassion, which means for me that science is of no value unless it is accompanied by social concern.

Although the years 1971 and 1972 were very difficult for me, they also were very exciting. I continued my life as part-time physicist and part-time hippie, doing research in particle physics at Imperial College while also pursuing my larger research in an organized and systematic way. I managed to get several part-time jobs—teaching high-energy physics to a group of engineers, translating technical texts from English into German, teaching mathematics to high school girls—which made enough money for me to survive but did not allow for any material luxury. My life during those two years was very much like that of a pilgrim; its luxuries and joys were not those of the material plane. What carried me through this period was a strong belief in my vision and a conviction that my persistence would eventually be rewarded. During those two years I always had a quote from the Taoist sage Chuang Tzu pinned to my wall: "I have sought a ruler who would employ me for a long time. That I have not found one shows the character of the time."

Physics and counterculture in Amsterdam

During the summer of 1971 an international physics conference was held in Amsterdam, one that I was very keen on attending for two reasons. I wanted to keep interacting with the leading researchers in my field; moreover, Amsterdam was famous in the counterculture as being the hippie capital of Europe, and I saw this as an excellent opportunity to find out more about the European movement. I applied to be invited to the conference as part of the team representing Imperial College but was told that the quota was already full. Having no money to pay for my transportation, hotel expenses, and the conference fee, I decided to travel to Amsterdam the way I had become accustomed to traveling in California—hitchhiking—first heading south to the Channel, then across to Ostend on the cheap ferry, and on through Belgium and Holland to Amsterdam.

I packed my suit, shirts, leather shoes, and physics papers in a bag, put on my patched jeans, sandals, and flowered shirt, and hit the road. The weather was superb and I greatly enjoyed traveling through Europe the slow way, meeting lots of people and visiting beautiful old towns on the way. My overriding experience on this trip, the first in Europe after two years of California, was the realization that European national borders are rather artificial divisions. I noticed that the language, customs, and physical characteristics of the people did not change abruptly at the borders, but rather gradually, and that the people on either side of the border often had much more in common with each other than, say, with the inhabitants of the capitals of their countries. Today, this recognition has been formalized in the political program of a "Europe of the regions" proposed by the European Green movement.

The week I spent in Amsterdam was the height of my schizophrenic life as hippie/physicist. During the day I would put on my suit and discuss problems of particle physics with my colleagues at the conference (sneaking in every day because I could not afford to pay the registration fee). In the evenings I would wear my hippie clothes and hang out in the cafés, squares, and houseboats of Amsterdam, and at night I would sleep in one of the parks in my sleeping bag together with hundreds of like-minded young people from all over Europe. I did so partly because I could not afford a hotel, but also because I wanted to participate fully in this exciting international community.

Amsterdam was a fabulous city in those days. The hippies were tourists of a new kind. They came to Amsterdam from all over Europe and the United States not to see the Royal Palace or the paintings of Rembrandt, but to be with one another. A great attraction was the fact that smoking marijuana and hashish was tolerated to the extent of being virtually legal in Amsterdam, but this beautiful city's attraction went far beyond that. There was a genuine desire among young people to meet one another and share radically new experiences and visions of a different future. One of the most popular meeting places was a large house called The Milky Way, which contained a health food restaurant and a discotheque plus an entire floor laid out with thick carpets, lit by candles and scented with incense, where people would sit in groups, smoke, and talk. In The Milky Way you could spend hours discussing Mahayana Buddhism, the teachings of Don Juan, the best places to buy glass beads in Morocco, or the latest play of the Living Theatre. The Milky Way could have been a place straight out of a Hesse novel, a place animated by the visitors' own creativity, cultural heritage, emotions, and fantasies.

One evening around midnight I was sitting on the steps to the entrance of The Milky Way with a couple of friends from Italy when suddenly the two separate realities of my life collided. A group of straight tourists was approaching the steps where I was sitting, and as they came nearer I recognized them, to my slight horror, as the physicists with whom I had had discussions the very same day. This clash of realities was more than I could handle. I pulled my Afghan jacket over my ears, put my head on the shoulder of the young woman sitting next to me, and waited until my colleagues, who were now standing just a few feet in front of me, finished their comments about "spaced-out hippies" and turned around to leave.

The Dance of Shiva

In the late spring of 1971 I felt ready to write my first article about the parallels between modern physics and Eastern mysticism. It revolved around my experience of the cosmic dance and the photomontage illustrating that experience, and I called it "The Dance of Shiva: The Hindu View of Matter in the Light of Modern Physics." The article was published in *Main Currents in Modern Thought*, a beautiful journal dedicated to promoting transdisciplinary and integrative studies.

While submitting my article to *Main Currents*, I also sent

copies to some of the leading theoretical physicists whom I expected to be open to philosophical considerations. The reactions I received were mixed, most of them cautious but some very encouraging. Sir Bernard Lovell, the famous astronomer, wrote: "I am entirely sympathetic with your thesis and conclusions. . . . The whole subject seems to me to be of fundamental importance." The physicist John Wheeler commented: "One has the feeling that the thinkers of the East knew it all, and if we could only translate their answers into our language we would have the answers to all our questions." The reply that delighted me most, however, came from Werner Heisenberg, who stated: "I have always been fascinated by the relations between the ancient teachings of the East and the philosophical consequences of the modern quantum theory."

Conversations with Heisenberg

Several months later I visited my parents in Innsbruck, and since I knew that Heisenberg lived in Munich, only an hour's drive away, and I had been very much encouraged by his letter, I wrote to him and asked whether I could visit him in Munich. I then called him from Innsbruck and he said that he would be very happy to receive me.

On April 11, 1972, I drove to Munich to meet the man who had had a decisive influence on my scientific career and my philosophical interests, the man who was considered one of the intellectual giants of our century. Heisenberg received me in his office at the Max Planck Institute, and when I sat down face to face with him at his desk I was immediately impressed. He was impeccably dressed in a suit and tie, his tie pinned to his shirt by a pin that formed the letter h, which is the symbol for Planck's constant, the fundamental constant of quantum physics. I noticed these details gradually during our conversation. What impressed me most right away was Heisenberg's clear blue-gray eyes, holding forth a gaze that showed clarity of mind, total presence, compassion, and serene detachment. For the first time I felt that I was sitting with one of the great sages of my own culture.

I began the conversation by asking Heisenberg to what extent he was still involved in physics, and he told me that he was pursuing a research program with a group of colleagues, that he came to the Institute every day, and that he was following the research in fundamental physics around the world with great interest. When I asked him what kind of results he still hoped to achieve, he gave me a brief outline of the goals of his research program, but he also said that he found as much pleasure in the process of research as in achieving those goals. I had the strong feeling that this man had pursued his discipline to the point of complete self-realization.

What was most astonishing about these first few minutes of our conversation was that I felt completely at ease. There was absolutely no trace of any posturing or pomp; Heisenberg never made me feel the difference in our status even for a second. We began to discuss recent developments in particle physics, and to my amazement I found myself contradicting Heisenberg only a few minutes into our discussion. My initial feelings of awe and reverence had quickly given way to the intellectual excitement felt in a good discussion. There was complete equality—two physicists discussing the ideas they found most exciting in the science they loved.

Naturally, our conversation soon drifted to the 1920s, and Heisenberg entertained me with many fascinating stories of that period. I realized that he loved to talk about physics and to reminisce about those exciting years. For example, he gave me a vivid description of discussions between Erwin Schrödinger and Niels Bohr that took place when Schrödinger visited Copenhagen in 1926 and presented his newly discovered wave mechanics, including the celebrated equation that bears his name, at Bohr's institute. Schrödinger's wave mechanics was a continuous formalism involving familiar mathematical techniques, while Bohr's interpretation of quantum theory was based on Heisenberg's discontinuous and highly unorthodox matrix mechanics, which involved so-called quantum jumps.

Heisenberg told me that Bohr tried to convince Schrödinger of the merits of the discontinuous interpretation in long debates that often took entire days. In one of these debates Schrödinger exclaimed in great frustration: "If one has to stick to this damned quantum jumping, then I regret having ever been involved in this thing." Bohr, however, pressed on and berated Schrödinger so intensely that Schrödinger finally got sick. "I remember well," Heisenberg continued with a smile, "how poor Schrödinger was lying in bed in Bohr's home and Mrs. Bohr was serving him a bowl of soup, while Niels Bohr was sitting on his bed insisting: 'But Schrödinger, you *must* admit . . .' "

When we talked about the developments that led Heisenberg to formulate the uncertainty principle, he told me an interesting detail that I had not found in any written account of the period. He said that in the early 1920s Niels Bohr suggested to him during one of their long philosophical conversations that they might have reached the limits of human understanding in the realm of the very small. Maybe, Bohr wondered, physicists would never be able to find a precise formalism to describe atomic phenomena. Heisenberg added with a fleeting smile, his gaze lost in reverie, that it was his great personal triumph to prove Bohr wrong on this account.

While Heisenberg was telling me these stories, I noticed that he had Jacques Monod's *Chance and Necessity* lying on his desk, and since I had just read this book myself with great interest I was very curious to hear Heisenberg's opinion. I told him that I thought Monod, in his attempt to reduce life to a game of roulette, governed by quantum-mechanical probabilities, had not really understood quantum mechanics. Heisenberg agreed with me and added that he found it sad that Monod's excellent popularization of molecular biology was accompanied by such bad philosophy.

This led me to discuss the broader philosophical framework underlying quantum physics and in particular its relation to that of Eastern mystical traditions. Heisenberg told me that he had repeatedly thought that the great contributions of Japanese physicists during recent decades might be owing to a basic similarity between the philosophical traditions of the East and the philosophy of quantum physics. I remarked that the discussions I had had with Japanese colleagues had not shown me that they were aware of this connection, and Heisenberg agreed: "Japanese physicists have a real taboo against speaking about their own culture, so much have they been influenced by the United States." Heisenberg believed that Indian physicists were somewhat more open in this respect, which had also been my experience.

When I asked Heisenberg about his own thoughts on Eastern philosophy, he told me to my great surprise not only that he had been well aware of the parallels between quantum physics and Eastern thought, but also that his own scientific work had been influenced, at least at the subconscious level, by Indian philosophy.

In 1929 Heisenberg spent some time in India as the guest of the celebrated Indian poet Rabindranath Tagore, with whom he had long conversations about science and Indian philosophy. This introduction to Indian thought brought Heisenberg great comfort, he told me. He began to see that the recognition of relativity, interconnectedness, and impermanence as fundamental aspects of physical reality, which had been so difficult for himself and his fellow physicists, was the very basis of the Indian spiritual traditions. "After these conversations with Tagore," he said, "some of the ideas that had seemed so crazy suddenly made much more sense. That was a great help for me."

At this point I could not help but pour out my heart to Heisenberg. I told him that I had come across the parallels between physics and mysticism several years ago, had begun to study them systematically, and was convinced that this was an important line of research. However, I could not find any financial support from the scientific community and found working without such support extremely difficult and draining. Heisenberg smiled: "I, too, am always accused of getting too much into philosophy." When I pointed out that our situations were rather different, he continued his warm smile and said: "You know, you and I are physicists of a different kind. But every now and then we just have to howl with the wolves."* These extremely kind words of Werner Heisenberg—"You and I are physicists of a different kind"—helped me, perhaps more than anything else, to keep my faith during the difficult times.

Writing The Tao of Physics

After my return to London I continued my studies of Eastern philosophies and their relation to the philosophy of modern physics with renewed enthusiasm. At the same time, I worked on presenting the concepts of modern physics to a lay audience. In fact, I pursued these two objectives separately at that time, because I thought that I might be able to publish my presentation of modern physics as a textbook before writing the book

* *A German expression equivalent to the English "run with the pack."*

about the parallels to Eastern mysticism. I sent the first few chapters of this manuscript to Victor Weisskopf, who is not only a famous physicist but also an outstanding popularizer and interpreter of modern physics. I received a very encouraging reply. Weisskopf told me that he was impressed by my ability to present the concepts of modern physics in nontechnical language, and he urged me to go on with this project, which he considered very important.

During the year 1972 I also had the opportunity of presenting my ideas about the parallels between modern physics and Eastern mysticism to several audiences of physicists, notably at an international physics seminar in Austria and at a special lecture I gave at CERN, the European research institute for particle physics in Geneva. The fact that I was invited to lecture on my philosophical ideas at such a prestigious institution meant a certain recognition of my work, but the response from most of my fellow physicists was hardly more than polite, slightly amused interest.

In April 1973, one year after I had visited Heisenberg, I returned to California for a visit of several weeks, during which I lectured at UC Santa Cruz and UC Berkeley and renewed my contacts with many friends and colleagues in California. One of those colleagues was Michael Nauenberg, a particle physicist at UC Santa Cruz whom I had met in Paris and who had invited me to join him on the faculty of UCSC in 1968. In Paris and during my first year at Santa Cruz Nauenberg and I had been quite close, working together on various research projects as well as keeping close personal contact. However, as I became more and more involved in the counterculture, we saw much less of each other, and during my first two years in London we had lost touch completely. Now each of us was glad to see the other again, and we went for a long walk in the redwood forest on the Santa Cruz campus.

During this walk, I told Nauenberg about my meeting with Heisenberg, and I was surprised that he got very excited when I mentioned Heisenberg's conversations with Tagore and his thoughts about Eastern philosophy. "If Heisenberg said that," Nauenberg exclaimed excitedly, "there must be something to it, and you should definitely write a book about it." At that time the keen interest of my colleague, whom I knew as a rather hard-headed and pragmatic physicist, caused me to change my priorities about which book should come first. As soon as I returned to London, I abandoned the textbook project and decided to incorporate the material I had already written into the text of *The Tao of Physics*.

Today *The Tao of Physics* is an international bestseller and is often praised as a classic that has influenced many other writers. But when I planned to write it, it was extremely difficult for me to find a publisher. Friends in London who were writers suggested that I should first look for a literary agent, and even that took considerable time. When I finally found an agent who agreed to take on this unusual project, he told me that he would need an outline of the book plus three sample chapters to offer to prospective publishers. This put me in a great dilemma. I knew that planning the entire book in detail, writing an outline of its contents, and then writing three chapters would take a lot of time and effort. Should I spend half a year or more on this work in the way I had done in the past, earning my living during the day with part-time jobs and beginning my real work in the evening when I was already tired? Or should I drop everything else and just concentrate on the book? And, in that case, where would I get the money to pay my rent and buy my food?

I remember leaving my agent's office and sitting down on a bench in Leicester Square in the center of London, weighing the possibilities and trying to find a solution. I felt, somehow, that I had to take the jump and make an all-out commitment to my vision regardless of the risks this would involve. And so I did. I decided to leave London temporarily and move to my parents' house in Innsbruck to write those three chapters, and to return to London only when this task was completed.

My parents were glad to have me in the house while I was writing, even though they were rather worried about the prospects of my career, and after two months of concentrated work I was ready to return to London and offer the manuscript to prospective publishers. I knew that this would not immediately resolve my financial dilemma, because I did not expect to get an advance from a publisher right away. But then an old friend of our family, a fairly wealthy Viennese lady, came to my rescue and offered me financial support that would tide me over for a few months. In the meantime, my agent offered the manuscript to the major publishers in London and New York, all of whom turned it down. After a dozen rejections, a small but enterprising London publishing firm, Wildwood House, accepted the proposal and paid me an advance that gave me sufficient support to write the entire book. Oliver Caldecott, who founded Wildwood House and who is now at Hutchinson, became not only my English publisher of this and subsequent books, but has also remained a good friend ever since those early days of *The Tao of Physics*. Throughout his long publishing career Caldecott has had a remarkable intuition for radical new ideas that would become key aspects of "new-paradigm" thinking many years later. He not only was the first publisher of *The Tao of Physics*—the best of his many hunches, as he has often told me proudly—but is also the British publisher of some of the most influential works mentioned in these pages.

From the day I signed the contract with Wildwood House my professional life took a decisive turn and has been successful and exciting ever since. I shall always remember the subsequent fifteen months, during which I wrote *The Tao of Physics*, as among the happiest in my life. I had enough money to continue the life-style I had become used to—modest as far as material luxury was concerned but rich in inner experiences. I had an exciting project to work on, and I had by now a large circle of very interesting friends—writers, musicians, painters, philosophers, anthropologists, and other scientists. My life and my work blended harmoniously in a rich and stimulating intellectual and artistic environment.

Discussions with Phiroz Mehta

When I first discovered the parallels between modern physics and Eastern mysticism the similarities between statements made by physicists and those made by mystics seemed very striking to me, but I was also skeptical. After all, I thought, these may just be similarities of words that will always occur when one compares different schools of thought, simply because we have a limited number of words at our disposal. In fact, I began my first article, "The Dance of Shiva," with this cautious remark. However, as I continued my systematic study of the relationship between physics and mysticism, and while I wrote *The Tao of Physics*, the parallels became deeper and more signifi-

cant the more I investigated them. I saw very clearly that I was
not dealing with any superficial similarity of words, but rather
with a profound harmony between two world views that had
been reached through quite different approaches. "The mystic
and the physicist," I wrote in that book, "arrive at the same conclusion; one starting from the inner realm, the other from the
outer world. The harmony between their views confirms the
ancient Indian wisdom that *Brahman*, the ultimate reality without, is identical to *Atman*, the reality within."

Two different developments led me to that realization. On
the one hand, the conceptual relationships I studied showed an
astonishing internal consistency. The more areas I explored, the
more consistently the parallels appeared. For example, in relativity theory the unification of space and time and the dynamic
aspect of subatomic phenomena are very closely related. Einstein recognized that space and time are not separate; they are
intimately connected and form a four-dimensional continuum—
space-time. A direct consequence of this unification of space
and time is the equivalence of mass and energy and, further,
the fact that subatomic particles must be understood as dynamic patterns, events rather than objects. In Buddhism the
situation is very similar. Mahayana Buddhists speak of the in-
terpenetration of space and time, a perfect expression to describe relativistic space-time, and they say that when it is realized that space and time are interpenetrating, objects will
appear as events rather than as things or substances. This kind
of consistency really struck me, and it appeared again and again
throughout my exploration.

The other development in my study was connected with
the fact that one cannot understand mysticism by reading books
about it; one has to practice it, to experience it, to "taste it," at
least to some extent, in order to have an idea of what the mystics are talking about. This involves following some discipline
and practicing some form of meditation that leads to the experience of an altered state of consciousness. Although I have
not gone very far in this kind of spiritual practice, my experiences nevertheless enabled me to understand the parallels I was
investigating not only intellectually but also at a deeper level
through intuitive insight. The two developments went hand in
hand. While I saw the internal consistency of the parallels with
increasing clarity, the moments of direct intuitive experience

occurred more frequently and I learned to use and harmonize these two complementary modes of cognition.

In both of these developments I was greatly helped by an old Indian scholar and sage, Phiroz Mehta, who lives in South London writing books about religious philosophies and teaching meditation classes. Mehta very kindly guided me through the large body of literature on Indian philosophy and religion, generously offered to let me consult his excellent personal library, and spent long hours with me discussing science and Eastern thought. I have very clear and beautiful memories of these regular visits, when we would sit in Mehta's library in the late afternoon, drinking tea and discussing the Upanishads, the writings of Sri Aurobindo, or some other Indian classic.

As the room gradually got darker our conversation would often give way to long moments of silence, which helped to deepen my insights, but I would also push for intellectual understanding and verbal expression. "Look at this teacup, Phiroz," I remember saying on one occasion. "In what sense does it become one with me in a mystical experience?" "Think of your own body," he replied. "When you are healthy, you are not aware of any of its myriads of parts. Your awareness is that of being one single organism. It is only when something goes wrong that you become aware of your eyelids or your glands. Similarly, the state of experiencing all of reality as a unified whole is the healthy state for the mystics. The division into separate objects, for them, is due to a mental disturbance."

Second visit to Heisenberg

In December 1974 I finished my manuscript and left London to return to California. This was another risk, because I had again run out of money, the book was nine months away from publication, I had no contract with any other publisher, nor had I any job. I borrowed $2,000 from a close friend, which amounted to most of her savings, packed my bags, put my manuscript in my shoulder bag, and booked a charter flight to San Francisco. Before leaving Europe, however, I went to say good-bye to my parents, and again I combined this trip with a visit to Werner Heisenberg.

At my second visit, Heisenberg received me as if we had known each other for years, and again we spent over two hours in animated conversation. Our discussion of current developments in physics this time was concerned mostly with the "bootstrap" approach to particle physics in which I had become interested in the meantime and about which I was very curious to hear Heisenberg's opinion. I shall return to this subject in the following chapter.

The other purpose of my visit, of course, was to find out what Heisenberg thought about *The Tao of Physics*. I showed the manuscript to him chapter by chapter, briefly summarizing the content of each chapter and emphasizing especially the topics related to his own work. Heisenberg was most interested in the entire manuscript and very open to hearing my ideas. I told him that I saw two basic themes running through all the theories of modern physics, which were also the two basic themes of all mystical traditions—the fundamental interrelatedness and interdependence of all phenomena and the intrinsically dynamic nature of reality. Heisenberg agreed with me as far as physics was concerned and he also told me that he was well aware of the emphasis on interconnectedness in Eastern thought. However, he had been unaware of the dynamic aspect of the Eastern world view and was intrigued when I showed him with numerous examples from my manuscript that the principal Sanskrit terms used in Hindu and Buddhist philosophy—*brahman*, *rita*, *lila*, *karma*, *samsara*, etc.—had dynamic connotations. At the end of my rather long presentation of the manuscript Heisenberg said simply: "Basically, I am in complete agreement with you."

As after our first meeting, I left Heisenberg's office in extremely high spirits. Now that this great sage of modern science had shown so much interest in my work and was so much in agreement with my results I was not afraid to take on the rest of the world. I sent Heisenberg one of the first copies of *The Tao of Physics* when it came out in November 1975, and he wrote to me right away that he was reading it and would write to me again once he had read more. This letter was to be our last communication. Werner Heisenberg died a few weeks later, on my birthday, while I was sitting on the sunny deck of my apartment in Berkeley consulting the *I Ching*. I shall always be grateful to him for writing the book that was the starting point of my search for the new paradigm and has given me continuing fascination with this subject, and for his personal support and inspiration.

2

No Foundation

GEOFFREY CHEW

The famous words of Isaac Newton, "I am standing on the shoulders of giants," are valid for every scientist. We all owe our knowledge and our inspiration to a "lineage" of creative geniuses. My own work within and beyond the field of science has been influenced by a large number of great scientists, several of whom play major roles in this story. As far as physics is concerned, my major sources of inspiration have been two outstanding men: Werner Heisenberg and Geoffrey Chew. Chew, who is now sixty, belongs to a different generation of physicists than Heisenberg, and although very well known within the physics community he is by no means as famous as the great quantum physicists. However, I have no doubt that future historians of science will judge his contributions to physics as equal to theirs. While Einstein revolutionized scientific thought with his theory of relativity, and Bohr and Heisenberg, with their interpretation of quantum mechanics, introduced changes so radical that even Einstein refused to accept them, Chew has made the third revolutionary step in twentieth-century physics. His "bootstrap" theory of particles unifies quantum mechanics and relativity theory into a theory that displays both the quantum and relativistic aspects of subatomic matter to their fullest extents and, at the same time, represents a radical break with the entire Western approach to fundamental science.

According to the bootstrap hypothesis, nature cannot be reduced to fundamental entities, like fundamental building blocks of matter, but has to be understood entirely through self-consistency. Things exist by virtue of their mutually consistent relationships, and all of physics has to follow uniquely from the requirement that its components be consistent with one another and with themselves. The mathematical framework of bootstrap physics is known as S-matrix theory. It is based on the concept of the S matrix, or "scattering matrix," which was originally proposed by Heisenberg in the 1940s and has been developed, over the past two decades, into a complex mathematical structure, ideally suited to combine the principles of quantum mechanics and relativity theory. Many physicists have contributed to this development, but Geoffrey Chew has been the unifying force and philosophical leader in S-matrix theory, much in the same way that Niels Bohr was the unifying force and philosophical leader in the development of quantum theory half a century earlier.

Over the past twenty years, Chew, together with his collaborators, has been using the bootstrap approach to develop a comprehensive theory of subatomic particles, along with a more general philosophy of nature. This bootstrap philosophy not only abandons the idea of fundamental building blocks of matter, but accepts no fundamental entities whatsoever—no fundamental constants, laws, or equations. The material universe is seen as a dynamic web of interrelated events. None of the properties of any part of this web is fundamental; they all follow from the properties of the other parts, and the overall consistency of their interrelations determines the structure of the entire web.

The fact that the bootstrap philosophy does not accept any fundamental entities makes it, in my opinion, one of the most profound systems of Western thought. At the same time, it is so foreign to our traditional scientific ways of thinking that it is pursued by only a small minority of physicists. Most physicists prefer to follow the traditional approach, which has always been bent on finding the fundamental constituents of matter. Accordingly, basic research in physics has been characterized by an ever-progressing penetration into the world of submicroscopic dimensions, down into the realms of atoms, nuclei, and subatomic particles. In this progression, the atoms, nuclei, and hadrons (i.e., the protons, neutrons, and other strongly interacting particles) were, in turn, considered to be "elementary particles." None of them, however, fulfilled that expectation. Each time, these particles turned out to be composite structures themselves, and each time physicists hoped that the next generation of constituents would finally reveal themselves as the ultimate components of matter. The most recent candidates for the basic material building blocks are the so-called quarks, hypothetical constituents of hadrons, which have not been observed so far and whose existence is made extremely doubtful by serious theoretical objections. In spite of these difficulties, most physicists still hang on to the idea of basic building blocks of matter, which is so deeply ingrained in our scientific tradition.

Bootstrap and Buddhism

When I first became aware of Chew's approach to understanding nature not as an assemblage of basic entities with certain fundamental properties, but rather as a dynamic web of interrelated events, in which no part is more fundamental than any other part, I was immediately attracted to it. At that time, I was in the midst of my study of Eastern philosophies, and I realized right away that the basic tenets of Chew's scientific philosophy stood in radical contrast to the Western scientific tradition but were in full agreement with Eastern, and especially Buddhist, thought. I immediately set out to explore the parallels between Chew's philosophy and that of Buddhism, and I summarized my results in a paper entitled "Bootstrap and Buddhism."

I argued in this paper that the contrast between "fundamentalists" and "bootstrappers" in particle physics reflects the contrast between two prevailing currents in Western and Eastern thought. The reduction of nature to fundamentals, I pointed out, is basically a Greek attitude, which arose in Greek philosophy together with the dualism between spirit and matter, whereas the view of the universe as a web of relationships is characteristic of Eastern thought. I showed how the unity and mutual interrelation of all things and events have found their clearest expression and most far-reaching elaboration in Mahayana Buddhism, and how this school of Buddhist thought is in complete harmony with bootstrap physics both in its general philosophy and in its specific picture of matter.

Before writing this paper I had heard Chew speak at several physics conferences and had met him briefly when he came to give a seminar at UC Santa Cruz, but I did not really know him. In Santa Cruz I was very impressed by his highly philosophical and thoughtful talk, but also rather intimidated. I would have loved to have a serious discussion with him, but I felt that I was far too ignorant for it and merely asked Chew a rather trivial question after the seminar. Two years later, however, after writing my paper, I was confident that my thinking had now evolved to a point where I could have a real exchange of ideas with Chew, and I sent him a copy of the paper and asked him for his comments. Chew's answer was very kind and extremely exciting to me. "Your way of describing the [bootstrap] idea," he wrote, "should make it more palatable to many and to some, perhaps, so esthetically appealing as to be irresistible."

This letter was the beginning of an association which has been a source of continuing inspiration to me and has decisively shaped my entire outlook on science. Later on Chew told me, to my great surprise, that the parallels between his bootstrap philosophy and Mahayana Buddhism had not been new to him when he received my article. In 1969, he told me, he and his family were preparing to spend a month in India, and during this preparation his son, half-humorously, pointed out the parallels between the bootstrap approach and Buddhist thought. "I was stupefied," said Chew. "I just couldn't believe it, but then my son went on and explained it to me, and it made a lot of sense." I wondered whether Chew, like so many physicists, felt threatened by having his ideas compared to those in mystical traditions. "No," he told me, "because I had already been accused of being on the mystical side. People had often commented that my approach to physics was not grounded in the same way that most physicists approached things. So it wasn't such a shock to me. It was a shock, but I quickly realized the appropriateness of the comparison."

Many years later, Chew described his encounter with Buddhist philosophy in a public lecture he gave in Boston, which was, to me, a beautiful demonstration of the depth and maturity of his thought:

> I remember very keenly my astonishment and chagrin—I think it was in 1969—when my son, who was then a senior in high school and had been studying Oriental philosophy, told me about Mahayana Buddhism. I was stunned, and there was a sense of embarrassment in discovering that my research had, somehow, become based on ideas that sounded terribly unscientific when they are associated with Buddhist teachings.
>
> Now, of course, other particle physicists, since they are working with quantum theory and relativity, are in the same position. However, most of them are reluctant to admit, even to themselves, what is happening to their discipline, which is, of course, beloved for its dedication to objectivity. But for me, the embarrassment that I felt in 1969 has gradually been replaced by a sense of awe, which is combined with a sense of gratitude that I am alive to see such a period of development.

During my visit to California in 1973, Chew invited me to give a lecture about the parallels between modern physics and Eastern mysticism at UC Berkeley, where he received me very graciously and spent most of the day with me. Since I had not made any significant contributions to theoretical particle physics for the previous couple of years and was well aware of the workings of the academic system, I knew very well that it was absolutely impossible for me to obtain a research position at the Lawrence Berkeley Laboratory, one of the most prestigious physics institutes in the world, where Chew headed the theory group. Nevertheless, I asked Chew at the end of the day whether he saw any possibility for me to come here and work with him. He told me, as I had expected, that he would not be able to get a research grant for me, but he added immediately that he would be delighted to have me here and to extend his hospitality and full access to the Lab's facilities whenever I chose to come. I was, of course, very excited and encouraged by this offer, which I accepted happily two years later.

When I wrote *The Tao of Physics*, I made the close correspondence between bootstrap physics and Buddhist philosophy its high point and finale. So, when I discussed the manuscript with Heisenberg, I was naturally very curious to hear his opinion about Chew's approach. I expected Heisenberg to be in sympathy with Chew, because in his writings he often emphasized the conception of nature as an interconnected network of events, which is also the starting point of Chew's theory. Moreover, it was Heisenberg who originally proposed the concept of the S matrix, which Chew and others developed into a powerful mathematical formalism twenty years later.

Indeed, Heisenberg told me that he was in complete agreement with the bootstrap picture of particles being dynamic patterns in an interconnected network of events. He did not believe in the quark model and even went so far as to call it nonsense. However, Heisenberg, like most physicists today, could not accept Chew's view that there should be *nothing* fundamental in one's theory, and in particular no fundamental equations. In 1958 Heisenberg had proposed just such an equation, which soon became known popularly as "Heisenberg's world formula," and he spent the rest of his life trying to derive the properties of all subatomic particles from this equation. So he was naturally very attached to the idea of a fundamental equation and unwilling to accept the bootstrap philosophy to its full, radical extent. "There is a fundamental equation," he told me, "whatever its formulation may be, from which the spectrum of elementary particles can be derived. One must not escape into the fog. Here I disagree with Chew."

Heisenberg did not succeed in deriving the spectrum of elementary particles from his equation, but Chew has recently succeeded in doing just that with his bootstrap theory. In particular, he and his collaborators have been able to derive results characteristic of quark models without any need to postulate the existence of physical quarks; to do, so to speak, quark physics without quarks.

Before that breakthrough, the bootstrap program had become severely mired in the mathematical complexities of

S-matrix theory. In the bootstrap view, every particle is related to every other particle, including itself, which makes the mathematical formalism highly nonlinear, and this nonlinearity was impenetrable until recently. In the mid-sixties, therefore, the bootstrap approach went through a crisis of faith, and the support for Chew's idea dwindled to a handful of physicists. At the same time, the quark idea gained momentum, and its adherents presented the bootstrappers with the challenge to explain the results achieved with the help of quark models.

The breakthrough in bootstrap physics was initiated in 1974 by a young Italian physicist, Gabriele Veneziano, but when I saw Heisenberg in January 1975 I was not aware of Veneziano's discovery. If I had been, I might have been able to show Heisenberg how the first outlines of a precise bootstrap theory were already emerging, out of the fog as it were.

The essence of Veneziano's discovery was the recognition that topology—a formalism well known to mathematicians but never before applied to particle physics—can be used to define categories of order in the interconnectedness of subatomic processes. With the help of topology, one can establish which interconnections are the most important and formulate a first approximation in which only those are taken into account, and then one can add the others in successive approximative steps. In other words, the mathematical complexity of the bootstrap scheme can be disentangled by incorporating topology into the S-matrix framework. When this is done, only a few special categories of ordered relationships turn out to be compatible with the well-known properties of the S matrix. These categories of order are precisely the quark patterns observed in nature. Thus, the quark structure appears as a manifestation of order and necessary consequence of self-consistency, without any need to postulate quarks as physical constituents of hadrons.

When I arrived in Berkeley in April 1975, Veneziano was visiting LBL (the Lawrence Berkeley Laboratory) and Chew and his collaborators were extremely excited about the new topological approach. For me, too, this was a very fortunate turn of events, as it gave me the opportunity to reenter active research in physics with relative ease after a lapse of three years. Nobody in Chew's research group knew anything about topology, and when I joined the group I had no research project on my hands; so I threw myself wholeheartedly into the study of topology and soon acquired some expertise in it, which made me a valuable member of the group. By the time everybody else caught up I had also reactivated my other skills and was able to participate fully in the topological bootstrap program.

Discussions with Chew

I have remained a member of Chew's research team at LBL ever since 1975 with greatly varying degrees of involvement, and this association has been extremely satisfying and enriching for me. Not only have I been very happy to be back in physics, I have had the unique privilege of a close collaboration and continual exchange of ideas with one of the truly great scientists of our time. My many interests beyond physics have kept me from doing research with Chew full time, and the University of California has never found it appropriate to support my part-time research, or to acknowledge my books and other publications as valuable contributions to the development and communication of scientific ideas. But I do not mind. Shortly after I returned to California, *The Tao of Physics* was published in the United States by Shambhala and then by Bantam Books, and has since become an international best-seller. The royalties from these editions and the fees for lectures and seminars, which I have given with increasing frequency, finally put an end to my financial difficulties, which had persisted through most of the seventies.

Over the past ten years I have seen Geoffrey Chew regularly and have spent hundreds of hours in discussion with him. The subject of our discussions was usually particle physics and, more specifically, the bootstrap theory, but we were in no way restricted by it and would often branch out quite naturally to discuss the nature of consciousness, the origin of space-time, or the nature of life. Whenever I was actively engaged in research, I would participate in all seminars and meetings of our research group, and when I was busy lecturing or writing I would see Chew at least every two or three weeks for a couple of hours of intensive discussions.

These sessions have been very useful for both of us. They have helped me enormously in keeping current with Chew's research and, more generally, with the important developments in particle physics. On the other hand, they have forced Chew to summarize the progress of his work at regular intervals, using the appropriate technical language to its full extent but concentrating on the principal developments without getting lost in unnecessary details or minor temporary difficulties. He has often told me that these discussions were a valuable aid for him in keeping his mind attentive to the grand design of the research program. Since I would enter the discussions with full knowledge of the main achievements and outstanding problems but unencumbered by the details of the day-to-day research routine, I was often able to pinpoint inconsistencies or ask for clarification in a way that would stimulate Chew and lead him to new insights. Over the years I got to know Geoff, as Chew is commonly called by his friends and colleagues, so well, and my thinking was so much influenced by his, that our interchanges would often generate a state of excitement and mental resonance that is very conducive to creative work. For me, these discussions will always belong among the high points of my scientific life.

Anybody who meets Geoff Chew will immediately find him a very kind and gentle person, and anybody who engages him in a serious discussion is bound to be impressed by the depth of his thinking. He has the habit of addressing every question or problem at the deepest possible level. Again and again I have heard him deal with questions for which I had ready-made answers as soon as I heard them, by saying slowly, after a few moments of reflection, "Well, you are asking a very important question," and then carefully mapping out the broad context of the question and advancing a tentative answer at its deepest and most significant level.

Chew is a slow, careful, highly intuitive thinker, and to watch him struggle with a problem has become a fascinating experience for me. I would often see an idea rising from the depth of his mind to the conscious level, and would watch him depict it in tentative gestures with his large, expressive hands before he would carefully and slowly formulate it in words. I have always felt that Chew has his S matrix in his bones; that he uses his body language to give these highly abstract ideas a tangible shape.

From the beginning of our discussions I had wondered

about Chew's philosophical background. I knew that Bohr's thinking was influenced by Kierkegaard and William James, that Heisenberg had studied Plato, that Schrödinger had read the Upanishads. I had always known Chew as a very philosophical person and, given the radical nature of his bootstrap philosophy, I was extremely curious about any influences of philosophy, art, or religion on his thinking. But whenever I talked to Chew I became so absorbed in our discussions of physics that it seemed a waste of time to break the flow of the discussion and ask Chew about his philosophical background. It took me many years to put that question to Chew, and when I finally did I was utterly surprised by his answer.

He told me that in his younger years he had tried to model himself after his teacher, Enrico Fermi, who was famous for his pragmatic approach to physics. "Fermi was an extreme pragmatist who was not really interested in philosophy at all," Chew explained. "He simply wanted to know the rules that would allow him to predict the results of experiments. I remember him talking about quantum mechanics and laughing scornfully at people who spent their time worrying about the interpretation of the theory, because he knew how to use those equations to make predictions. And for a long time I tried to think that I was going to behave as much as possible in the spirit of Fermi."

It was only much later, Chew told me, when he started to write and give talks, that he began to think about philosophical questions. When I asked him to tell me about people who had influenced his thinking, all the names he mentioned were those of physicists, and when I wondered in great surprise whether he had been influenced by any school of philosophy, or anything outside physics, he simply replied, "Well, I am certainly not aware of any. I can't identify anything like that."

It seems, then, that Chew is a truly original thinker who derived his revolutionary approach to physics and his profound philosophy of nature from his own experience of the world of subatomic phenomena; an experience which, of course, can only be indirect, through complicated and delicate instruments of observation and measurement, but which, for Chew, nevertheless is very real and meaningful. One of Chew's secrets may be that he immerses himself completely in his work and is capable of intense concentration for prolonged periods of time. In fact, he told me that his concentration is virtually continuous: "One aspect of the way I operate is that I almost never stop thinking about the problem of the moment. I rarely turn off, unless something is very immediate, like driving a car when it's dangerous. Then I will stop thinking, but for me continuity is crucial; I have to keep going."

Chew also told me that he very rarely reads anything outside his domain of research, and he said that he remembered an anecdote about Paul Dirac, one of the famous quantum physicists, who once replied to the question whether he had read a certain book with absolute and straightforward seriousness: "I never read. It prevents me from thinking." "Now, I *will* read things," Chew said laughingly as he recounted the anecdote, "but I have to have a very specific motivation for doing so."

One might think that Chew's continuous and intense concentration on his conceptual world would make him a rather cold and somewhat obsessed person, but just the opposite is true. He has a warm and open personality; he hardly ever appears to be tense or frustrated and will often laugh happily and spontaneously during a discussion. As long as I have known Geoff Chew, I have experienced him as being very much at peace with himself and the world. He is extremely kind and considerate and manifests in his everyday life the tolerance that he considers to be characteristic of his bootstrap philosophy. "A physicist who is able to view any number of different, partially successful models without favoritism," he wrote in one of his papers, "is automatically a bootstrapper." I have always been impressed by the harmony between Chew's science, his philosophy, and his personality, and although he considers himself a Christian and is close to the Catholic tradition, I cannot help feeling that his approach to life shows, basically, a Buddhist attitude.

Bootstrapping space-time

Since bootstrap physics is not based on any fundamental entities, the process of theoretical research differs in many ways from that of orthodox physics. In contrast to most physicists, Chew does not dream of a single decisive discovery that will establish his theory once and for all, but rather sees his challenge in constructing, slowly and patiently, an interconnected network of concepts, none of which is any more fundamental than the others. As the theory progresses, the interconnections in this network become more and more precise; the entire network comes more and more into focus, as it were.

In this process, the theory also becomes ever more exciting as more and more concepts are "bootstrapped"—that is, explained through the overall self-consistency of the conceptual web. According to Chew, this bootstrapping will include the basic principles of quantum theory, our conception of macroscopic space-time, and, eventually, even our conception of human consciousness. "Carried to its logical extreme," writes Chew, "the bootstrap conjecture implies that the existence of consciousness, along with all other aspects of nature, is necessary for self-consistency of the whole."

At present, the most exciting part of Chew's theory is the prospect of bootstrapping space-time, which appears to be feasible in the near future. In the bootstrap theory of particles, there is no continuous space-time. Physical reality is described in terms of isolated events that are causally connected but are not embedded in continuous space and time. Space-time is introduced macroscopically, in connection with the experimental apparatus, but there is no implication of a microscopic space-time continuum.

The absence of continuous space and time is, perhaps, the most radical and most difficult aspect of Chew's theory, for physicists as well as for lay people. Chew and I recently discussed the question of how our everyday experience of separate objects moving through continuous space and time can be explained by such a theory. Our conversation was triggered by a discussion of the well-known paradoxes of quantum theory.

"I think that this is one of the most puzzling aspects of physics," Chew began, "and I can only state my own point of view, which I don't think is shared by anybody else. My feeling is that the principles of quantum mechanics, as they are stated, are not satisfactory and that the pursuit of the bootstrap program is going to lead to a different statement. I think that the form of this statement will include such things as: you should not try to express the principles of quantum mechanics in an a priori accepted space-time. That is the flaw of the present situation. Quantum mechanics has something intrinsically discrete about it, whereas the idea of space-time is continuous. I believe that if you try to state the principles of quantum mechanics after having accepted space-time as an absolute truth, then you will get into difficulties. My feeling is that the bootstrap approach is going to eventually give us simultaneous explanations for space-time, quantum mechanics, and the meaning of Cartesian reality. All these will come together, somehow, but you will not be able to begin with space-time as a clear, unambiguous basis and then put these other ideas on top of it."

"Nevertheless," I argued, "it seems evident that atomic phenomena *are* embedded in space-time. You and I are embedded in space and time, and so are the atoms we consist of. Space-time is a concept that is extremely useful, so what do you mean by the statement that one should not embed atomic phenomena in space-time?"

"Well, first of all, I take it as obvious that the quantum principles render inevitable the idea that objective Cartesian reality is an approximation. You cannot have the principles of quantum mechanics and, at the same time, say that our ordinary ideas of external reality are an exact description. You can produce enough examples, showing how a system subject to quantum principles begins to exhibit classical behavior when it becomes sufficiently complex. That is something which people have repeatedly done. You can actually show how classical behavior emerges as an approximation to quantum behavior. So the classical Cartesian notion of objects and all of Newtonian physics are approximations. I don't see how they can be exact. They have to depend on the complexity of the phenomena which are being described. A high degree of complexity, of course, can end up averaging out in such a way that it produces effective simplicity. This effect makes classical physics possible."

"So you have a quantum level at which there are no solid objects and at which classical concepts do not hold; and then, as you go to higher and higher complexity, the classical concepts somehow emerge?"

"Yes."

"And you are saying, then, that space-time is such a classical concept?"

"That's right. It emerges along with the classical domain and you should not accept it at the beginning."

"And now you have also some ideas about how space-time will emerge at high complexity?"

"Right. The key notion is the idea of gentle events, and the whole idea is uniquely associated with photons."

Chew then went on to explain that photons—the particles of electromagnetism and light—have unique properties, including that of being massless, which allow them to interact with other particles in events that cause only very slight disturbances. There can be an infinite number of these "gentle events," and as they build up, they result in an approximate localization of the other particle interactions, and thus the classical notion of isolated objects emerges.

"But what about space and time?" I asked.

"Well, you see, the understanding of what a classical object is, of what an observer is, of what electromagnetism is, of what space-time is—all these are tied together. Once you have the idea of gentle photons in the picture, you can begin to recognize certain patterns of events as representing an observer looking at something. In this sense, I would say, you can hope to make a theory of objective reality. But the meaning of space-time will come at the same moment. You will not start with space-time and then try to develop a theory of objective reality."

Chew and David Bohm

It became clear to me from this conversation that Chew's plan is an extremely ambitious one. He hopes to achieve nothing less than to derive the principles of quantum mechanics (including, for example, the Heisenberg uncertainty principle), the concept of macroscopic space-time (and with it the basic formalism of relativity theory), the characteristics of observation and measurement, and the basic notions of our everyday Cartesian reality—to derive all this from the overall self-consistency of the topological bootstrap theory.

I had been vaguely aware of this program for several years, because Chew kept mentioning various aspects of it even before the bootstrapping of space-time became a concrete possibility. And whenever he talked about his grand design, I had to think of another physicist, David Bohm, who is pursuing a similarly ambitious program. I had been aware of David Bohm, who was well known as one of the most eloquent opponents of the standard, so-called Copenhagen interpretation of quantum theory, since my student days. In 1974 I met him personally at the Brockwood meeting with Krishnamurti and had my first discussions with him. I noticed quickly that Bohm, like Chew, was a deep and careful thinker and that he was involved, as Chew would be several years later, in the forbidding task of deriving the basic principles of both quantum mechanics and relativity theory from a deeper, underlying formalism. He also placed his theory in a broad philosophical context, but, unlike Chew, Bohm has been strongly influenced by a single philosopher and sage, Krishnamurti, who, over the years, became his spiritual mentor.

Bohm's starting point is the notion of "unbroken wholeness," and his aim is to explore the order he believes to be inherent in the cosmic web of relations at a deeper, "nonmanifest" level. He calls this order "implicate," or "enfolded," and describes it with the analogy of a hologram, in which each part, in some sense, contains the whole. If any part of a hologram is illuminated, the entire image will be reconstructed, although it will show less detail than the image obtained from the complete hologram. In Bohm's view the real world is structured according to the same general principles, with the whole enfolded in each of its parts.

Bohm realizes that the hologram is too static to be used as a model for the implicate order at the subatomic level. To express the essentially dynamic nature of subatomic reality he has coined the term "holomovement." In his view the holomovement is a dynamic phenomenon out of which all forms of the material universe flow. The aim of his approach is to study the order enfolded in this holomovement, not by dealing with the structure of objects, but rather with the structure of movement, thus taking into account both the unity and the dynamic nature of the universe.

Bohm's theory is still tentative, but there seems to be an intriguing kinship, even at this preliminary stage, between his theory of the implicate order and Chew's bootstrap theory. Both approaches are based on a view of the world as a dynamic web of relations; both attribute a central role to the notion of order; both use matrices to represent change and transformation, and topology to classify categories of order.

Over the years, I gradually became aware of these similarities and was very eager to arrange a meeting between Bohm and Chew, who had virtually no contact with each other, so that they could become familiar with each other's theories and discuss their similarities and differences. Several years ago, I was indeed able to facilitate such a meeting at UC Berkeley, which led to a very stimulating exchange of ideas. Since that meeting, which was followed by further discussions between Chew and Bohm, I have not been very much in touch with David Bohm and do not know to what extent his thinking was affected by Chew's. What I do know is that Geoff Chew has become quite familiar with Bohm's approach, has been influenced by it to some extent, and has come to believe, as I do, that the two approaches have so much in common that they might well merge in the future.

A network of relationships

Geoffrey Chew has had an enormous influence on my world view, my conception of science, and my way of doing research. Although I have repeatedly branched out very far from my original field of research, my mind is essentially a scientific mind, and my approach to the great variety of problems I have come to investigate has remained a scientific one, albeit within a very broad definition of science. It was Chew's influence, more than anything else, that helped me to develop such a scientific attitude in the most general sense of the term.

My continuing association and intensive discussions with Chew, together with my studies and practice of Buddhist and Taoist philosophy, have allowed me to become completely comfortable with one of the most radical aspects of the new scientific paradigm—the lack of any firm foundation. Throughout the history of Western science and philosophy, there has always been the belief that any body of knowledge had to be based on firm foundations. Accordingly, scientists and philosophers throughout the ages have used architectural metaphors to describe knowledge.* Physicists looked for the "basic building blocks" of matter and expressed their theories in terms of

* I owe this insight to my brother, Bernt Capra, who is an architect by training.

"basic" principles, "fundamental" equations, and "fundamental" constants. Whenever major scientific revolutions occurred it was felt that the foundations of science were moving. Thus Descartes wrote in his celebrated *Discourse on Method:*

> In so far as [the sciences] borrow their principles from philosophy, I considered that nothing solid could be built on such shifting foundations.

Three hundred years later, Heisenberg wrote in his *Physics and Philosophy* that the foundations of classical physics, that is, of the very edifice Descartes had built, were shifting:

> The violent reaction to the recent development of modern physics can only be understood when one realizes that here the foundations of physics have started moving; and that this motion has caused the feeling that the ground would be cut from under science.

Einstein, in his autobiography, described his feelings in terms very similar to Heisenberg's:

> It was as if the ground had been pulled out from under one, with no firm foundation to be seen anywhere, upon which one could have built.

It appears that the science of the future will no longer need any firm foundations, that the metaphor of the building will be replaced by that of the web, or network, in which no part is more fundamental than any other part. Chew's bootstrap theory is the first scientific theory in which such a "web philosophy" has been formulated explicitly, and he agreed in a recent conversation that abandoning the need for firm foundations may be the major shift and deepest change in natural science:

"I think that is true, and it is also true that because of the long tradition of Western science the bootstrap approach has not become reputable yet among scientists. It is not recognized as science precisely because of its lack of a firm foundation. The whole idea of science is, in a sense, in conflict with the bootstrap approach, because science wants questions which are clearly stated and which can have unambiguous experimental verification. Part of the bootstrap scheme, however, it that no concepts are regarded as absolute and you are always expecting to find weaknesses in your old concepts. We are constantly downgrading concepts that in the recent past would have been considered fundamental and would have been used as the language for questions.

"You see," Chew went on to explain, "when you formulate a question, you have to have some basic concepts that you are accepting in order to formulate the question. But in the bootstrap approach, where the whole system represents a network of relationships without any firm foundation, the description of our subject can be begun at a great variety of different places. There isn't any clear starting point. And the way our theory has developed in the last few years, we quite typically don't know what questions to ask. We use consistency as the guide, and each increase in the consistency suggests something that is incomplete, but it rarely takes the form of a well-defined question. We are going beyond the whole question-and-answer framework."

A methodology that does not use well-defined questions and recognizes no firm foundation of one's knowledge does indeed seem highly unscientific. What turns it into a scientific endeavor is another essential element of Chew's approach, which represents another major lesson I learned from him— recognition of the crucial role of approximation in scientific theories.

When physicists began to explore atomic phenomena at the beginning of the century, they became painfully aware of the fact that all the concepts and theories we use to describe nature are limited. Because of the essential limitations of the rational mind, we have to accept the fact that, as Heisenberg has phrased it, "every word or concept, clear as it may seem to be, has only a limited range of applicability." Scientific theories can never provide a complete and definitive description of reality. They will always be approximations to the true nature of things. To put it bluntly, scientists do not deal with truth; they deal with limited and approximate descriptions of reality.

This recognition is an essential aspect of modern science, and it is especially important in the bootstrap approach, as Chew has emphasized again and again. All natural phenomena are seen as being ultimately interconnected, and in order to explain any one of them we need to understand all the others, which is obviously impossible. What makes science so successful is the fact that approximations are possible. If one is satisfied with an approximate understanding of nature, one can describe selected groups of phenomena in this way, neglecting other phenomena which are less relevant. Thus one can explain many phenomena in terms of a few, and consequently understand different aspects of nature in an approximate way without having to understand everything at once. The application of topology to particle physics, for example, resulted in an approximation of precisely that kind, which led to the recent breakthrough in Chew's bootstrap theory.

Scientific theories, then, are approximate descriptions of natural phenomena, and according to Chew it is essential that one should always ask, as soon as a certain theory is found to work: Why does it work? What are its limits? In what way, exactly, is it an approximation? These questions are seen by Chew as the first step toward further progress, and the whole idea of progress through successive approximative steps is for him a key element of the scientific method.

The most beautiful illustration of Chew's attitude, for me, was an interview he gave to British television a few years ago. When asked what he would see as the greatest breakthrough in science in the next decade, he did not mention any grand unifying theories or exciting new discoveries, but said simply: "the acceptance of the fact that all our concepts are approximations."

This fact is probably accepted in theory by most scientists today but is ignored by many in their actual work, and it is even less known outside of science. I vividly remember an after-dinner discussion which illustrated the great difficulty most people have in accepting the approximate nature of all concepts, and which, at the same time, was for me another beautiful example of the depth of Chew's thinking. The discussion took place in the home of Arthur Young, the inventor of the Bell helicopter, who is a neighbor of mine in Berkeley, where he founded the Institute for the Study of Consciousness. We were sitting around the dinner table of our hosts—Denyse and Geoff Chew, my wife Jacqueline and I, and Ruth and Arthur Young. As the conversation turned to the notion of certainty in science, Young brought up one scientific fact after another, and Chew showed him through careful analysis how all of these "facts" were really approximate notions. Finally,

Young cried out, rather frustrated: "Look, there *are* some absolute facts. There are six people sitting around this table right now. This is absolutely true." Chew just smiled gently and looked at Denyse, who was pregnant at that time. "I don't know, Arthur," he said quietly. "Who can tell precisely where one person begins and the other ends?"

The fact that all scientific concepts and theories are approximations to the true nature of reality, valid merely for a certain range of phenomena, became evident to physicists at the beginning of the century in the dramatic discoveries that led to the formulation of quantum theory. Since that time, physicists have learned to see the evolution of scientific knowledge in terms of a sequence of theories, or "models," each more accurate and comprehensive than the previous one but none of them representing a complete and final account of natural phenomena. Chew has added a further refinement to this view that is typical of the bootstrap approach. He believes that the science of the future may well consist of a mosaic of interlocking theories and models of the bootstrap type. None of them would be any more fundamental than the others, and all of them would have to be mutually consistent. Eventually, a science of this kind would go beyond the conventional disciplinary distinctions, using whatever language becomes appropriate to describe different aspects of the multileveled, interrelated fabric of reality.

Chew's vision of a future science—an interconnected network of mutually consistent models, each of them being limited and approximate and none of them being based on firm foundations—has helped me enormously in applying the scientific method of investigation to a wide variety of phenomena. Two years after I joined Chew's research group I began to explore the new paradigm in several fields beyond physics—in psychology, health care, economics, and others. In doing so, I had to deal with a disconnected and often contradictory collection of concepts, ideas, and theories, none of which seemed developed sufficiently to provide the conceptual framework I was looking for. Very often, it was not even clear which questions I should ask to increase my understanding, and I certainly could not see any theory that seemed more fundamental than the others.

In this situation, it was natural for me to apply Chew's

approach to my work, and so I spent several years patiently integrating ideas from different disciplines into a slowly emerging conceptual framework. During this long and arduous process it was especially important to me that all the interconnections in my network of ideas were mutually consistent, and I spent many months checking the entire network, sometimes by drawing large nonlinear conceptual maps to make sure all the concepts were hanging together consistently.

I never lost confidence that a coherent framework would eventually emerge. I had learned from Chew that one can use different models to describe different aspects of reality without regarding any one of them as fundamental, and that several interlocking models can form a coherent theory. Thus the bootstrap approach became a living experience for me not only in my research in physics but also in my much broader investigation of the change in paradigms, and my ongoing discussions with Geoff Chew have been a continuing source of inspiration for my entire work.

3

The Pattern Which Connects

GREGORY BATESON

The Tao of Physics was published at the end of 1975 and was received enthusiastically in England and the United States, generating an enormous interest in the "new physics" among a wide range of people. As a consequence of this strong interest I traveled extensively, lecturing to professional and lay audiences and discussing with men and women from all walks of life the concepts of modern physics and their implications. In these discussions I was often told by people from various disciplines that a change of world view similar to the one that occurred in physics was now happening in their fields; that many of the problems they were facing in their disciplines were connected, somehow, with the limitations of the mechanistic world view.

These discussions prompted me to take a closer look at the influence of the Newtonian paradigm* on various disciplines, and in early 1977 I planned to write a book on the subject with the working title "Beyond the Mechanistic World View." The basic idea was that all our sciences—the natural sciences as well as the humanities and social sciences—were based on the mechanistic world view of Newtonian physics; that serious limitations of this world view were now becoming apparent; and that scientists in various disciplines would therefore be forced to go beyond the mechanistic world view, as we have done in physics. In fact, I saw the new physics—the conceptual framework of quantum theory, relativity theory, and especially of bootstrap physics—as the ideal model for new concepts and approaches in other disciplines.

This thinking contained a major flaw, which I realized only gradually and which took me a long time to overcome. By presenting the new physics as a model for a new medicine, new psychology, or new social science, I had fallen into the very Cartesian trap that I wanted scientists to avoid. Descartes, I would learn later, used the metaphor of a tree to present human knowledge, its roots being metaphysics, the trunk physics, and the branches all the other sciences. Without knowing it, I had adopted this Cartesian metaphor as the guiding principle for my investigation. The trunk of my tree was no longer Newtonian physics, but I still saw physics as the model for the other sciences and hence physical phenomena, somehow, as the primary reality and basis for everything else. I did not think so explicitly, but these ideas were implicit when I advocated the new physics as a model for other sciences.

Over the years I experienced a profound change of perception and thought in this respect, and in the book that I finally wrote, *The Turning Point*, I no longer presented the new physics as a model for other sciences but rather as an important special case of a much more general framework, the framework of systems theory.

The important change in my thought from "physics thinking" to systems thinking occurred gradually and as a result of many influences, but more than anything else it was the influ-

---

* *It was only later that I appreciated the pivotal role of Descartes in the development of the mechanistic world view and hence adopted the term "Cartesian paradigm."*

ence of one individual, Gregory Bateson, that changed my perspective. Shortly after we met, Bateson said jokingly to a common friend: "Capra? The man is crazy! He thinks we are all electrons." This comment gave me the initial jolt and my subsequent contacts with Bateson over two years changed my thinking in profound ways and provided me with the key elements of a radically new view of nature, which I came to call "the systems view of life."

Gregory Bateson will be regarded as one of the most influential thinkers of our time by future historians. The uniqueness of his thought came from its broad range and its generality. In an age characterized by fragmentation and overspecialization, Bateson challenged the basic assumptions and methods of several sciences by looking for patterns behind patterns and for processes beneath structures. He declared that relationship should be the basis of all definition and his main aim was to discover the principles of organization in all the phenomena he observed, "the pattern which connects," as he would put it.

Conversations with Bateson

I met Gregory Bateson in the summer of 1976 in Boulder, Colorado, where I was giving a course at a Buddhist summer school when he came to give a lecture. This lecture was my first contact with Bateson's ideas; I had heard quite a lot about him before—he had become a sort of cult figure at UC Santa Cruz—but I had never read his book, *Steps to an Ecology of Mind.* During the lecture I was extremely impressed by Bateson's vision and his uniquely personal style; but most of all I was amazed by the fact that his central message—the shift from objects to relationships—was virtually identical with the conclusions I had drawn from the theories of modern physics. I spoke to him briefly after the lecture, but I would not really get to know him until two years later, during the last two years of his life, which he spent at the Esalen Institute on the Big Sur coast. I went there quite frequently to give seminars and to visit people in the Esalen community who had become my friends.

Bateson was a very imposing figure: a giant intellectually

and also physically; very tall and very big, very imposing at all levels. For many people he was quite intimidating, and I, too, was somewhat overawed by Bateson, especially at the beginning. I found it very difficult to just engage in casual conversation with him; I always felt that I had to prove myself, to say something intelligent or ask some intelligent question, and it was only very slowly that I could have some small talk with him. Even then, that did not happen too often.

It also took me quite a while to call Bateson "Gregory." In fact, I don't think I would have ever called him by his first name had he not lived at Esalen, which is an extremely informal place. Even there it took me quite a while and, actually, Bateson himself seemed to have a hard time calling himself Gregory. He usually referred to himself as Bateson. He liked to be called Bateson, maybe because of his upbringing in British academic circles, where this is customary.

When I got to know Bateson in 1978, I knew he did not care too much about physics. Bateson's main interest, his intellectual curiosity, and the strong passion he brought to his science were concerned with living matter, with "living things," as he would say. In *Mind and Nature* he wrote:

> In my life I have put the descriptions of sticks and stones and billiard balls and galaxies in one box . . . and have left them alone. In the other box, I put living things: crabs, people, problems of beauty . . .

This "other box" is what Bateson studied; this is where his passion was. So, when he met me he knew that I came from the discipline that studied those sticks and stones and billiard balls, and he had a kind of intuitive mistrust of physicists, I think. Bateson's lack of interest in physics could also be seen from the fact that he was prone to making errors of the kind nonphysicists often make when they talk about physics; confusion between "matter" and "mass" and similar errors.

So when I met Bateson I knew that he had a prejudice against physics, and I was very eager to show him that the kind of physics I was engaged in was, in fact, extremely close to his own thinking. I had an excellent opportunity to do so shortly after I met him, when I gave a one-day seminar at Esalen to which he came. With Bateson in my audience I felt very inspired, although I don't think he said anything during the whole day. I tried to present the basic concepts of twentieth-century physics, without distorting them in any way, in such a manner that the close kinship with Bateson's thinking was obvious. I must have managed pretty well because I heard afterward that Bateson was very impressed by my seminar. "What a bright boy!" he said to a friend.

After that day I always felt that Bateson respected my work; more than that, I felt he began to genuinely like me and to develop a certain fatherly affection for me.

During these last two years of his life I had many very animated conversations with Gregory Bateson: in the dining lodge of the Esalen Institute, on the terrace of his house overlooking the ocean, and in other places on this beautiful mesa on the Big Sur coast. He gave me the manuscript of *Mind and Nature* to read, and I vividly remember sitting for hours in the grass high above the Pacific Ocean on a clear, sunny day, hearing the waves break as they rolled in regular rhythms, being visited by beetles and spiders, while reading Bateson's manuscript:

> What pattern connects the crab to the lobster and the orchid
> to the primrose and all four of them to me? And me to you?

When I came to Esalen to give seminars, I would often meet Bateson in the dining lodge, and he would beam at me: "Hello, Fritjof; did you come to do a show?" After the meal he would ask: "Coffee?" and bring coffee for both of us, and we would continue our conversation.

My conversations with Gregory Bateson were of a very special kind, owing to the special way in which he himself presented his ideas. He would lay out a network of ideas in the form of stories, anecdotes, jokes, and seemingly scattered observations, without spelling anything out in full. Bateson did not like to spell out things in full, knowing, perhaps, that a better understanding is reached when you are able to grasp the connections yourself, in a creative act, without being told. He would spell out things minimally, and I remember very well the gleam in his eye and the pleasure in his voice when he saw that I was able to follow him through this web of ideas. I was by no means able to follow him all the way through, but maybe a little further, every now and then, than other people, and that gave him great pleasure.

In this way, Bateson would lay out his web of ideas and I would check certain nodes in this network against my own understanding with brief remarks and quick questions. He would be especially pleased when I was able to jump ahead of him and skip a link or two in the network. His eyes would light up on those rare occasions indicating that our minds resonated.

I have tried to reconstruct a typical conversation of that kind from my memory.* One day we were sitting on the deck outside the Esalen lodge and Bateson was talking about logic. "Logic is a very elegant tool," he said, "and we've got a lot of mileage out of it for two thousand years or so. The trouble is, you know, when you apply it to crabs and porpoises, and butterflies and habit formation"—his voice trailed off, and he added after a pause, looking out over the ocean—"you know, to all those pretty things"—and now, looking straight at me—"logic won't quite do."

"No?"

"It won't do," he continued animatedly, "because that whole fabric of living things is not put together by logic. You see, when you get circular trains of causation, as you always do in the living world, the use of logic will make you walk into paradoxes. Just take the thermostat, a simple sense organ, yes?"

He looked at me, questioning whether I followed and, seeing that I did, he continued.

"If it's on, it's off; if it's off, it's on. If yes, then no; if no, then yes."

With that he stopped to let me puzzle about what he had said. His last sentence reminded me of the classical paradoxes of Aristotelian logic, which was, of course, intended. So I risked a jump.

"You mean, do thermostats lie?"

Bateson's eyes lit up: "Yes-no-yes-no-yes-no. You see, the cybernetic equivalent of logic is oscillation."

He stopped again, and at that moment I suddenly had an insight, making a connection to something I had been interested in for a long time. I got very excited and said with a provocative smile:

"Heraclitus knew that!"

"Heraclitus knew that," Bateson repeated, answering my smile with one of his.

* The ideas touched upon in this conversation are spelled out in greater detail below.

"And so did Lao Tzu," I pushed on.

"Yes, indeed; and so do the trees over there. Logic won't do for them."

"So what do they use instead?"

"Metaphor."

"Metaphor?"

"Yes, metaphor. That's how this whole fabric of mental interconnections holds together. Metaphor is right at the bottom of being alive."

Stories

Bateson's way of presenting his ideas was an essential and intrinsic part of his teaching. Because of his special technique of blending his ideas with the style of presentation, very few people understood him. In fact, as R. D. Laing pointed out at a seminar he gave at Esalen in honor of Bateson: "Even the few people who *thought* they understood him, *he* did not think understood him. Very, very few people, he thought, understood him."

This lack of understanding also applied to Bateson's jokes. He was not only inspiring and enlightening; he was also wonderfully entertaining, but his jokes, again, were of a special kind. He had a very keen English sense of humor, and when he was joking he would only spell out 20 percent of the joke and you were supposed to guess the rest; sometimes he would even tone it down to 5 percent. As a consequence, many of the jokes Bateson made in his seminars were met with complete silence, punctuated only by his own chuckle.

Shortly after I met Bateson he told me a joke of which he was very fond, a joke which he told many times to many audiences. I think that this joke can serve as a key to understanding Bateson's thinking and his way of presenting ideas. Here is how he would tell it:

There was a man who had a powerful computer, and he wanted to know whether computers could ever think. So he asked it, no doubt in his best Fortran: "Will you ever be able to think like a human being?" The computer clicked and rattled and blinked, and finally it printed out its answer on a piece of paper, as these machines do. The man ran to pick up the printout, and there, neatly typed, read the following words: "THAT REMINDS ME OF A STORY."

Bateson considered stories, parables, and metaphors to be essential expressions of human thinking, of the human mind. Although he was a very abstract thinker, he would never deal with any idea in a purely abstract way but would always present it concretely by telling a story.

The important role of stories, in Bateson's thinking, is intimately connected with the importance of relationships. If I had to describe Bateson's message in one word, it would be "relationships"; that was what he always talked about. A central aspect of the emerging new paradigm, perhaps *the* central aspect, is the shift from objects to relationships. According to Bateson, relationship should be the basis of all definition; biological form is put together of relations and not of parts, and this is also how people think; in fact, he would say, it is the only way in which we can think.

Bateson often emphasized that in order to describe nature accurately one should try to speak nature's language. Once he illustrated this rather dramatically by asking: "How many fingers do you have on your hand?" After a puzzled pause several people said timidly, "Five," and Bateson shouted, "No!"; then some tried four and again he said no. Finally, when everybody gave up, he said: "No! The correct answer is you should not ask such a question; it is a stupid question. That is the answer a plant would give you, because in the world of plants, and of living beings in general, there are no such things as fingers; there are only relationships."

Since relationships are the essence of the living world one would do best, Bateson maintained, if one spoke a language of relationships to describe it. This is what stories do. Stories, Bateson would say, are the royal road to the study of relationships. What is important in a story, what is true in it, is not the plot, the things, or the people in the story, but the relationships between them. Bateson defined a story as "an aggregate of formal relations scattered in time," and this is what he was after in all his seminars, to develop a web of formal relations through a collection of stories.

So Bateson's favorite method was to present his ideas in terms of stories, and he loved to tell stories. He would approach his subject from all kinds of angles, spinning out time after time variations on the same theme. He would touch on this and touch on that, making jokes in between, switching from the description of a plant to that of a Balinese dance, to the play of dolphins, to the difference between Egyptian and Judeo-Christian religion, to a dialogue with a schizophrenic, and on and on. This style of communication was highly entertaining and fascinating to watch, but it was very difficult to follow. To the uninitiated, to somebody who could not follow the complex patterns, Bateson's style of presentation often sounded like pure rambling, but it was much more than that. The matrix of his collection of stories was a coherent and precise pattern of relationships, a pattern which for him embodied great beauty. The more complex the pattern became, the more beauty it exhibited. "The world gets much prettier as it gets more complicated," he would say.

Bateson was very taken by the beauty manifest in the complexity of patterned relationships, and he derived a strong esthetic pleasure from describing these patterns. In fact, that pleasure was often so strong that he would get carried away. He would tell a story and while telling it would be reminded of another link in the pattern, which led him into another story. Thus he would end up presenting a system of stories within stories involving subtle relationships, laced with jokes that further elaborated these relationships.

Bateson could also be very theatrical, and it was not without reason that he jokingly referred to his Esalen seminars as "shows." And so it would often happen that he got so carried away by the poetic beauty of the complex patterns he was describing, by making all kinds of jokes and stringing together anecdotes, that in the end he did not have enough time left to pull everything together. When the threads he had spun during a seminar would not come together to form the whole web in the end, it was not because they did not connect, or because Bateson was unable to bring them together; it was simply because he got so carried away that he ran out of time. Or he would get bored after speaking for an hour or two and would think that the connections he had shown were so obvious that everybody should be able to pull them together into an integrated whole without his further help. At those times he would simply say: "I guess that's it—time for questions," whereupon he would generally refuse to give straight answers to the questions asked but would reply with yet another collection of stories.

"What it's all about"

One of the central ideas in Bateson's thought is that the structure of nature and the structure of mind are reflections of each other, that mind and nature are of a necessary unity. Thus epistemology—"the study of how it is that you can know something," or, as he sometimes put it, "what it's all about"—ceased to be abstract philosophy for Bateson and became a branch of natural history.*

One of Bateson's main aims in his study of epistemology was to point out that logic was unsuitable for the description of biological patterns. Logic can be used in very elegant ways to describe linear systems of cause and effect, but when causal sequences become circular, as they do in the living world, their description in terms of logic will generate paradoxes. This is true even for nonliving systems involving feedback mechanisms, and Bateson often used the thermostat as an illustration of his point.

When the temperature drops, the thermostat switches on the heating system; this causes the temperature to rise, which causes the thermostat to switch off the heating system, thereby causing the temperature to drop, and so on. The application of logic will turn the description of this mechanism into a paradox: if the room is too cold, then the heater will come on; if the heater is on, then the room will get too hot; if the room gets too hot, then the heater will be turned off, etc. In other words, if the switch is on, then it is off; if it is off, then it is on. This, Bateson says, is because logic is timeless, whereas causality involves time. If time is introduced, the paradox turns into an oscillation. Similarly, if you program a computer to solve one of the classical paradoxes of Aristotelian logic—e.g., a Greek says: "Greeks always lie." Does he tell the truth?—the computer will give the answer YES-NO-YES-NO-YES-NO . . . turning the paradox into an oscillation.

I remember being very impressed when Bateson presented this insight to me, because it further illuminated something I had often noticed myself. Philosophical traditions which have

---

* Bateson often preferred to use the term "natural history," rather than "biology," probably in order to avoid associations with the mechanistic biology of our time.

a dynamic view of reality, a view containing the notions of time, change, and fluctuation as essential elements, tend to emphasize paradoxes. They will often use these paradoxes as a teaching tool to make students aware of the dynamic nature of reality, in which the paradoxes dissolve into oscillations. Lao Tzu in the East and Heraclitus in the West are, perhaps, the best known examples of philosophers who made extensive use of this method.

In his study of epistemology, Bateson emphasized again and again the fundamental role of metaphor in the living world. To illustrate this point he would often write down on the blackboard the following two syllogisms.

Men die.	Men die.
Socrates is a man.	Grass dies.
Socrates will die.	Men are grass.

The first of these syllogisms is known as the Socrates syllogism; the second I will call the Bateson syllogism.* The Bateson syllogism is not valid in the world of logic; its validity is of a very different nature. It is a metaphor and is found in the language of poets.

Bateson pointed out that the first syllogism is concerned with a type of classification that establishes class membership by identification of subjects ("Socrates is a man"), whereas the second syllogism does so by identifying predicates ("Men die—Grass dies"). In other words, the Socrates syllogism identifies items, the Bateson syllogism identifies patterns. And this is why metaphor, according to Bateson, is the language of nature. Metaphor expresses structural similarity or, better still, similarity of organization, and metaphor in this sense was the central concern of Bateson's work. Whatever field he worked in, he would look for nature's metaphors, for "the pattern which connects."

Metaphor, then, is the logic upon which the entire living world is built, and since it is also the language of poets Bateson was very fond of mixing his factual statements with poetry. In one of his Esalen seminars, for example, he quoted from mem-

---

* A critic once remarked that this syllogism was not logically sound, but that this was the way Bateson thought. Bateson agreed and was very proud of this observation.

ory, almost exactly, these beautiful lines from William Blake's "Marriage of Heaven and Hell":*

> Dualistic religions hold that man has two real existing principles, a body and a soul; that energy is alone from the body, while reason is alone from the soul; and that God will torment man in eternity for following his energies. The truth is that man has no body distinct from his soul, the so-called body being a portion of soul discerned by the five senses; that energy is the only life and is from the body; that reason is the outward bound or circumference of energy; and that energy is eternal delight.

Although Bateson sometimes liked to present his ideas in poetic form, his way of thinking was that of a scientist and he always emphasized that he was working inside of science. He clearly saw himself as an intellectual—"My job is thinking," he would say—but he also had a very strong intuitive side, which was manifest in the way he observed nature. He had a unique ability to glean things from nature by very intense observation. This was not just ordinary scientific observation. Bateson was able, somehow, to observe a plant or animal with his whole being, with empathy and with passion. And when he talked about it he would describe that plant in minute and loving detail, using what he considered to be the plant's own language to talk about the general principles he had derived from his direct contact with nature.

Bateson thought of himself primarily as a biologist, and he considered the many other fields he was involved in—anthropology, epistemology, psychiatry, and others—as branches of biol-

---

* Blake's original reads as follows:

> All Bibles or sacred codes have been the causes of the following Errors.
> 1. That Man has two real existing principles Viz: a Body & a Soul.
> 2. That Energy, called Evil, is alone from the Body, & that Reason, called Good, is alone from the Soul.
> 3. That God will torment Man in Eternity for following his Energies.
> But the following Contraries to these are True:
> 1. Man has no Body distinct from his Soul for that called Body is a portion of Soul discerned by the five Senses, the chief inlets of Soul in this age.
> 2. Energy is the only life and is from the Body and Reason is the bound or outward circumference of Energy.
> 3. Energy is Eternal Delight.

ogy. However, he did not mean this in a reductionist sense; his biology was not mechanistic. His field of study was the world of "living things" and his aim was to discover the principles of organization in this world.

Matter, for Bateson, was always organized—"I know nothing about unorganized matter, if there be any," he wrote in *Mind and Nature*—and its patterns of organization became more and more beautiful to him as their complexity increased. Bateson would always insist that he was a monist, that he was developing a scientific description of the world which did not split the universe dualistically into mind and matter, or into any other separate realities. He often pointed out that Judeo-Christian religion, while boasting of monism, was essentially dualistic because it separated God from His creation. Similarly, he insisted that he had to exclude all other supernatural explanations because they would destroy the monistic structure of his science.

This does not mean that Bateson was a materialist. On the contrary, his world view was deeply spiritual, infused with the kind of spirituality that is the very essence of ecological awareness. Accordingly, he took very strong positions on ethical questions, being especially alarmed by the arms race and the destruction of the environment.

A new concept of mind

Bateson's most outstanding contributions to scientific thought, in my view, were his ideas about the nature of mind. He developed a radically new concept of mind, which represents for me the first successful attempt to really overcome the Cartesian split that has caused so many problems in Western thought and culture.

Bateson proposed to define mind as a systems phenomenon characteristic of "living things." He listed a set of criteria that systems have to satisfy for mind to occur. Any system that satisfies these criteria will be able to process information and develop the phenomena we associate with mind—thinking, learning, memory, etc. In Bateson's view, mind is a necessary and inevitable consequence of a certain complexity which begins long before organisms develop a brain and a higher nervous system. He also emphasized that mental characteristics were manifest not only in individual organisms but also in social systems and ecosystems, that mind was immanent not only in the body but also in the pathways and messages outside the body.

Mind without a nervous system? Mind being manifest in all systems that satisfied certain criteria? Mind immanent in pathways and messages outside the body? These ideas were so new to me, at first, that I could not make any sense of them. Bateson's notion of mind did not seem to have anything to do with the things I associated with the word "mind," and it took several years for this radical new idea to seep into my consciousness and permeate my awareness and my world view at all levels. The more I was able to integrate Bateson's concept of mind into my world view, the more liberating and exhilarating it became for me, and the more I realized its tremendous implications for the future of scientific thought.

My first breakthrough in understanding Bateson's notion of mind came when I studied Ilya Prigogine's theory of self-organizing systems. According to Prigogine, physicist, chemist, and Nobel laureate, the patterns of organization characteristic of living systems can be summarized in terms of a single dynamic principle, the principle of self-organization. A living organism is a self-organizing system, which means that its order is not imposed by the environment but is established by the system itself. In other words, self-organizing systems exhibit a certain degree of autonomy. This does not mean that they are isolated from their environment; on the contrary, they interact with it continually, but this interaction does not determine their organization; they are self-organizing.

Over the last fifteen years, a theory of self-organizing systems has been developed in considerable detail by a number of researchers from various disciplines under the leadership of Prigogine. My understanding of this theory was helped enormously by extensive discussions with Erich Jantsch, a systems theorist who was one of Prigogine's principal disciples and interpreters. Jantsch lived in Berkeley, where he died in 1980, the same year that Bateson died, at the age of fifty-two. His book *The Self-Organizing Universe* was one of my main sources in my study of living systems, and I vividly remember our long and intensive discussions, which also gave me special pleasure because they were held in German, Jantsch being Austrian like myself.

It was Erich Jantsch who pointed out to me the connection between Prigogine's concept of self-organization and Bateson's concept of mind. Indeed, when I compared Prigogine's criteria for self-organizing systems to Bateson's criteria of mental process, I found that the two sets of criteria were very similar; in fact, they seemed close to being identical. I realized immediately that this meant that mind and self-organization were merely different aspects of one and the same phenomenon, the phenomenon of life.

I was extremely excited by this insight, which meant for me not only my first real understanding of Bateson's concept of mind but also an entirely new perspective on the phenomenon of life. I could not wait to see Bateson again, and I took the first opportunity to visit him and try out my new understanding on him. "Look, Gregory," I said as we sat down for a cup of coffee, "your criteria for mind seem identical to me to the criteria for life." Without any hesitation he looked straight into my eyes and said: "You're right. Mind is the essence of being alive."

From that moment on my understanding of the relationship between mind and life, or mind and nature, as Bateson would put it, continued to deepen, and with it came an increased appreciation of the richness and beauty of Bateson's thought. I realized fully why it was impossible for him to separate mind and matter. When Bateson looked at the living world, he saw its principles of organization as being essentially mental, with mind being immanent in matter at all levels of life. He thus arrived at a unique synthesis of notions of mind with notions of matter; a synthesis that was, as he liked to point out, neither mechanical nor supernatural.

Bateson distinguished clearly between mind and consciousness, and he made it clear that consciousness was not, or not yet, included in his concept of mind. I often tried to coax him into making some statement about the nature of consciousness, but he would always refuse to do so, saying only that this was the great untouched question, the next big challenge. The nature of consciousness and the nature of a science of consciousness—if there could indeed be such a science—would become central themes in my discussions with R. D. Laing. It was only through these discussions, which took place several months after Bateson's death, that I came to understand why Bateson so adamantly refused to make rash statements about the nature of consciousness. And later still, when Laing gave his Bateson seminar at Esalen, I was not surprised at the passage he had chosen to read from *Mind and Nature:*

> Everybody keeps wanting me to rush in. It is monstrous— vulgar, reductionist, sacrilegious—call it what you will—to rush in with an oversimplified question. It is a sin against . . . aesthetics and against consciousness and against the sacred.

Discussions with Robert Livingston

During the spring and summer of 1980, the outlines of my chapter "The Systems View of Life," which was to become the core of my presentation of the new paradigm in *The Turning Point,* slowly emerged. To sketch the outlines of a new framework that might serve as a basis for biology, psychology, health care, economics, and other fields of study was a tremendous task, and it would have overwhelmed me had I not been fortunate to receive help from several outstanding scientists.

One who patiently watched my knowledge and self-confidence grow and who helped me along with advice and stimulating discussions at every turn was Robert Livingston, professor of neuroscience at UC San Diego. It was Bob Livingston who challenged me to incorporate Prigogine's theory into my conceptual framework and it was he, more than anybody else, who helped me explore the multiple aspects of the new systems biology. Our first long discussion took place in a small boat in the Yacht Harbor at La Jolla, where we sat for hours swaying with the waves and discussing the differences between machines and living organisms. Later I would alternate between discussions with Livingston and with Jantsch, measuring the increase of my understanding against their knowledge, and it was Bob Livingston again who was of tremendous help in my struggle to integrate Bateson's concept of mind into the framework I was developing.

Bateson's legacy

The integration of ideas from different disciplines at the leading edge of science into a coherent conceptual framework was a long and laborious endeavor. Whenever questions arose that I could not answer myself I would contact experts in the relevant fields, but sometimes I would encounter questions that I could not even associate with any particular discipline or school of thought. In those cases I would often make a note in the margin of my manuscript, "Ask Bateson!", and I would bring up the subject with Bateson at my next visit.

Unfortunately, some of these questions are still unanswered. Gregory Bateson died in July 1980 before I could show him any part of my final manuscript. I wrote the first few paragraphs of "The Systems View of Life," which he had so strongly influenced, on the day after Bateson's funeral at the place where his ashes had been scattered, the cliffs where the Esalen River joins the Pacific Ocean, a sacred burial ground to the Indian tribe that gave the Esalen Institute its name.

It is strange that I got closest to Bateson during the week before he died, although I did not even see him during that week. I was working very intensely on my notes about his concept of mind and, in doing so, I not only absorbed his ideas but also heard his characteristic voice and felt his presence. Sometimes I felt as if Bateson was peering over my shoulder to watch what I was writing, and I found myself engaged in a very intimate dialogue with him, much more intimate than any of our actual conversations.

I knew at that time that Bateson was ill and in the hospital, but I did not realize how serious his condition was. However, one night during this intense period of work I dreamed that he had died. I was so upset by that dream that I called Christina Grof at Esalen the next day, and she told me that Bateson had indeed died the day before.

The funeral ceremony for Gregory Bateson was one of the most beautiful ceremonies I have ever witnessed. A large group of people—the Bateson family, friends, and members of the Esalen community—sat in a circle on a lawn above the ocean, with a little altar in the center of the circle carrying Bateson's ashes, his picture, incense, and loads of fresh flowers. During the ceremony playing children, dogs, birds, and other animals filled the air with noise against the background of the ocean waves, as if to remind us of the oneness of all life. The ceremony progressed seemingly without any plan or schedule. Nobody seemed to direct it and, somehow, everybody knew what to contribute—a self-organizing system. There was a Benedictine monk from a nearby hermitage, which Bateson had often visited, who offered prayers; Zen monks from the San Francisco Zen Center who chanted and performed various rituals; people who sang and played music; others who recited poetry; and others still who spoke about their relationships with Bateson.

When it was my turn I spoke briefly about Bateson's concept of mind. I expressed my belief that it would have a strong impact on future scientific thinking, and I added that it could also help us, at that very moment, to cope with Bateson's death. "Part of his mind," I said, "has certainly disappeared with his body, but a large part is still around and will be around for a long time. It is the part that participates in our relationships with each other and with the environment; relationships which have been profoundly influenced by Gregory's personality. As you know, one of Gregory's favorite phrases was 'the pattern which connects.' I believe that Gregory himself has become such a pattern. He will continue to connect us with each other and with the cosmos, and in this way he will live on in each of us and in the cosmos. I feel that if any of us next week walked into each other's houses, we would not feel like total strangers. There would be a pattern which connects—Gregory Bateson."

Two months later I was traveling in Spain on my way to an international conference near Saragossa. I had to change trains in Aranjuez, a town whose name held magic for me because of the music it had inspired, and since I had some time I left the train station and went for a walk. It was early in the morning but getting hot already, and I ended up in a small marketplace where merchants were just beginning to fill their stands with fruits and vegetables for their first customers.

I sat down at a table in the shade near a kiosk where I bought myself an espresso and a copy of *El Pais*, the Spanish national newspaper. As I was sitting there watching the merchants and their customers, I reflected on the fact that I was a complete stranger in this environment. I did not even know exactly where in Spain I was; I could not understand any of the conversations I heard; I could hardly tell the age I lived in from what I observed, the activities around me being part of a traditional market scene that must have taken place more or less like this for hundreds of years. I enjoyed this reverie as I leafed through my newspaper, which I could not read too well either, having bought it in an attempt at inconspicuousness rather than for actual information.

But when I came to the center pages of the paper the whole world changed for me. Across the top, in large black letters, a message was written that I understood immediately: GREGORY BATESON (1904–1980). It was a long eulogy and review of Bateson's work, and looking at it I suddenly no longer felt like a foreigner. The small marketplace, Aranjuez, Spain, the Whole Earth—all that was my home. I felt a deep sense of belonging—physically, emotionally, and intellectually—and with it a direct realization of the ideal I had expressed several weeks before: Gregory Bateson—the pattern which connects.

4

Swimming in the Same Ocean

STANISLAV GROF and R. D. LAING

When I decided to write a book about the limitations of the mechanistic world view and the emergence of a new paradigm in various fields, it was clear to me that I could not undertake this enterprise all by myself. It would have been impossible for me to evaluate the voluminous literature of even one discipline other than my own in order to find out where major changes were occurring and where significant new ideas were emerging, let alone attempt this in several disciplines. From the very beginning, therefore, I saw my book as the result of some kind of collaborative effort.

At first, I planned it as a multi-author book, modeled after a seminar, "Beyond the Mechanistic World View," that I had given at UC Berkeley in the spring quarter of 1976 and to which I had invited several guest lecturers. But then I changed my mind and decided to write the entire book myself with the help of a group of advisers who would write background papers for me in their fields of expertise, suggest the literature I should read, and help me when conceptual problems would arise during the writing of the book. I chose to concentrate on four disciplines—biology, medicine, psychology, and economics—and in early 1977 I began to look for advisers in those fields.

At that time, my life and style of working were very much influenced by Taoist philosophy. I sought to heighten my intuitive awareness and to recognize "the patterns of the Tao"; I was practicing the art of *wu-wei*, that is, of not working "against the grain of things," of waiting for the right moment without forcing anything unduly. Castaneda's metaphor of the cubic centimeter of chance that pops out from time to time and is picked up by the "warrior" who leads a disciplined life and has sharpened his intuition was ever present in my mind.

When I started to look for advisers I did not undertake a systematic search, or anything like it, but saw this task as being part of my Taoist practice. I knew that all I had to do was remain alert and focused on my purpose, and sooner or later the right people would cross my path. I knew whom I was looking for: people who had sound and comprehensive knowledge of their areas of expertise; who were deep thinkers and shared my holistic vision; who had made significant contributions to their fields of study but had broken out of the narrow confines of academic disciplines; people who, like myself, were rebels and innovators.

This Taoist way of choosing my advisers worked beautifully. Over the next three years I met many outstanding men and women who made a deep impact on my thinking and helped me enormously in putting my book together, and four of them agreed to work with me as my special advisers in the way I had envisioned. As I explored the conceptual shifts in various fields and discovered fascinating connections and relationships between them, I did it much more through discussions with people than through reading books. In fact, I developed an acute intuitive sense for recognizing people who were exploring these new ways of thinking, sometimes merely from a casual comment or a question raised in a seminar. As I got to know them and engaged them in intensive discussions, I also developed a knack for drawing them out and stimulating them to go further than they had before in their formulation of new ideas.

Those years were extremely rich in intellectual adventures and expanded my knowledge tremendously. The greatest expansion, perhaps, occurred in my understanding of psychology, a discipline about which I knew very little and which became for me a fascinating field of learning, experience, and personal growth. During the sixties and early seventies I had been engaged in prolonged explorations of multiple levels of consciousness, but the framework for these explorations was that of Eastern spiritual traditions. I had learned from Alan Watts that these traditions, and especially Buddhism, could be seen as the Eastern equivalent to Western psychotherapy, and I had also expressed this view in *The Tao of Physics*. However, I had done so without really knowing psychotherapy. I had read only one essay by Freud and, perhaps, two or three by Jung, who appealed to me because he was very much in accord with the values of the counterculture. As far as the field of psychiatry was concerned, it was completely foreign to me. I had only had some glimpses of psychotic states through discussions of psychedelic drugs during the sixties and, in some way, through the intense performances of experimental theater that I attended with great enthusiasm during my four years in London.

Paradoxically, psychologists and psychotherapists soon became my keenest and most enthusiastic professional audiences when I traveled around the country lecturing about *The Tao of Physics*, in spite of my ignorance of their fields. Naturally, I had numerous discussions with them that went far beyond physics and Eastern philosophy, with Jung's work very often being the point of departure, and thus my knowledge of psychology increased and deepened gradually over the years. These discussions, however, were only the prelude to my exchanges with two extraordinary men who would continually challenge my mind and push my thinking to its limits; two men to whom I owe most of my insights into the multiple realms of human consciousness—Stanislav Grof and R. D. Laing.

Grof and Laing are both psychiatrists, trained in the psychoanalytic tradition, and they are both brilliant and original thinkers who have far transcended the Freudian framework and have radically changed the conceptual boundaries of their discipline. Both share a deep interest in Eastern spirituality and a fascination with "transpersonal" levels of consciousness, and both have great respect for each other's work. Beyond these similarities, however, they are totally different, even diametrically opposed, personalities.

Grof is a large, heavily built, serene person; Laing is small and gaunt, with a lively and expressive body language reflecting a rich repertoire of changing moods. Grof's demeanor inspires confidence, Laing's often intimidates people. Grof tends to be diplomatic and engaging, Laing uninhibited and combative; Grof calm and serious, Laing capricious and full of sarcastic humor. At our first meeting I felt immediately comfortable with Grof. By contrast, I had great difficulty, at first, in understanding Laing, who comes from Glasgow and has never lost his Scottish brogue, and although he fascinated me immediately, it took me a long time to feel at ease with him.

Over the next four years, my intensive alternating interactions with these two outstanding and dramatically differing personalities would broaden my entire conceptual framework and would deeply affect my consciousness.

The politics of experience

My first contact with R. D. Laing's work was in the summer of 1976 at the Naropa Institute in Boulder, Colorado, the Buddhist summer school where I also met Gregory Bateson. During that summer I spent six weeks at Naropa teaching a course about *The Tao of Physics*, and while doing so I attended two other courses: a poetry workshop given by Allen Ginsberg and a course on "madness and culture" taught by Steve Krugman, a psychologist and social worker from Boston. Laing's classic text, *The Divided Self*, was part of the reading assignment for Krugman's class, and through reading selected parts of this book and attending the lectures I became familiar with the basic ideas of Laing's work.

Before that, I really had no understanding of what was meant by psychosis or schizophrenia, nor did I know the difference between psychiatry and psychotherapy. However, I did know who R. D. Laing was. His *Politics of Experience* had become a cult book in the sixties and, although I had not read it, many of my friends had and I was somewhat familiar with Laing's social critique.

Laing's ideas found a strong resonance in the countercul-

ture of the sixties, as they forcefully expressed the two major
themes that dominated the decade: the questioning of authority
and the expansion of consciousness. With great eloquence and
passion Laing questioned the authority of psychiatric institutions to deprive mental patients of their basic human rights:

> The "committed" person labeled as patient, and specifically
> as "schizophrenic," is degraded from full existential and
> legal status as human agent and responsible person to some-
> one no longer in possession of his own definition of himself,
> unable to retain his own possessions, precluded from the ex-
> ercise of his discretion as to whom he meets, what he does.
> His time is no longer his own and the space he occupies is
> no longer of his choosing. After being subjected to a deg-
> radation ceremonial known as psychiatric examination, he
> is bereft of his civil liberties in being imprisoned in a total
> institution known as a "mental" hospital. More completely,
> more radically than anywhere else in our society, he is
> invalidated as a human being.

Laing in no way denied the existence of mental illness. But
he insisted that, in order to understand a patient, the psychiatrist had to understand him in the context of his relations with
other human beings, which included very centrally the relationship between the patient and the psychiatrist himself. Traditional psychiatry, by contrast, has followed a Cartesian approach
in which the patient is isolated from his or her environment—
conceptually as well as physically—and labeled in terms of a
well-defined mental disease. Laing emphasized that no one *has*
schizophrenia like having a cold and went on to make the radical assertion that in many of the classic psychiatric texts the
very psychopathology projected onto the person called "patient"
can clearly be seen manifested in the mentality of the psychiatrist.

Conventional psychiatry is plagued by a confusion that
lies at the very center of the conceptual problems of all modern, scientific medicine: the confusion between disease process
and disease origins. Instead of asking why a mental illness
occurs, medical researchers try to understand the biological
mechanisms through which the disease operates. These mechanisms, rather than the true origins, are seen as the causes of the
illness. Accordingly, most current psychiatric treatments are
limited to suppressing symptoms with psychoactive drugs. Al-

though they have been very successful in doing so, this approach has not helped psychiatrists understand mental illness any better, nor has it allowed their patients to solve the underlying problems.

This is where Laing parted company with most of his colleagues. He concentrated on the origins of mental illness by looking at the human condition—at the individual embedded in a network of multiple relationships—and thus addressed psychiatric problems in existential terms. Instead of treating schizophrenia and other forms of psychosis as diseases, he regarded them as special strategies that people invent in order to survive in unlivable situations. This view amounted to a radical change in perspective, which led Laing to see madness as a sane response to an insane social environment. In *The Politics of Experience* he articulated a trenchant social critique that resonated strongly with the critique of the counterculture and is as valid today as it was twenty years ago.

While most psychologists and psychiatrists studied human *behavior* and tried to relate it to physiological and biochemical phenomena, Laing immersed himself in the study of the subtleties and distortions of human *experience*. Here again he was fully in tune with the spirit of the sixties. Guided by philosophy, music, poetry, meditation, and mind-expanding drugs, he went on a journey through the multiple realms of human consciousness, and with great intensity and tremendous literary skill he depicted mental landscapes in which thousands of readers recognized their own experiences.

Realms of the human unconscious

My initial contacts with the work of R. D. Laing in the summer of 1976 awakened my curiosity about Western psychology. From that time on I would take every opportunity to expand my knowledge about the human psyche in discussions with psychologists and psychotherapists. In many of these discussions, the name of Stan Grof was mentioned, and it was often suggested to me that I should meet this man who was an important figure in the human potential movement and entertained ideas about science and spirituality that were very close to my own. Following my *wu-wei* approach of waiting for the right moment, I did not make any efforts to contact Grof and was delighted when I received an invitation, in February 1977, to a small gathering in San Francisco in his honor.

When I met Grof at that reception I was very surprised. I had always heard people refer to him as "Stan" and it had never occurred to me that his full name was Stanislav. I expected to meet a California psychologist, and when I shook hands with him I realized to my great surprise not only that he was European but that he came from a cultural background very close to my own. His native Prague and my native Vienna are a mere one hundred miles apart, and our countries share a long common history during which the two cultures blended considerably. Meeting Grof, therefore, felt somewhat like meeting a distant cousin, which created an immediate bond that would later turn into a close friendship.

My sense of familiarity and ease was further enforced by Grof's personality. He is very warm, easily approachable, and inspires confidence and trust. He speaks slowly, carefully, and with great concentration, and he impresses his audience not only by the extraordinary nature of his ideas but also by the great depth of his personal involvement. In lectures and seminars he can—and often does—speak literally for hours without any notes. At these times he remains totally centered and a strong radiance often shines through his eyes and keeps his audience entranced.

At the reception, Grof gave a brief summary of his research with psychedelic drugs, which I found utterly amazing and fascinating. I knew that he was an authority in the field, but I had no idea of the extent of his research. During the sixties I had read several books on LSD and other psychedelics, had been deeply affected by Aldous Huxley's *Doors of Perception* and by Alan Watts's *Joyous Cosmology*, and had experimented with mind-expanding substances myself. His clinical experience in the use of LSD for psychotherapy and psychological exploration was by far the vastest that any single individual had accumulated. Grof began his clinical work in 1956 at the Psychiatric Institute in Prague and continued it in the United States from 1967 to 1973 at the Maryland Psychiatric Research Center. During those seventeen years he personally guided over 3,000 sessions with LSD and had access to more than 2,000 records of sessions conducted by his colleagues in Czechoslovakia and the United States. In 1973 he joined the Esalen Institute as scholar-in-residence, where he has now spent over a decade evaluating and expanding his massive research. When we met at the reception in 1977, Grof had written two books about his findings and was planning to write two more, which he has since completed.

When I realized the vast extent and great depth of Grof's research, I naturally asked him the question that had fascinated an entire generation during the sixties: "What is LSD, and what is its essential effect on the human mind and body?"

"This is a key question which I asked myself for many years," Grof replied. "The search for typical, mandatory pharmacological effects of LSD was an important aspect of my early analytical work on the LSD data. And the result of this search, which went on for many years, was extremely surprising. After analyzing over three thousand records from LSD sessions, I have not found a single symptom that would be an absolutely mandatory and invariant component of the LSD experience. The absence of any distinct drug-specific effects and the enormous range of phenomena that occur during these sessions have convinced me that LSD is best understood as a powerful unspecific amplifier, or catalyst, of mental processes, which facilitates the emergence of unconscious material from different levels of the human psyche. The richness and enormous variability of the LSD experience can be explained in this way by the fact that the entire personality of the subject and the structure of his or her unconscious play a decisive role.

"This conclusion resulted in a tremendous shift of my perspective," Grof continued. "I realized with great excitement that, rather than studying the specific effects of a psychoactive drug on the brain, I would be able to use LSD as a powerful research tool for the exploration of the human mind. The capacity of LSD and other psychedelics to expose otherwise invisible phenomena and processes to scientific investigation gives these substances a unique potential. It does not seem exaggerated to me to compare their significance for psychiatry and psychology to that of the microscope for medicine or the telescope for astronomy."

Grof then went on to summarize his evaluation of the LSD data. Emphasizing the magnitude of the task he had set himself, he said simply: "It involved nothing less than drawing the first maps of unknown and uncharted territories of the human mind." The result was a new psychological cartography, which Grof published in his first book, *Realms of the Human Unconscious.*

I was deeply impressed by Grof's brief account of his research, but the greatest surprise of the evening was still to come. When somebody asked him about the effect of his work on contemporary psychology and psychotherapy, Grof explained how his observations may help to bring some clarity into "the jungle of competing systems of psychotherapy."

"Even a cursory look at Western psychology," he began, "will reveal controversies of enormous proportions about the dynamics of the human mind, the nature of emotional disorders, and the basic principles of psychotherapy. In many instances, disagreements of a very fundamental nature can be seen even among researchers who originally started from the same basic assumptions." To illustrate his point, Grof then briefly outlined the differences between the theories of Freud and his original disciples Adler, Rank, Jung, and Reich.

"Observations of systematic changes in the content of psychedelic sessions have helped to eliminate some of the most striking contradictions between these schools," he continued. "When you compare material from consecutive LSD sessions of the same person, it becomes evident that there is a definite continuity, a successive unfolding of deeper and deeper levels of the unconscious. On this inner journey a person may first move through a Freudian phase, then pass through a death-rebirth experience that can be loosely referred to as Rankian, and the advanced sessions of the same person may have a mythological and religious quality that can best be described in Jungian terms. All these psychotherapeutic systems can therefore be useful for certain stages of the LSD process.

"Much of the confusion in contemporary psychotherapy," Grof concluded, "comes from the fact that individual researchers have focused their attention primarily on a certain level of the unconscious and have then tried to generalize their findings to the human mind in its totality. Many of the controversies among the different schools can be reconciled by this simple realization. All the systems involved may represent more or less accurate descriptions of the aspect or level of the unconscious which they are describing. What we need now is a 'bootstrap psychology' that would integrate the various systems into a collection of maps covering the entire range of human consciousness."

I was stunned by this remark. I had come to the reception to meet a famous psychiatrist and learn more about the human psyche, and in the back of my mind was also the question whether Stan Grof could be my adviser for psychology. During the whole evening, his fascinating account of his research had greatly surpassed my expectations, and now he had clearly outlined an important part of the very task I was engaged in—the integration of different schools of thought into a new conceptual framework—advocating the very same philosophy, Chew's bootstrap approach, that had become an essential aspect of my own work. I naturally felt that Grof would be an ideal adviser for me and was very eager to get to know him better. At the end of the evening he told me that *The Tao of Physics* had been an important discovery for him and invited me very kindly to visit him at his home at Big Sur, near Esalen, for a long discussion and exchange of ideas. I left the meeting in very high spirits, feeling that I had made an important step toward advancing my understanding of psychology and realizing my project.

A cartography of consciousness

A few weeks after meeting Grof and before I visited him at Big Sur, I saw him again in Canada, where we both spoke at a conference on new models of reality and their applications to medicine, sponsored by the University of Toronto. In the meantime, I had read his *Realms of the Human Unconscious* with great excitement, and Grof's lecture at the conference gave me additional insights into his work.

Grof's discovery that psychedelics act as powerful catalysts of mental processes is supported by the fact that the phenomena he observed in LSD sessions are in no way limited to psychedelic experimentation. Many of them have been observed in meditative practice, trance states, shamanic healing ceremonies, in near-death situations and other biological emergencies, and in a variety of other non-ordinary states of consciousness. Even though Grof constructed his "cartography of the unconscious" on the basis of his clinical research with LSD, he has since corroborated it with many years of careful studies of other non-ordinary states of consciousness, which may occur spontaneously or may be induced by special techniques without any drugs.

Grof's cartography encompasses three major domains: the domain of "psychodynamic" experiences, involving complex reliving of emotionally relevant memories from various periods of the individual's life; the domain of "perinatal" experiences, related to the biological phenomena involved in the process of birth; and an entire spectrum of experiences going beyond individual boundaries and transcending the limitations of time and space, for which Grof has coined the term "transpersonal."

The psychodynamic level is clearly autobiographical in origin and can be understood, to a large extent, in terms of basic psychoanalytic principles. "If psychodynamic sessions were the only type of LSD experience," writes Grof, "the observations from LSD psychotherapy could be considered to be laboratory proof of the basic Freudian premises. The psychosexual dynamics and the fundamental conflicts of the human psyche as described by Freud are manifested with unusual clarity and vividness."

The domain of perinatal experiences may be the most fascinating and most original part of Grof's cartography. It exhibits a variety of rich and complex experiential patterns related to the problems of biological birth. Perinatal experiences involve an extremely realistic and authentic reliving of various stages of one's actual birth process—the serene bliss of existence in the womb in primal union with the mother; the "no exit" situation of the first stage of delivery, when the cervix is still closed while uterine contractions encroach on the fetus, creating a claustrophobic situation accompanied by intense physical discomfort; the propulsion through the birth canal, involving an enormous struggle for survival under crushing pressures; and, finally, the sudden relief and relaxation, the first breath, and the cutting of the umbilical cord, completing the physical separation from the mother.

In perinatal experiences the sensations and feelings associated with the birth process may be relived in a direct, realistic way and may also emerge in the form of symbolic, visionary experiences. For example, the experience of enormous tensions that is characteristic of the struggle in the birth canal is often accompanied by visions of titanic fights, natural disasters, and various images of destruction and self-destruction. To facilitate an understanding of the great complexity of physical symptoms, imagery, and experiential patterns, Grof has grouped them into four clusters, called perinatal matrices, which correspond to consecutive stages of the birth process. Detailed studies of the interrelations among the various elements of these matrices have led him to profound insights into many psychological conditions and patterns of human experience. I remember once asking Gregory Bateson, after we had both attended one of Grof's seminars, what he thought of Grof's work on the psychological impact of the birth experience. Bateson, as he often liked to do, responded with a clipped phrase: "Nobel caliber."

The last major domain of Grof's cartography of the unconscious is that of transpersonal experiences, which seem to offer deep insights into the nature and relevance of the spiritual dimension of consciousness. Transpersonal experiences involve an expansion of consciousness beyond the conventional boundaries of the organism and, correspondingly, a larger sense of identity. They may also involve perceptions of the environment transcending the usual limitations of sensory perception, often approaching direct mystical experience of reality. Since the transpersonal mode of consciousness generally transcends logical reasoning and intellectual analysis, it is extremely difficult, if not impossible, to describe in factual language. Indeed, Grof has found that the language of mythology, which is much less restricted by logic and common sense, often seems more appropriate to describe experiences in the transpersonal domain.

His detailed explorations of the perinatal and transpersonal domains convinced Grof that Freudian theory had to be expanded considerably to accommodate the new concepts he had developed. This conclusion coincided with his moving in 1967 to the United States, where he found a very vital movement in American psychology, known as humanistic psychology, which had already expanded the discipline far beyond the Freudian framework. Under the leadership of Abraham Maslow, humanistic psychologists endeavored to study healthy individuals as integral organisms; were deeply concerned with personal growth and "self-actualization," recognizing the potential inherent in all human beings; and focused their attention on experience rather than intellectual analysis. Accordingly, numerous new psychotherapies and "bodywork" schools had been developed, which were referred to collectively as the human potential movement.

Although Grof's work was received by the human potential movement with great enthusiasm, he soon found that even the framework of humanistic psychology was too narrow for him, and in 1968 he founded, together with Maslow and several others, the school of transpersonal psychology, which is concerned specifically with the recognition, understanding, and realization of transpersonal states of consciousness.

Visiting Grof at Big Sur

In March 1977, on a beautiful hot day, I drove south along the sparkling Pacific coastline to visit Stan Grof at his home in Big Sur. During the sixties, I had often been to the Big Sur area, either driving or hitchhiking, and as I approached it on the winding, rocky road—on my right the deep blue ocean; on my left the smooth, sensuous hills covered with lush green grass that would soon turn into gold—I vividly remembered the magic of those days. Together with the "flower children" of the counterculture I had hiked through the dry heat of the Big Sur hills; climbed up the narrow, shady gulches of many creeks, swimming naked in their ponds and showering under their waterfalls; I had spent many nights in my sleeping bag on secluded beaches, and solitary days in meditation high up in the hills, with Castaneda's *Teachings of Don Juan* or Hesse's *Steppenwolf* as my companions.

Ever since those days Big Sur had had a special fascination for me, and now, as I caught glimpses of magnificent vistas of the ragged coast, fanning out before my eyes and disappearing into shades of gray at the horizon, my body relaxed and my mind expanded. I felt inspired and excited by my memories and even more excited by the expansion of consciousness which, I knew, was in store for me on this trip.

When I arrived at Grof's home, he greeted me warmly, introduced me to his wife, Christina, and showed me around the house. It is one of the most beautiful and inspiring places I have ever seen: a simple redwood frame with a spectacular view of the Pacific Ocean, perched on the edge of a cliff a couple of miles north of Esalen. The exterior walls of the living room are almost entirely of glass, with doors leading out to a wooden deck overhanging the breaking waves. One wall of the room is dominated by a huge Huichol yarn painting in brilliant colors, depicting people and animals on a sacred vision quest. There is a large fireplace, built of rough stones, in one corner; a comfortable couch surrounded by shelves of art books and encyclopedias in the other; and throughout the room there are objects of religious art, pipes, drums, and other implements of shamanistic rituals, which Grof collected on his journeys around the world. The entire house mirrors Grof's personality—highly artistic, calm and peaceful, and yet exciting and inspiring. Since my first visit I have spent many days in that house, with the Grofs and also alone, which I will always remember as among the happiest moments of my life.

After showing me the house and telling me several anecdotes relating to his art collection, Stan offered me a glass of wine on the sundeck, and we sat down in this magnificent spot for our first long conversation. He began by telling me again that *The Tao of Physics* had been a very important book for him. He said that he had always encountered tremendous resistance among his colleagues when he talked about psychedelic therapy. Not only was there a lot of confusion, caused by the abuses of LSD and the resulting legal restrictions; the entire framework he had developed was so radically different from that of conventional psychiatry that it was considered incompatible with his colleagues' scientific views about reality and thus, by implication, unscientific. In *The Tao of Physics* Grof had found for the first time a detailed description of a conceptual framework in which he recognized many similarities to his own and which, moreover, was based on discoveries in physics, the most respected of the sciences. "I believe," he concluded, "that in the future there will be tremendous support for consciousness research if we find solid bridges between the material that is coming from the study of altered states of consciousness and the theoretical speculations of modern physicists."

Grof then proceeded to outline the similarities between the perceptions of reality he had observed in psychedelic experiences and those emerging from modern physics. He did so by going through the three domains of his cartography of the unconscious, and to explain the experiences of the first, psychodynamic domain he gave me a lucid and concise summary of Freud's psychoanalytic theory.

I took this opportunity to ask Grof about some "Newtonian" aspects of psychoanalysis of which I had recently become aware, for example, the notion of internal "objects," located in psychological space, and of psychological forces with definite directions driving the "mechanisms and machineries" of the mind. These aspects had been pointed out to me by Stephen Salenger, a psychoanalyst in Los Angeles with whom I had had several inspiring discussions and who had invited me to give a talk to the Los Angeles Psychoanalytic Society.

Grof confirmed my suspicion that psychoanalysis, like most scientific theories of the nineteenth and early twentieth centuries, had been modeled after Newtonian physics. In fact, he showed me that the four basic perspectives from which psychoanalysts have traditionally approached and analyzed mental life—the so-called topographic, dynamic, economic, and genetic perspectives—correspond, one by one, to four sets of concepts that form the basis of Newtonian mechanics. However, Grof also emphasized that to recognize the limitations of the psychoanalytic approach could in no way diminish the genius of its founder. "Freud's contribution was truly extraordinary," he said admiringly. "Almost single-handedly Freud discovered the unconscious and its dynamics. He also discovered the interpretation of dreams. He created a dynamic approach to psychiatry, studying the forces that lead to psychological disorders. He emphasized the importance of childhood experiences for the future development of the individual. He identified the sexual drive as one of the principal psychological forces. He introduced the notion of infantile sexuality and outlined the principal stages of early psychosexual development. Any one of these discoveries would be impressive as the product of an entire lifetime."

Coming back to the psychodynamic domain of the LSD experience, I asked Grof whether any changes of world view occurred at that level.

"At that level," he explained, "the major consequence seems to be that people regard certain aspects of their perceptions of who they are, of what the world is, and of what society is as inauthentic. They begin to see these perceptions as direct derivatives of childhood experiences, as comments on their individual history. And as they are able to relive their past experiences, their opinions and views become more open and more flexible, instead of being rigidly categorized."

"But there wouldn't be really profound changes in their world view at that level?"

"No, the really fundamental changes begin at the perinatal level. One of the most striking aspects of that domain is the close relationship between the experiences of birth and death. The encounter with suffering and struggle, and the annihilation of all previous reference points in the birth process, are so close to the experience of death that the entire process may be regarded as a death-rebirth experience. The perinatal level is the level of both birth and death. It is a domain of existential experiences which exerts a crucial influence on a person's mental and emotional life and on his or her world view.

"Once people confront death and the impermanence of everything on an experiential level," Grof continued, "they frequently start seeing *all* of their present life strategies as being erroneous and the totality of their perceptions as some kind of fundamental illusion. The experiential encounter with death often amounts to a true existential crisis that forces people to reexamine the meaning of their lives and the values they live by. Worldly ambitions, competitive drives, the longing for status, power, or material possessions all tend to fade away when they are viewed against the background of potentially imminent death."

"And what happens then?"

"Well, out of the death-rebirth process emerges the feeling that life is constant change, that it is a process, and that it doesn't make any sense to hang on to specific goals or concepts. People begin to feel that the only sensible thing to do is to focus on change itself, which is the only constant aspect of existence."

"You know, that's exactly the basis of Buddhism. As I hear you describe these experiences, I get the feeling that there is a spiritual quality to them."

"That's right. The complete death-rebirth process always represents a spiritual opening. People who go through that experience invariably appreciate the spiritual dimension of existence as being extremely important, if not fundamental. And at the same time their image of the physical universe changes.

People lose the feeling of separateness; they stop thinking of solid matter and begin to think of energy patterns."

With that remark we had reached one of the bridges between consciousness research and modern physics that Grof had mentioned at the beginning of our conversation, and we spent considerable time discussing the details of the views of physical reality emerging from the two disciplines. This discussion led me to ask Grof whether the changes in perceptions occurring in LSD sessions included changes in people's perceptions of space and time. I had noticed that so far he had not mentioned the concepts of space and time, which had changed so radically in modern physics.

"Not at the perinatal level," he answered. "Although the world is seen as energy patterns when the spiritual dimension enters into the experience, there is still an objective, absolute space, in which everything is happening, and there is linear time. But this changes in a very fundamental way when people begin to experience the next level, the transpersonal domain. At that level, the image of three-dimensional space and of linear time is shattered completely. People get experiential evidence that these notions are not mandatory; that under certain special circumstances they can be transcended in many ways. In other words, there are alternatives not only to conceptual thinking about the world but to actual experience of the world."

"What would these alternatives be?"

"Well, you can experience any number of spaces in psychedelic sessions. You may be sitting here at Big Sur, and suddenly there may be an intrusion of the space of your bedroom in Berkeley, or of a space from your childhood, or from the distant past of human history. You may experience any number of transformations; even simultaneous experiences of different spatial arrangements. Similarly, you may experience different modes of time—circular time, time running backwards, time 'tunnels'—and with that you become aware that there are alternatives to the causal way of looking at things."

Indeed, I could see plenty of parallels to modern physics but, somehow, I was less interested in exploring these further than in touching on a question that is a central issue in spiritual traditions—the nature of consciousness and its relation to matter.

"This is a question which comes up again and again in

psychedelic sessions at the transpersonal level," Grof explained, "and there is a fundamental shift of perception. The question of conventional Western science—Where is the moment at which consciousness originates? When does matter become conscious of itself?—is turned upside down. The question now becomes: How does consciousness produce the illusion of matter? You see, consciousness is seen as something primordial, which cannot be explained on the basis of anything else; something that is just there and which, ultimately, is the only reality; something that is manifest in you and me, and in everything around us."

Grof paused and I, too, remained silent. We had talked for a long time, and now the sun was almost setting, sending a streak of gold across the ocean as it approached the horizon. It was a scene of extraordinary beauty and serenity, punctuated by the slow, rhythmic breathing of the Pacific—wave after wave rolling in with a low rumble and crashing on the rocks below us.

Grof's comments on the nature of consciousness were not new to me. I had read them many times, in different variations, in the classic texts of Eastern mysticism. Yet, in his description of the psychedelic experience they seemed more direct and more vivid to me. And as I looked out over the ocean, my awareness of the unity of all things became very real and compelling.

Grof followed my gaze and, somehow, must have picked up on my thoughts. "One of the most frequent metaphors that you find in psychedelic reports," he continued, "is that of the circulation of water in nature. The universal consciousness is likened to the ocean—a fluid, undifferentiated mass—and the first stage of creation to the formation of waves. A wave can be viewed as an individual entity, and yet it is obvious that the wave is the ocean and the ocean is the wave. There is no ultimate separation."

Again, this was a familiar image, one that I had used myself in *The Tao of Physics* when I described how Buddhists and quantum physicists alike used the analogy of water waves to illustrate the illusion of separate entities. But then Grof went on to refine the metaphor in a way that was new and very impressive to me.

"The next stage of creation would be a wave breaking on

the rocks and spraying droplets of water into the air, which will exist as individual entities for a short time before they are swallowed again by the ocean. So, there you have fleeting moments of separate existence.

"The next stage in this metaphoric thinking," he continued, "would be a wave that hits the rocky shore and withdraws again but leaves a small pool of tidal water. It may take a long time until the next wave comes and reclaims the water that was left there. During that time, the tidal pool is a separate entity, and yet it is an extension of the ocean which, eventually, will return to its source."

I looked down to the tidal pools in the crevices of the rocks below us, appreciating the many playful variations that were possible within Grof's metaphor. "What about evaporation?" I asked.

"That's the next stage," Grof replied. "Imagine water evaporating and forming a cloud. Now the original unity is obscured and concealed by an actual transformation, and it takes some knowledge of physics to realize that the cloud is the ocean and the ocean is the cloud. Yet the water in the cloud will eventually reunite with the ocean in the form of rain.

"The final separation," Grof concluded, "where the link with the original source appears to be completely forgotten, is often illustrated by a snowflake that has crystallized from the water in the cloud, which had originally evaporated from the ocean. Here you have a highly structured, highly individual, separate entity which bears, seemingly, no resemblance to its source. Now you really need some sophisticated knowledge about water to recognize that the snowflake is the ocean and the ocean is the snowflake. And in order to reunite with the ocean, the snowflake has to give up its structure and individuality; it has to go through an ego death, as it were, to return to its source."

Again we both fell silent, as I reflected on the manifold meanings of Grof's beautiful metaphor. The sun had set in the meantime; the wisp of clouds on the horizon had turned from gold to deep red; and as I gazed across the ocean, thinking of its numerous manifestations in the endless cycles of water circulation, I suddenly had a deep insight. After some contemplation I broke our silence.

"You know, Stan, I just realized a profound connection

between ecology and spirituality. Ecological awareness, at the deepest level, is the intuitive awareness of the oneness of all life, the interdependence of its multiple manifestations and its cycles of change and transformation. But your description of transpersonal experiences just made it clear to me that such awareness can also be called spiritual awareness.

"In fact," I continued with great excitement, "spirituality, or the human spirit, could be defined as the mode of consciousness in which we feel connected to the cosmos as a whole. This makes it evident that ecological awareness is spiritual in its deepest essence. And it is then no surprise that the new vision of reality emerging from modern physics, which is a holistic and ecological vision, is in harmony with the visions of spiritual traditions."

Grof slowly nodded in agreement without saying anything. There was no need for further conversation, and we sat in silence for a long time, until it was almost dark and the air became so chilly that we went inside.

I stayed overnight in the Grofs' guest room and spent the next day with them, exchanging stories and getting to know them on a personal level. Stan invited me to give a joint seminar with him at Esalen later in the year, and before I left he went to his library, and to my great surprise he pulled out a beautifully bound and illustrated German edition of the *Fritjof Saga*, a celebrated Swedish legend, which had led my mother to give me my name. He presented the book to me as a token of our new friendship—a generous present from an extraordinary man.

Experiencing R. D. Laing

My first meeting with R. D. Laing took place in May 1977 when I returned to London for the first visit since my move to California after finishing *The Tao of Physics*. I had left London and my large circle of friends in December 1974 with the completed manuscript in my shoulder bag and with great hopes of establishing myself in California as a physicist and writer. Now, two and a half years later, I had achieved most of what I had hoped for. *The Tao of Physics* had been published in England and in the United States, had been received enthusiastically in both countries, and was being translated into several other languages. I was a member of Geoffrey Chew's research team at Berkeley, working closely with one of the deepest scientific thinkers of our time. My financial difficulties were finally over, and I had embarked on an exciting new project—the exploration of the change of paradigms in the sciences and in society—which brought me in contact with many extraordinary people.

So when I returned to London I was naturally in very high spirits. I spent three weeks celebrating with my friends, who received me with great affection and joy; I gave two lectures about *The Tao of Physics* at the Architectural Association, a school of architecture that served as a forum for the artistic and intellectual avant-garde during the sixties and seventies; I made a short television film with the BBC about my book, in which my old friend Phiroz Mehta spoke the Hindu texts; and I visited several outstanding scholars to discuss my ideas and future projects with them. For three weeks I had an absolutely fabulous time.

One of the scholars I visited was the physicist David Bohm, with whom I discussed the new breakthrough in bootstrap physics and the relations I saw between Chew's and Bohm's theories. Another memorable visit was one with Joseph Needham at Cambridge. Needham is a biologist who has become one of the leading historians of Chinese science and technology. His monumental work *Science and Civilisation in China* greatly influenced my thinking when I wrote *The Tao of Physics*, but I had never dared to visit him. Now I felt secure enough to contact Needham and he very graciously invited me to dinner at his college, Gonville and Caius, where I spent a very inspiring evening with him.

Both of these visits were highly stimulating for me but, somehow, they were overshadowed by two other visits, which were directly connected with my new project: one to E. F. Schumacher (to be recounted in Chapter 6), the author of *Small Is Beautiful*, and the other to R. D. Laing. Visiting Laing was one of my main purposes when I arrived in London. A close friend of mine, Jill Purce, who is a writer and editor with many connections in London's artistic, literary, and spiritual circles, had met Laing through the anthropologist Francis Huxley, whom I also knew. So I sent Laing, via Jill and Francis,

an article of mine that summarized *The Tao of Physics*, together with a note saying that I would be very excited and honored to meet him, that I was now expanding my research into
new areas, and that I had a few questions regarding psychology
and psychotherapy. Would he be so kind as to spend some time
with me to discuss these matters? I also wanted to ask Laing
what he thought about Grof's work, and I even played with the
idea of asking him to be one of my advisers.

Laing sent word back that he could see me and that I
should meet him on a certain day at 11:00 A.M. in his house in
Hampstead, not far from where I had lived before leaving London. So on that day, a beautiful, warm, clear spring day—one
of those rare sparkling London days that are especially exhilarating after the long English winter—I rang the bell at R. D.
Laing's home. Being well aware of his reputation for being ec-
centric, unpredictable, and often difficult to deal with, I was
slightly nervous about this meeting. However, I had had conversations with very unusual people before; I was seriously
interested in hearing Laing's ideas; I knew what I wanted to
ask him; and I trusted my ability to engage people in stimulating intellectual discussions. So even though I was a little
nervous, I was also quite confident.

Laing opened the door and peered at me with half-closed,
curious eyes, his head bent and slightly tilted, his shoulders
hunched. He was wearing a scarf around his neck and looked
gaunt and frail. Recognizing who I was, he ushered me in
with a quizzical smile and a somewhat exaggerated bow, shy
but friendly. He fascinated me right from the first moment.
He inquired whether I had had breakfast and when I told him
I had, he asked me whether I would mind going to a nearby
restaurant with a nice garden where *he* could have breakfast
and I could join him for coffee or a glass of wine.

While we walked to the restaurant, I told Laing that I
was very grateful to him for this meeting and asked him
whether he had had a chance to look at my book or read the
article I had sent him. He said that he had not been able to
read either; he had only glanced at the article. I then told him
that my book was about parallels between the concepts of
modern physics and the basic ideas in the mystical traditions
of the East and asked him whether he himself had ever given
any thought to such parallels. I knew that Laing had spent

some time in India but I did not know whether he had any knowledge of quantum physics.

"I'm not surprised at all about these parallels," he began in a somewhat impatient tone. "When you think of Heisenberg's emphasis on the observer . . ."—and with that he launched into a forceful and concise summary of the concepts of modern physics in one of those long monologues which, I would learn later, are very characteristic of him. His synopsis of the philosophy of quantum mechanics and relativity theory was very close to the way I had presented it in *The Tao of Physics* and made the parallels to Eastern mysticism quite obvious. I was absolutely overwhelmed by this brilliant summary, by Laing's ability to grasp the essential aspects of a field that must have been quite foreign to him, and by his concise resumé of the main points.

When we arrived at the restaurant, Laing ordered an omelet and asked me whether I would like to join him in ordering a glass of wine. I nodded in agreement and he ordered a bottle of red wine, which he recommended as the specialty of the house. Sitting in a lovely garden on that beautiful, sunny, late morning, we then engaged in an animated, wide-ranging conversation that would last for over two hours. For me, this conversation was not only highly stimulating intellectually; it was a fascinating experience altogether, sustained by Laing's extremely expressive way of speaking. He always makes his points with passion, and while he speaks a rich gamut of emotions plays itself out in his face and body language—disgust, scorn, mocking sarcasm, charm, tenderness, delicacy, aesthetic pleasure, and much more. His speech can, perhaps, be best compared to a piece of music. Its tone is often incantatory, its rhythm always distinctive; its sentences are long and probing, like variations on a musical theme, with changing emphasis and intensity. Laing likes to use language to *depict* things, rather than to describe them, freely mixing casual language with sophisticated quotations from literature, philosophy, and religious texts. In doing so, he displays the extraordinary range and depth of his background: He has a thorough education in Greek and Latin, has done extensive studies in philosophy and theology in addition to his long training in psychiatry, is an accomplished pianist, writes poetry, and has spent considerable time studying mystical traditions, Eastern as well as Western,

and honing his awareness through yoga and Buddhist meditation. In our long first conversation this rich world of Laing's
knowledge and experience slowly began to unfold and to cast
a lasting spell on me. During the entire conversation, Laing
was extremely kind to me. Even though he often spoke with
great intensity, he was never aggressive or sarcastic toward me,
but always very gentle and friendly.

Laing began the conversation by talking about India, continuing some of the thoughts he had expressed during our walk
to the restaurant. I had not yet been to India at that time,
and Laing told me that he was disgusted to see so many self-
appointed, fake gurus exploiting the romantic longings of naive
Western disciples. He spoke of these pseudo-gurus with great
scorn and did not tell me that during his stay in India he had
become deeply inspired by true spiritual masters. It was not
until several years later that I learned how much he had been
affected by Indian spirituality, especially by Buddhism. In this
connection we also talked about Jung, and again Laing was
critical. He said that he felt Jung was very patronizing in some
of his forewords to books on Eastern mysticism, projecting his
psychiatric Swiss outlook on the Eastern traditions. This was
"absolutely insupportable" to Laing, even though he had great
respect for Jung as a psychotherapist.

At this point I presented the basic theme of my new book
to Laing, starting with the idea that the natural sciences, as
well as the humanities and the social sciences, had all modeled
themselves after Newtonian physics, that more and more scientists were now becoming aware of the limitations of the mechanistic, Newtonian world view, and that they would have to
change their underlying philosophies in radical ways in order
to participate in the current cultural transformation. In particular, I mentioned the parallels between Newtonian physics
and psychoanalysis, which I had discussed with Grof.

Laing agreed with my basic thesis and he also confirmed
the idea of the Newtonian framework of psychoanalysis. Indeed, he told me that the critique of Freud's mechanistic thinking was even more relevant when it came to interpersonal relations. "Freud had no constructs for any system consisting of
more than one person," Laing explained. "He had his mental apparatus, his psychic structures, his internal objects, his
forces—but he had no idea of how two of these mental ap-

paratuses, each with its own constellation of internal objects, can relate to each other. For Freud, they interacted simply mechanically, like two billiard balls. He had no concept of experience shared by human beings."

Laing then went on to talk about his broader critique of psychiatry, emphasizing especially his conviction that psychoactive drugs should never be forced on a patient. "What right do we have to interfere with anybody's confusion?" he asked. He affirmed that a much more subtle drug approach was needed. It was all right for him to calm down a patient with drugs, but beyond that one should follow a kind of "homeopathic approach" to mental illness, "dancing with the body" and only "slightly nudging the brain." He also told me that the original sense of the word "therapist," in its Greek form *therapeutes*, was that of an attendant. A therapist, Laing maintained, should therefore be a specialist in attentiveness and awareness.

As our conversation proceeded, I became more and more delighted by the extent to which Laing confirmed my basic thesis and agreed with my approach. At the same time, I realized that his personality and style were so different from mine that we would probably not work well together. Besides, I had virtually made up my mind that I would ask Stan Grof to be my adviser for psychology and so I asked Laing what he thought of Grof's work. He spoke very highly of Grof, saying that his work on LSD therapy and, in particular, his ideas on the influence of the birth experience on a person's psyche were something he himself was very interested in and had the highest respect for. Later in the conversation, when I mentioned my plan of assembling a group of advisers, Laing said simply: "If you have Grof, you can't find anyone better."

Encouraged by Laing's sympathetic comments and suggestions and by his far-reaching agreement with my ideas, I finally put the question to him that I was most curious about: What is the essence of psychotherapy? How does it work? In my recent discussions with psychotherapists, I told him, I had often asked this question, and I remembered in particular a conversation with Jungian analysts in Chicago, including Werner Engel and June Singer, which gave me the vague idea that there had to be some kind of "resonance" between therapist and patient to initiate the healing process. To my great surprise and delight, Laing told me that he himself saw something like that as the very essence of psychotherapy. "Essentially," he said, "psychotherapy is an authentic meeting between human beings," and to illustrate the meaning of this beautiful definition he proceeded to tell me about one of his therapy sessions: A man came to see him and told him about some problems related to his job and his family situation. The man told him a story that seemed to have no outstanding features—married, two children, some office job; there was really nothing unusual in his life, no drama, no complex interplay of special circumstances. "I listened to him," said Laing; "I asked him a few questions; and at the end the man burst into tears and said: 'For the first time, I have felt like a human being.' After that, it was a handshake, and that was it."

This story was quite mysterious to me. I really could not see what point Laing wanted to make, and it would take me several years to understand it. As I pondered the meaning of the story, Laing noticed that we had emptied our bottle and asked me whether I felt like having more wine. He told me that the restaurant actually had an even better wine, which he could highly recommend. I had had a very light breakfast early in the morning and had drunk half of our first bottle practically on an empty stomach, but I made no objection to his ordering a second. I was willing to become totally intoxicated, rather than risk a break in the flow of our conversation.

When the second bottle came, Laing went through an elaborate ritual of tasting the wine, and after a quick toast—the wine was indeed excellent—he launched into a series of stories about therapeutic encounters and psychotic healing journeys that became more and more convoluted and bizarre, culminating in the story of a woman who was healed by spontaneously turning into a hound and back again into a woman in a dramatic three-day episode that lasted from Good Friday to Easter Monday—from death to resurrection—while she was all by herself in a large, remote country house.*

I had had some difficulty in understanding Laing right from the beginning because I was not used to his Scottish brogue. Now, as the wine had its effect on me, his accent seemed to get more exotic, his speech more captivating, and everything—the reality of the garden restaurant and the re-

* *Several years later, Laing published this extraordinary story in his book* The Voice of Experience.

ality of his extraordinary stories—became more of a haze. All
that added up to a very unusual experience during which I felt
somewhat like Alice in Wonderland, traveling on a guided tour
through the strange and fantastic world of R. D. Laing.

What actually happened was that Laing, at this first meeting, put me in an altered state of consciousness to talk about
altered states of consciousness, skillfully blending our discussions of these experiences with actual experience. In doing so,
he helped me to understand that my question "What is the
essence of psychotherapy?" did not have the clear answer I
had expected. Through his fantastic stories Laing conveyed a
message to me that he had encapsulated in a single sentence in
The Politics of Experience: "The really decisive moments in
psychotherapy, as every patient or therapist who has ever experienced them knows, are unpredictable, unique, unforgettable, always unrepeatable and often indescribable."

The paradigm shift in psychology

My first meetings with Stan Grof and R. D. Laing provided
me with the outline of a basic framework for studying the paradigm shift in psychology. My starting point had been the idea
that "classical" psychology, like classical physics, was shaped
by the Newtonian model of reality. I could see myself that this
was quite evident in the case of behaviorism, and both Grof
and Laing confirmed my thesis for psychoanalysis.*

At the same time, Grof's "bootstrap" approach to psychology showed me how different psychological schools can be integrated into a coherent system if one realizes that they are
dealing with different levels and dimensions of consciousness.
According to Grof's cartography of the unconscious, psychoanalysis is the appropriate model for the psychodynamic domain; the theories of Freud's "renegade" disciples Adler, Reich,
and Rank can be associated with different aspects of Grof's
perinatal matrices; various schools of humanistic and existential psychology can be related to the existential crisis and the
spiritual opening of the perinatal level; and, finally, Jung's

* Later on, I learned that structuralism, the third important current of
"classical" psychological thinking, also incorporated Newtonian concepts
into its theoretical framework.

analytic psychology is clearly associated with the transpersonal level. The transpersonal level also provides the important link to spirituality and to Eastern approaches to consciousness. Moreover, my conversations with Grof revealed an essential connection between spirituality and ecology.

During my visit at Big Sur, Grof also showed me an article by Ken Wilber, a transpersonal psychologist who has developed a very comprehensive "spectrum psychology," which unifies numerous approaches, both Western and Eastern, into a spectrum of psychological models and theories reflecting the entire range of human consciousness. Wilber's system is fully consistent with Grof's. It comprises several major levels of consciousness—essentially Grof's three levels, which Wilber calls the ego level, the existential level, and the transpersonal level, plus a fourth "biosocial" level reflecting aspects of a person's social environment. I was very impressed by the clarity and scope of Wilber's system when I read his article, "Psychologia Perennis: The Spectrum of Consciousness" (which he later enlarged to a book, *The Spectrum of Consciousness*), and I realized immediately that Laing's work was an important approach to the biosocial domain.

Laing had not only clarified several questions regarding psychology in our first conversation, but had also pointed out an approach to psychotherapy, and to therapy in general, which went beyond the mechanistic conception of health. The notion of the therapist as an attendant seemed to imply the recognition of some sort of natural potential for self-healing inherent in the human organism, and I felt that this was an important idea that I should explore further. It also seemed to be related to another idea Laing and I had discussed, that of a certain "resonance" between therapist and patient as a decisive factor in psychotherapy. In fact, when I returned to California from my trip to London, I planned to visit Stan Grof specifically to discuss the nature of psychotherapy.

Conversations at Esalen

During the summer and fall of 1977 I saw Stan Grof quite often. We gave several joint seminars, spent time together at his Big Sur home, and got to know each other very well. During that time I also came to appreciate the graciousness and warmth of his wife, Christina, who facilitates Stan's workshops and whose vivacious humor often lightened up our conversations. In July Stan and I both participated in the annual conference of the Association of Transpersonal Psychology at Asilomar, near Monterey, and at that meeting we designed a joint seminar, "Journeys Beyond Space and Time." We planned to talk in this seminar about an outer journey into the realms of subatomic matter and an inner journey into the realms of the unconscious, and then to compare the world views emerging from these two adventures. Stan also told me that he would try to convey the results from his LSD research experientially with a slide show, showing a multitude of images from the visual arts underlined by powerful, evocative music, which would guide the viewer through a simulated experience of the death-rebirth process and subsequent spiritual opening. We were both very excited about this joint project and planned to give the seminar first at Esalen and then, if it worked, on college campuses.

The seminar at Esalen was very successful. We explored the parallels between modern physics and consciousness research with a group of about thirty participants during a long day of presentations and intensive discussions. Grof's slide show was most impressive—a powerful emotional counterpoint to our intellectual exploration. Several months later we repeated our seminar twice, once in Santa Cruz and once in Santa Barbara. Both of these events were sponsored by "university extensions," that is, institutes for adult education attached to universities. In contrast to the universities themselves, these "extensions" have always shown great interest in new ideas and have sponsored many interdisciplinary seminars and courses.

The story of my getting to know Stan Grof is also the story of my association with Esalen, which has been a place of inspiration and support for me for a full decade. The Esalen Institute was founded by Michael Murphy and Richard Price on a magnificent piece of property belonging to the Murphy family. A large coastal mesa forms several tree-lined terraces, separated by a creek where the Esalen Indians used to bury their dead and hold their sacred rites. Hot mineral springs flow out of the rocks on a cliff overlooking the ocean. Murphy's grandfather had bought this enchanting piece of land in 1910 and had built a large house, known today affectionately as the Big House in the Esalen community. In the early sixties Murphy took over the family property and, together with Price, started a center where people from different disciplines could meet and exchange ideas. With Abraham Maslow, Rollo May, Fritz Perls, Carl Rogers, and many other pioneers of humanistic psychology giving "workshops," Esalen soon became an influential center of the human potential movement and has remained a forum where people with open minds are able to exchange ideas in an informal and extremely beautiful setting.

I very well remember my first extended visit to Esalen, in August 1976, on my way back home from the Naropa Institute in Boulder. I had driven my old Volvo through the hot and dusty deserts of Arizona and Southern California and was traveling up the coast, enjoying the first fresh breeze in days and the sight of green meadows, when I suddenly remembered that the Esalen Institute was located somewhere along my way. I did not know anybody at Esalen then and had been there only once, during the sixties, together with over a thousand other people attending a rock festival. But the thought of walking barefoot on the lush green lawns, breathing the invigorating ocean air, and soaking in the mineral baths was so tempting after the long, hot drive that I could not resist stopping at the gate when I reached the Esalen sign.

I gave my name to the guard and told him that I was on my way home from Colorado, where I had given a course on *The Tao of Physics*. Would they mind if I spent a few hours relaxing on their grounds and enjoying the baths? The guard passed on the request to Dick Price, who immediately sent word back that I was welcome to stay as long as I wanted, and that he was looking forward to meeting me.

From that day until his death in 1985 in a tragic accident in the mountains of Big Sur, Dick was extremely kind and generous to me, graciously offering me his hospitality innumerable times. His generosity has been equaled by the entire Esalen community, a fluctuating tribe of a few dozen people spanning several generations, who have always received me with genuine friendship and affection.

Over the last ten years, Esalen has been the ideal place for me to unwind and replenish my energies after long travels and exhausting work. But it has been much more than that to me—

a place where I have met a large number of unusual and fascinating men and women, and where I had the unique opportunity to test new ideas in small, informal circles of highly educated and experienced people. Most of these opportunities were provided by Stan and Christina Grof, who regularly offer a unique kind of four-week seminar, widely known simply as "the Grof monthlong."

During these four weeks, a group of two dozen participants live together in the Big House and interact with a string of outstanding guest lecturers who come for two or three days each, often overlapping and interacting with one another. The seminar is organized around a central theme, the emerging new vision of reality and the corresponding expansion of consciousness. The unique feature of the Grof monthlongs is that Stan and Christina offer their participants not only intellectual enrichment through stimulating and challenging discussions but, at the same time, experiential contact with the ideas discussed through art, meditative practice, ritual, and other nonrational modes of cognition. Ever since I met the Grofs I have participated in their seminars whenever I could, and this has helped me enormously in formulating and testing my ideas.

After our seminar on "Journeys Beyond Space and Time" in the fall of 1977, I stayed at Esalen for a few more days, primarily to talk with Stan at length about the nature of mental illness and of psychotherapy.

When I asked Grof what his observations from LSD research had taught him about the nature of mental illness, he began by telling me the story of a lecture he had given at Harvard in the late sixties shortly after arriving in the United States. During that lecture he described how patients in a psychiatric hospital in Prague had made tremendous improvements after going through LSD therapy, and how some of them had radically changed their world views as a result of the therapy, becoming seriously interested in yoga, meditation, and the realm of myth and archetypal images. During the discussion a Harvard psychiatrist remarked: "It seems to me that you helped these patients with their neurotic problems, but you made them psychotic."

"This comment," Grof explained, "is typical of a misunderstanding that is widespread and very problematic in psychiatry. The criteria used to define mental health—sense of identity, recognition of time and space, perception of the environment, and so on—require that a person's perceptions and views conform to the Cartesian-Newtonian framework. The Cartesian world view is not merely the principal frame of reference; it is regarded as the only valid description of reality. Anything else is considered to be psychotic by conventional psychiatrists."

His observations of transpersonal experiences had shown him, Grof continued, that human consciousness seems to be capable of two complementary modes of awareness. In the Cartesian-Newtonian mode, we perceive everyday reality in terms of separate objects, three-dimensional space, and linear time. In the transpersonal mode, the usual limitations of sensory perception and of logical reasoning are transcended and our perception shifts from solid objects to fluid energy patterns. Grof emphasized that he used the term "complementary" to describe the two modes of consciousness on purpose, because the corresponding modes of perception may be called "particle-like" and "wave-like" in analogy to quantum physics.

I was fascinated by this comment, as I suddenly saw a closed loop of influences in the history of science. I pointed out to Grof that Niels Bohr had been inspired by psychology when he chose the term "complementarity" to describe the relationship between the particle and wave aspects of subatomic matter. In particular, he had been impressed by William James's description of complementary modes of consciousness in schizophrenic persons. Now Grof was bringing the concept back into psychology, enriching it further through the analogy with quantum physics.

Since James had used the notion of complementarity in connection with schizophrenics, I was naturally curious to hear Grof's views on the nature of schizophrenia and of mental illness in general.

"There seems to be a fundamental dynamic tension between the two modes of consciousness," he explained. "To perceive reality exclusively in the transpersonal mode is incompatible with our normal functioning in the everyday world, and to experience the conflict and clash of the two modes without being able to integrate them is psychotic. You see, the symptoms of mental illness may be viewed as manifestations of an interface noise between the two modes of consciousness."

As I reflected on Grof's remarks, I asked myself how one would characterize a person functioning exclusively in the Cartesian mode, and I realized that this would also be madness.

As Laing would say, it is the madness of our dominant culture.

Grof agreed: "A person functioning exclusively in the Cartesian mode may be free from manifest symptoms but cannot be considered mentally healthy. Such individuals typically lead ego-centered, competitive, goal-oriented lives. They tend to be unable to derive satisfaction from ordinary activities in everyday life and become alienated from their inner world. For people whose existence is dominated by this mode of experience no level of wealth, power, or fame will bring genuine satisfaction. They become infused with a sense of meaninglessness, futility, and even absurdity that no amount of external success can dispel.

"A frequent error of current psychiatric practice," Grof concluded, "is to diagnose people as psychotics on the basis of the content of their experiences. My observations have convinced me that the idea of what is normal and what is pathological should not be based on the content and nature of people's experiences but on the way in which they are handled and on the degree to which a person is able to integrate these unusual experiences into his or her life. Harmonious integration of transpersonal experiences is crucial to mental health, and sympathetic support and assistance in this process is of critical importance to a successful therapy."

With this remark, Grof had broached the subject of psychotherapy, and I told him about the idea of a resonance between therapist and patient, which had emerged in my conversations with Laing and other psychotherapists. Grof agreed that such a "resonance" phenomenon is often a crucial element but added that there are other "catalysts" as well for inducing the healing process. "I myself believe that LSD is the most powerful catalyst of this kind," he said, "but other techniques have been developed to stimulate the organism, or energize it in some special way, so that its potential to heal itself becomes active.

"Once the therapeutic process has been initiated," Grof went on, "the role of the therapist is to facilitate the emerging experiences and help the client overcome resistances. You see, the idea here is that the symptoms of mental illness represent frozen elements of an experiential pattern that needs to be completed and fully integrated if the symptoms are to disappear. Rather than suppressing symptoms with psychoactive drugs, this kind of therapy will activate and intensify them to bring about their full experience, integration, and resolution."

"And this integration may include the transpersonal experiences you mentioned before?"

"Yes, it often will. In fact, the full unfolding of experiential patterns can be extremely dramatic and challenging for both client and therapist, but I believe that one should encourage and support the therapeutic process no matter what form and intensity it assumes. To do so, both therapist and client should suspend as much as possible their conceptual frameworks and expectations during the experiential process, which will often take the form of a kind of healing journey. My experience has shown me that if the therapist is willing to encourage and support such a venture into unknown territory, and if the client is open to it, they will often be rewarded by extraordinary therapeutic achievements."

Grof then told me that many new therapeutic techniques had been developed during the sixties and seventies to mobilize blocked energy and transform symptoms into experiences. In contrast to the traditional approaches, which are mostly limited to verbal exchanges, the new, so-called experiential therapies encourage nonverbal expression and emphasize direct experience involving the total organism. I knew that Esalen had been one of the principal centers of experimentation with these experiential therapies, and over the following years I would come to experience several of them myself in my search for holistic approaches to health and healing.

In fact, in the years following our conversation Stan himself, together with Christina, integrated hyperventilation, evocative music, and bodywork into a therapeutic method that can induce surprisingly intense experiences after a relatively short period of fast, deep breathing. After experimenting for many years with this method, which has since become widely known as "Grof breathing," Stan and Christina are convinced that it represents one of the most promising approaches to psychotherapy and self-exploration.

Discussions with June Singer

My explorations of the paradigm shift in psychology were dominated and shaped decisively by my recurrent interactions with Stan Grof and R. D. Laing. Between these conversations, however, I also had many discussions with other psychiatrists, psychologists, and psychotherapists. One of the most stimulating exchanges was a series of discussions with June Singer, a Jungian analyst whom I met in Chicago in April 1977. Singer had just published a book, *Androgyny*, on psychosexual manifestations of the masculine/feminine interplay and its numerous mythological representations. Since I had been interested for a long time in the Chinese concept of *yin* and *yang* as two archetypal complementary poles, which she had used extensively in her book, there was much common ground between us and many ideas to discuss. However, our conversations soon shifted to Jungian psychology and its parallels to modern physics.

At that time, I knew about the Cartesian-Newtonian framework of psychoanalysis from my first conversation with Stan Grof but I knew very little about Jungian psychology. What emerged from the conversations with June Singer was the remarkable observation that many of the differences between Freud and Jung parallel those between classical and modern physics. Singer told me that Jung himself, who was in close contact with several of the leading physicists of his time, was well aware of these parallels.

While Freud never abandoned the basic Cartesian orientation of his theory and tried to describe the dynamics of psychological processes in terms of specific mechanisms, Jung attempted to understand the human psyche in its totality and was especially concerned with its relations to the wider environment. His concept of the collective unconscious, in particular, implies a link between the individual and humanity as a whole, which cannot be understood within a mechanistic framework. Jung also used concepts that are surprisingly similar to the ones used in quantum physics. He saw the unconscious as a process involving "collectively present dynamic patterns," which he called archetypes. These archetypes, according to Jung, are embedded in a web of relationships, in which each archetype, ultimately, involves all the others.

Naturally, I was fascinated by these similarities and we decided that we would explore them further in a joint seminar, which Singer arranged at Northwestern University for the late fall. I have found this way of getting to know somebody's ideas, through giving joint seminars, extremely stimulating, and I have been fortunate to be able to participate in such exchanges many times throughout my intellectual journey.

The seminar with June Singer took place in November, that is, after my long conversations and joint workshops with Stan Grof. Thus I had a much better grasp of the innovative ideas in contemporary psychology and psychotherapy, and our discussions of the parallels between physics and Jungian psychology were very animated and productive. We continued them in the evening with a group of Jungian analysts who held regular training sessions with Singer, and there our conversation soon focused on Jung's notion of psychic energy. I was very curious as to whether Jung had the same concept of energy in mind that is used in the natural sciences (i.e., energy as a quantitative measure of activity) when he used that term. But I could not get a clear answer from this group of Jungians even after prolonged discussions. I recognized what the problem was only a few years later when I read Jung's essay "On Psychic Energy," and looking back on it today I can see this recognition as an important step in the development of my own ideas.

Jung used the term "psychic energy" in the quantitative, scientific sense, but in order to make contact with the natural sciences he drew numerous analogies to physics in his article, analogies which are often quite inappropriate for the description of living organisms and make his theory of psychic energy rather confusing. At the time of our discussions in Chicago I still saw the new physics as an ideal model for new concepts in other disciplines, and thus I was unable to pinpoint the problem in Jung's theory and in our discussion. It was only several years later, owing to the influence of Gregory Bateson and other systems theorists, that my thinking changed significantly. Once I had put the systems view of life in the center of my synthesis of the new paradigm, it became relatively easy to see that Jung's theory of psychic energy could be reformulated in modern systems language and thus made consistent with the most advanced current developments in the life sciences.

The roots of schizophrenia

In April 1978, I made another trip to England to give several lectures, and again I met with R. D. Laing. By that time, about one year after our first meeting, I had not only had many discussions with Stan Grof and other psychologists and psychotherapists, but had also become very interested in studying the conceptual framework of medicine and had given several lectures comparing the paradigm shifts in physics and medicine. I sent Laing several articles I had written on these subjects and asked him whether he would have another discussion with me during my visit to London. I specifically wanted to discuss the nature of mental illness, and especially of schizophrenia, with Laing, and I had prepared a rather precise agenda for this discussion.

This time I saw Laing at first at a party given by my friend Jill Purce. During most of the evening he was sitting on the floor, the center of attention, with about a dozen people gathered around him. In later years I often saw Laing in such situations. He loves to have an audience and this "holding court" often brings forth his brilliance, wit, and theatrical expressiveness. At Jill's party, my encounters with Laing were brief and rather unpleasant for me. I was eager to know what he thought of the material I had sent him, but he refused to enter into any serious discussion. Instead, he kept provoking me, teasing me, and playing all kinds of games. "Well, Dr. Capra," he would say sarcastically, "here we have a puzzle for you. How do you explain this one?" I felt very uncomfortable during the whole evening, which went on until quite late. Laing was one of the last to leave, and as he walked out the door he looked at me with a mischievous smile and said: "Okay, Thursday, one o'clock," which was the appointment we had made. I thought to myself: Oh my God, this is going to be so unpleasant! What am I going to do?

Two days later I met Laing at one o'clock at his home, and to my great surprise I saw immediately that he was totally different from the way he had been at the party. As at our first meeting, he was very kind, and he also was much more open than before. We went to a nearby Greek restaurant for lunch, and on the way Laing told me: "I read the material you sent me, and I agree with everything you say; so we can just take it from there." I was overjoyed. Once again Laing, a great authority in the medical field, and in particular on the subject of mental illness, had confirmed my first tentative steps, which gave me tremendous encouragement.

Throughout the meal Laing was extremely cooperative and helpful, and our discussion, in contrast to the first one, was very focused and quite systematic. My aim was to explore the nature of mental illness further. I had learned from Stan Grof that symptoms of mental illness may be viewed as "frozen" elements of an experiential pattern that needs to be completed for the healing to occur. Laing agreed completely with this view. He told me that most psychiatrists today never see the natural history of their patients because it is frozen by tranquilizers. In this frozen state, the patient's personality is bound to appear broken and his behavior unintelligible.

"But madness need not only be break*down*," said Laing; "it can also be break*through!*" He emphasized that a systemic and experiential perspective was needed to see that the behavior of a psychotic patient is by no means irrational but, on the contrary, quite sensible when viewed from the patient's existential position. From that perspective, he explained, even the most complex psychotic behavior may appear as a sensible strategy for survival.

When I asked Laing to give me an example of such psychotic strategies, he introduced me to Bateson's double-bind theory of schizophrenia, which, he told me, had greatly influenced his own thinking. According to Bateson, the "double-bind" situation is the central characteristic in the communication patterns of families of diagnosed schizophrenics. The behavior labeled as schizophrenic, Laing explained, represents the person's strategy for living in what he has come to experience as an unlivable situation, "a situation in which he cannot make a move, or make no move, without feeling pushed and pulled, both from within himself and from the people around him, a situation in which he can't win, no matter what he does." For example, the double bind may be set up for a child by contradictory verbal and nonverbal messages, either from one or from both parents, with both kinds of messages implying punishment or threats to the child's emotional security. When these situations occur frequently, Laing explained, the double-bind structure may become a habitual expectation in the child's mental life and may generate schizophrenic experiences and behavior.

Laing's description of the roots of schizophrenia made it quite clear to me why he believed that mental illness could only be understood by studying the social system in which the patient is embedded. "The behavior of the diagnosed patient," he insisted, "is part of a much larger network of disturbed behavior, of disturbed and disturbing patterns of communication. There is no schizophrenic person; there is only a schizophrenic system."

Even though our conversation often went into technical details, it was much more than just a scholarly discussion. Laing knows how to create drama and unusual experiences and, as in our first meeting, did so for me this time. When he explained something to me, he tried not merely to convey information but to create an experience as well. Experience, I would learn later, has been a subject of great fascination for Laing, and he maintains that it is something one cannot describe. So he tries to *generate* experience by illustrating his points with passion, intensity, and great theatrical flair.

For example, when he described the double bind to me, he illustrated it with the example of a child receiving conflicting messages from the parent: "Imagine a child in a state of mind where he never knows, when his mother approaches him and reaches out, whether she will caress him or hit him." While saying that, Laing looked at me with great intensity and slowly raised his hand until it was right in front of my face. For several seconds, I really did not know what would happen next, and I felt a sudden rush of anxiety combined with great uncertainty and confusion. This, of course, was exactly the effect he wanted to produce, and, naturally, he neither caressed nor hit me but relaxed after a few seconds and took a sip of wine. He had illustrated his point with perfect intensity and timing.

A little while later, Laing showed me how psychological patterns can manifest themselves as physical symptoms. He explained that somebody who is always holding back his emotions would tend also to hold in his breath and might develop an asthmatic condition. Laing demonstrated with very expressive gestures how this may come about, and he ended up mimicking an asthma attack with such realistic intensity that people in the restaurant began to turn around and look at him, thinking that there was really something wrong. All this made me feel quite uncomfortable, but again he had created a strong experience to illustrate his point.

From the nature of mental illness our conversation then

shifted to the therapeutic process, and here Laing emphasized very strongly that the best therapeutic approach was often to provide a supportive environment in which the patient's experiences are allowed to unfold. To do so, he said, required the help of sympathetic people with experience of such frightening journeys. "Instead of mental hospitals," he insisted, "we need initiation ceremonies in which the person will be guided through inner space by people who have been there and back again."

Laing's remark about a healing journey through inner space reminded me of the very similar conversation I had had with Stan Grof, and I was especially interested in hearing Laing's view on the similarities between the journeys of schizophrenics and mystics. I told him that Grof had pointed out to me that psychotic people often experience reality in transpersonal states of consciousness that are strikingly similar to those of mystics. Yet mystics, clearly, are not insane. According to Grof, our notions of what is normal and what is pathological should not be based on the content and nature of one's experience, but rather on the degree to which one is able to integrate these unusual experiences into one's life. Laing fully agreed with this view and confirmed that the experiences of schizophrenics, in particular, were often indistinguishable from those of mystics. "Mystics and schizophrenics find themselves in the same ocean," he said solemnly, "but the mystics swim whereas the schizophrenics drown."

Work and meditation at Big Sur

My second meeting with Laing in London marked a closure of my studies of the paradigm shift in psychology. During the rest of 1978 I turned to other fields—to medicine and health care on the one hand, to economics and ecology on the other. My friendship with Stan Grof, however, continued to play an important role in those activities. During the summer of 1978 I spent several weeks alone in his house working on my manuscript, while he and Christina were on lecture tours.

These weeks were the most perfect blending of work and meditation I have ever experienced. I slept on the couch in the Grofs' living room, enveloped in the slow, soothing rhythm of the ocean. I would get up long before the sun came over the mountains, do my *Tai Ji* exercises facing the gray expanse of the Pacific, make breakfast, and eat it on the balcony as the first rays of sun touched the deck. I would then begin to work in one corner of the room, wrapped in warm and comfortable clothes while the fresh morning breeze came in through the open balcony doors. As the sun rose higher, I would move my small table across the floor to remain in the shade, shedding my clothes in layers as the house heated up, ending up in shorts and T-shirt sweating in the blazing afternoon sun. I would continue to work with great concentration as the sun went down and the air cooled off, retracing my path across the room and gradually putting my clothes back on until, fully clothed, I would end up where I had started out, enjoying the cool breeze of the evening. At sunset I would pause for long contemplative moments, and at night I would light a fire and retire to the couch with books from Stan's extensive library.

I worked steadily in this way day after day, sometimes fasting for several days, sometimes interrupting my work to go over to Esalen for conversations with Gregory Bateson. I built a sundial to keep track of the passing hours and immersed myself completely in the cyclical rhythms that shaped my activities—the recurring passages of night and day, the ebb and flow of cool sea breezes and blazing summer sun, and in the background the endless rhythm of waves crashing against the rocks, waking me up in the morning and sending me to sleep at night.

The Saragossa conference

Two years later, in September 1980, I had my third, longest, and most intensive encounter with R. D. Laing. It was at a conference in Spain on "The Psychotherapy of the Future," sponsored by the European Association for Humanistic Psychology. By that time I had already written a sizable portion of *The Turning Point* and had decided to draw a firm line and not accept any further information for the manuscript. However, my meeting with Laing was so disturbing and challenging that I altered my decision and incorporated some essential aspects of our conversations into the text.

The conference took place near Saragossa at the Monasterio de Piedra, a beautiful twelfth-century monastery which had been converted into a hotel. The array of participants was very impressive. In addition to Laing, there were Stan Grof, Jean Houston, and Rollo May, and the group would also have included Gregory Bateson had he not died two months earlier. The entire conference lasted three weeks, but I stayed for only one week because I was in the midst of writing and did not want to interrupt my work for a longer period. During that week I experienced a wonderful feeling of community and adventure generated by the extraordinary group of participants and the magnificent setting of the conference. Lectures were held in the old refectory of the monastery, often by candlelight; there were seminars in the cloister and in the garden, and informal discussions on a large balcony until late at night.

Laing was the animating spirit of the entire conference. Most of the discussions and happenings revolved around his ideas and the many facets of his personality. He had come to the conference with a large entourage of family, friends, former patients, and disciples, including even a small film crew. He was active day and night and never seemed to tire. He gave lectures and seminars, and arranged filmed dialogues with other participants. He spent many evenings in intensive discussions with small groups of people, which usually ended in long monologues when everybody else had become too tired to continue the conversation; and he would often end up at the piano, long after midnight, and reward those who had held out that long with superb renditions of Cole Porter and Gershwin.

During that week I really got to know Laing. Up to then our relationship had been cordial and our discussions very inspiring for me, but it was not until the Saragossa conference that I really got close to Laing on a personal level. When I arrived at the Monasterio, I ran into him right away in the cloister. I had not seen him in two years and he greeted me very warmly with a big, affectionate hug. I was surprised and very touched by this spontaneous expression of affection. On the same evening, after dinner, Laing invited me to join him and a group of friends for a glass of cognac and discussions. We all sat down on the balcony, surrounded by the balmy breezes of that beautiful Mediterranean summer evening, Laing and I side by side, leaning against the white stucco wall with a fairly large circle of people in front of us.

Ronnie (as I had begun to call Laing, following the example of his friends) asked me what I had been up to in the past two years, and I told him that I was working on my book and that, lately, I had become very interested in the nature of mind and consciousness. The next thing I knew Laing was attacking me extremely vigorously. "How dare you, as a scientist, even ask about the nature of consciousness," he scowled indignantly. "You have absolutely no right to ask that question, to even use words like 'consciousness,' or 'mystical experience.' It is preposterous of you to dare mention science and Buddhism in the same breath!" This was not a joking, teasing attack like that at the London party. It was the beginning of a serious, vigorous, and sustained attack on my position as a scientist, voiced passionately in an angry and accusing tone.

I was shocked. I was not prepared at all for such an outburst. Laing was supposed to be on my side! Indeed, he had been; and I was especially taken aback by his attacking me like this on the day I had arrived and just a few hours after his warm welcome. At the same time, I felt his intellectual challenge, and my shock and confusion soon gave way to intense mental activity, as I tried to understand Laing's position, evaluate it in relation to my own, and prepare myself for responding. In fact, as he continued his passionate diatribe against science, which he saw me as representing, I found myself becoming very excited. I have always enjoyed intellectual challenge, and this was the most dramatic challenge I had ever encountered. Once again, Laing had placed our dialogue in a spectacular setting. Not only was I leaning against the wall of the balcony facing Ronnie's tribe of friends and disciples; I also felt pushed against the wall metaphorically by his relentless attack. But I did not mind. In my state of excitement all traces of embarrassment and discomfort had disappeared.

The main point of Laing's attack was that science, as it is practiced today, has no way of dealing with consciousness, or with experience, values, ethics, or anything referring to quality. "This situation derives from something that happened in European consciousness at the time of Galileo and Giordano Bruno," Laing began his argument. "These two men epitomize two paradigms—Bruno, who was tortured and burned for saying that there were infinite worlds; and Galileo, who said that the scientific method was to study this world as if there were no consciousness and no living creatures in it. Galileo made the statement that only quantifiable phenomena were admitted to the domain of science. Galileo said: 'Whatever cannot be measured and quantified is not scientific'; and in post-Galilean science this came to mean: 'What cannot be quantified is not real.' This has been the most profound corruption from the Greek view of nature as *physis*, which is alive, always in transformation, and not divorced from us. Galileo's program offers us a dead world: Out go sight, sound, taste, touch, and smell, and along with them have since gone esthetic and ethical sensibility, values, quality, soul, consciousness, spirit. Experience as such is cast out of the realm of scientific discourse. Hardly anything has changed our world more during the past four hundred years than Galileo's audacious program. We had to destroy the world in theory before we could destroy it in practice."

Laing's critique was devastating, but as he paused and reached for his glass of cognac, and before I could say anything in reply he leaned over me and whispered under his breath so that nobody else could hear it: "You don't mind me setting you up like that, do you?" With that aside he instantly created a conspiratorial mood and shifted the whole context of his attack. I just had time to whisper back, "Not at all!" and then I had to concentrate fully on my response.

I defended myself as well as I could, being put on the spot with hardly any time for reflection. I said that I agreed with Laing's analysis of Galileo's role in the history of science, realizing at the same time that I had concentrated much more on Descartes and had not sufficiently appreciated the importance of Galileo's emphasis on quantification. I also agreed with Laing that there was no room for experience, values, and ethics in the science of today. However, I then went on to say that my own endeavor was precisely to help change today's science in such a way that these considerations could be incorporated into the scientific framework of the future. To do so, I emphasized, the first step had to be the shift from the mechanistic and fragmented approach of classical science to a holistic paradigm, in which the main emphasis was no longer on separate entities but on relationships. This would make it possible to introduce context and meaning. Only when one had that holistic framework, I concluded, could one begin to take further steps in response to Laing's concerns.

Laing was not immediately satisfied with my response. He

wanted a more radical approach, going beyond the intellect altogether. "The universe was a vast machine yesterday," he said sarcastically; "it is a hologram today. Who knows what intellectual rattle we'll be shaking tomorrow." Thus the argument went back and forth for quite a while, and in the midst of it Ronnie leaned over to me once more and said softly, in a confidential tone: "You realize, the questions I am asking you are all questions I am asking myself. I am not just attacking you, or other scientists out there. I am tarred with the same brush. I could not get so curled up over this if it were not a personal struggle."

The discussion went on until very late that night, and when I finally went to bed I still could not sleep for a long time. Laing had presented me with a tremendous challenge. I had spent the previous two years studying and integrating various attempts to expand the framework of science, including Laing's own approaches in addition to those of Grof, Jung, Bateson, Prigogine, Chew, and many others. After long months of carefully structuring my voluminous notes I had sketched the outlines of a radically new conceptual framework and had just begun to mold all that work into the text of the book. At that critical stage Laing was challenging me to expand my framework even further—further than anything I had attempted—in order to incorporate quality, values, experience, consciousness. Did I want to go that far? Could I do it and, if not, how was I to deal with Laing's challenge? The impact of that first Saragossa evening was too strong for me to simply drop the entire subject. Somehow, I *had* to deal with Laing's argument, both in my mind and in my book. But how was I going to handle it?

I spent most of the following day pondering my problem, and in the evening I was ready to see Laing again. "I have thought a lot about what you said last night, Ronnie," I told him at dinner, "and I would like to respond to your critique in a more complete and systematic way tonight, if you feel like sitting down with me for another glass of cognac." Laing agreed, and so we settled down on the balcony again after dinner in the same setting as the night before.

"I would like to present to you tonight," I began, "as completely and systematically as I can, the view of mind and consciousness that I see emerging from the conceptual framework that I am now developing and which I shall present in my book. This is not a framework in which your critique can be fully satisfied, but I believe, as I said last night, that it is a necessary first step toward that goal. From the vantage point of my new framework, you can actually begin to see how experience, values, and consciousness might be incorporated in the future."

Laing simply nodded his head and kept listening attentively with intense concentration. I then proceeded to give him a concise but nevertheless fairly extensive presentation of my ideas. I began with the view of living organisms as self-organizing systems, explained Prigogine's notion of dissipative structures, and emphasized especially the view of biological forms as manifestations of underlying processes. I then wove in Bateson's concept of mind as the dynamics of self-organization and related it to Jung's notion of the collective unconscious. Finally, having carefully prepared the ground, I addressed the issue of consciousness. To do so, I first specified that what I meant by "consciousness" was the property of mind characterized by self-awareness. "Awareness," I argued, "is a property of mind at all levels of complexity. Self-awareness, as far as we know, manifests itself only in higher animals and fully unfolds in the human mind; and it is this property of mind that I mean by consciousness."

"Now, if we look at theories of consciousness," I continued, "we can see that most of them are variations of two seemingly opposite views. One of these views I will call the Western scientific view. It considers matter as primary and consciousness as a property of complex material patterns, which emerges at a certain level of biological evolution. Most neuroscientists today subscribe to this view."

I paused for a moment, and seeing that Laing had no intention of interjecting anything, I proceeded: "The other view of consciousness may be called the mystical view, since it is generally held in mystical traditions. It regards consciousness as the primary reality, as the essence of the universe, the ground of all being, and everything else—all forms of matter and all living beings—as manifestations of that pure consciousness. This mystical view of consciousness is based on the experience of reality in non-ordinary modes of awareness, and such mystical experience, they say, is indescribable. It is . . ."

"Any experience!" Laing shouted, interrupting me force-fully, and when he saw my puzzled look, he repeated: "Any experience! Any experience of reality is indescribable! Just look around you for a moment and see, hear, smell, and feel where you are."

I did as he told me, becoming fully aware of the mild summer night, the white walls of the balcony against the outlines of trees in the park, the sound of crickets, the half moon hanging in the sky, the faint strains of a Spanish guitar in the distance, and the closeness and attention of the crowd surrounding us—experiencing a symphony of shades, sounds, smells, and feelings, while Laing continued: "Your consciousness can partake of all that is in one single moment, but you will never be able to describe the experience. It's not just mystical experience; it's *any* experience." I knew that Laing was right, and I also knew immediately that his point needed much further thought and discussion, even though it did not directly affect my argument, which I was about to conclude.

"Okay, Ronnie, *any* experience," I agreed. "Now, since the mystical view of consciousness is based on direct experience, we should not expect science, at its present stage, to confirm or contradict it. Nevertheless, I feel that the systems view of mind seems to be perfectly consistent with both views and could therefore provide an ideal framework for unifying the two."

Again I paused briefly to collect my thoughts, and as Laing remained silent I went on to clinch my argument: "The systems view agrees with the conventional scientific view that consciousness is a property of complex material patterns. To be precise, it is a property of living systems of a certain complexity. On the other hand, the biological structures of these systems are manifestations of underlying processes. What processes? Well, the processes of self-organization, which we have identified as mental processes. In this sense, biological structures are manifestations of mind. Now, if we extend this way of thinking to the universe as a whole, it is not too far-fetched to assume that *all* its structures—from subatomic particles to galaxies and from bacteria to human beings—are manifestations of the universal dynamics of self-organization, which means of the cosmic mind. And this, more or less, is the mystical view. Now, I realize that there are several leaps in this argument. Still, I feel that the systems view of life provides a meaningful framework for unifying the traditional approaches to the age-old questions of the nature of life, mind, and consciousness."

Now I fell silent. My long monologue had been a tremendous effort for me. For the first time I had laid out, as clearly and concisely as I could, my entire framework for approaching the questions of life, mind, and consciousness. I had presented it to the most knowledgeable and forceful critic I knew and had been as inspired, spontaneous, and alert as I would ever be. So this was my answer to Laing's challenge of the previous evening, and after a while I asked him: "How does that sound to you, Ronnie? What do you think of it?"

Laing lit a cigarette, took a sip of cognac, and finally made the most encouraging comment I could have hoped for. "I will have to think about it," he said simply. "This is not something I can address myself to right away. You have introduced quite a few new ideas and I will have to think about them."

With this comment the tension that had persisted for the last hour was broken and we spent the rest of the evening in a very relaxed and warm conversation in which Laing and I were joined by many of our group. Again the conversation went on until very late, with Laing quoting freely from Thomas Aquinas, Sartre, Nietzsche, Bateson, and many others. As the night drew on I got more and more tired, while Laing kept stringing together long monologues that became more and more convoluted. Noticing my fatigue and lack of concentration after a while, he turned to me and said with an affectionate smile: "You see, Fritjof, the main difference between us is that you are an Apollonian thinker and I am a Dionysian thinker."

During the next two days, I spent most of my time with Ronnie and his friends in a relaxed and playful mood without ever mentioning our discussion. However, Laing lent me an early draft of the manuscript of his book *The Voice of Experience*, in which I found the forceful accusation of post-Galilean science that he had thrown at me during our first evening on the balcony. I was so impressed by this powerful passage that I copied it down to quote it in *The Turning Point*. I remember that one year later, when I had finished writing my book, Laing showed me the final version of his manuscript, and to my great disappointment I noticed that it no longer contained that passage. When I told Laing about my disappointment, he smiled: "Fritjof, if you cited that passage, I am going to put it back."*

After a couple of days of relaxation and some more thinking, I found a way in which quality and experience might possibly be incorporated into a future science, and the next day after lunch I invited Laing to join me for coffee in a café next to the hotel. When we sat down and I asked him what I could order for him, he said: "If you don't mind, I'll have a black coffee, a beer, and a cognac." When this unusual combination arrived, Laing drank the beer and then the coffee but left the cognac untouched for the time being.

I began to elaborate on what I had presented to him the other evening by reviewing the methodology of conventional science, in which data are gathered by observation and measurement, and are then interconnected with the help of conceptual models that are expressed, whenever possible, in mathematical language. I emphasized that the quantification of all statements has traditionally been seen as a crucial criterion of the scientific approach, and I agreed with Laing that such a science is inadequate for understanding the nature of consciousness and will not be able to deal with any qualities or values.

Laing lit a cigarette and reached for his cognac; swirling it in the glass, he savored its aroma but did not drink it.

"A true science of consciousness," I went on, "would have to be a new type of science dealing with qualities rather than quantities and being based on shared experience rather than verifiable measurements. The data of such a science would be patterns of experience that cannot be quantified or analyzed. On the other hand, the conceptual models interconnecting the data would have to be logically consistent, like all scientific models, and might even include quantitative elements. Such a new science would quantify its statements whenever this method is appropriate, but would also be able to deal with qualities and values based on human experience."

"I would add to this," Laing replied, the untouched glass of cognac still in his hand, "that the new science, the new epistemology, has got to be predicated upon a change of heart, upon a complete turning around; from the intent to dominate and control nature to the idea of, for example, Francis of Assisi,

---

* He actually never did; the passage quoted in The Turning Point is from the first draft of Laing's manuscript.

that the whole creation is our companion, if not our mother. That is part of your turning point. Only then can we address ourselves to alternative perceptions that will come into view."

Laing then went on to speculate about a new kind of language that would be appropriate for the new science. He pointed out to me that conventional scientific language is descriptive, whereas language to share experience needs to be *depictive*. It would be a language more akin to poetry, or even to music, which would depict an experience directly, conveying, somehow, its qualitative character. "I have become more doubtful about language as a necessary paradigm for thinking," he mused. "If we think in terms of music, is that a language?"

As I reflected on these comments, several of our friends entered the café, and Laing asked me whether I minded if they joined us. Of course I did not mind, and Ronnie invited them to sit down. "Let me just tell these people what you and I have been talking about," he continued. "If you don't mind, let me just reiterate what you have been saying." He then proceeded to give a brilliant summary of what I had said three nights before and during the last hour. He summarized the entire conceptual framework in his own words, in his highly idiosyncratic style, with all the intensity and passion that are characteristic of him. After this discourse, which amounted to an exhortation, there was no more doubt in my mind about whether Laing had accepted my ideas. I felt very strongly that we were now indeed, in his own metaphor, swimming in the same ocean.

We had been sitting in the café for a couple of hours when Laing suddenly remembered that he was scheduled to lecture that afternoon. So we all moved to the refectory of the Monasterio where Laing delivered an inspired lecture on his new book, *The Voice of Experience*. He spoke for over an hour without any notes, standing easily and underlining his words with eloquent gestures, the untouched glass of cognac, that most elegant of props, still in his hand. I spent the remainder of the evening in Laing's company, yet I never saw him drink that cognac.

My stay in Saragossa was by then coming to an end, and it ended on a very high note. During my last two days, at the end of the second week of the conference, Stan and Christina Grof arrived at the Monasterio. I had presented a brief introduction to their work a few days before, based on my discussions with Stan and on my own experiences of "Grof breathing," and their arrival had been awaited very eagerly. Being in the same place with both of my mentors, Grof and Laing, for the first time, I could not resist the temptation to arrange a three-way conversation, and I suggested a public panel discussion on the question "What is the nature of consciousness?" The discussion, in which the three of us were joined by another psychiatrist, Roland Fischer, took place in the afternoon in the packed dining room, with Laing playing the master of ceremonies.

This was an excellent opportunity for me to review, test, and solidify what I had learned from my long conversations with Laing during the whole week and, at the same time, to see how he and Grof would respond to each other's ideas. To begin the discussion, Laing asked the three of us for brief opening statements, and Grof and Fischer responded by outlining the scientific and mystical views of consciousness, much as I had done in my conversation with Laing several days before. I then added a brief outline of the systems view of mind and carefully specified my terminology. I emphasized in particular that I saw awareness as a property of mind at all levels of life and self-awareness as the crucial characteristic of that level where consciousness is manifest.

After a moment of reflection, Laing turned to me: "You were very careful to unfold these terms—mind, consciousness, awareness, self-awareness. Would you care to add to your definitions a definition of matter?"

I realized immediately that he had put his finger on a very difficult question. I responded by contrasting the Newtonian view of matter as consisting of basic building blocks, all of which in turn are made of the same material substance, with the Einsteinian view of mass being a form of energy and matter consisting of patterns of energy continually transforming themselves into one another. However, I also had to admit that, while it is understood that all energy is a measure of activity, physicists do not have an answer to the question: What is it that is active?

Laing now turned to Grof and asked him whether he accepted my definitions. "I grew up with the scientific view, which I learned in medical school," Stan began. "But as I began my LSD research, I found this view increasingly untenable, and my observations would also present many problems for Fritjof's definitions. For example, in psychedelic sessions there seems to be a continuous line from human consciousness to very authentic experiences of animal consciousness, to experiences of plant consciousness, and all the way to the consciousness of inorganic phenomena; for example, consciousness of the ocean, of a tornado, or even of a rock. At all these levels people may have access to information that definitely is beyond anything they would normally know."

Laing turned back to me: "How do you accommodate experiences of that kind, which are also reported by people in deep meditation, in shamanism, and so forth? Do you accept these experiences on their own terms, or do you feel that some other form of accounting has to be given? How do you integrate that sort of thing into your world view?"

I agreed that, from the scientific point of view, I would certainly have great difficulties with the notion of a rock being conscious. I added, however, that I also believed in the possibility of a future synthesis between the scientific and the mystical views of consciousness, and I outlined once more my framework for such a synthesis. "As far as the rock is concerned," I concluded, "I cannot ascribe any consciousness to it from the perspective of seeing it as a distinct entity. But from the perspective of seeing it as part of a larger system, the universe, which is mindful and conscious, I would say that the rock, like everything else, participates in that larger consciousness. Mystics and people with transpersonal experiences, typically, would place themselves in that larger perspective."

Grof agreed: "When people experience the consciousness of a plant or a rock, they do not see the world as being full of objects and then add consciousness to that Cartesian universe. They would start out from a fabric of conscious states out of which the Cartesian reality is then, somehow, orchestrated."

At this point, Roland Fischer introduced a third perspective by reminding us that what we perceive is largely created through interactional processes. "For example," he explained, "the sweetness we taste in a piece of sugar is neither a property of the sugar nor a property of ourselves. We are producing the experience of sweetness in the process of interacting with the sugar."

"This is exactly the kind of observation Heisenberg made

about atomic phenomena, which were thought to have independent, objective properties in classical physics," I interjected.
"Heisenberg showed that an electron, for example, may appear
as a particle or a wave depending on how you look at it. If you
ask it a particle question, it will give you a particle answer; if
you ask it a wave question, it will give you a wave answer.
'Natural science,' writes Heisenberg, 'does not simply describe
and explain nature; it is part of the interplay between nature
and ourselves.' "

"If the whole universe is like the sweet taste," Laing replied, "which is neither in the observer nor in the observed but
in the relationship between the two, how can you then talk
about the universe as though it were an observed object? You
seem to talk as if there were a universe which then evolves in
some way."

"It is very difficult to talk about the evolution of the entire
universe," I conceded, "because the concept of evolution implies
a sense of time, and when you talk about the universe as a
whole, you have to go beyond the conventional notion of linear
time. For the same reason, it does not make much sense to say,
'first there was matter and then consciousness,' or 'first consciousness and then matter,' because those statements, too, imply a linear concept of time, which is inappropriate at the cosmic level."

Now Laing turned to Grof with a sweeping question: "Stan,
all of us here know that you have spent the greater part of your
life studying different states of consciousness; unusual, altered
states as well as ordinary states of mind. What is your testi-
mony? What do your studies of experience and your own experiences have to tell us that we wouldn't know otherwise?"

Grof began slowly after some reflection: "Many years ago,
I went through thousands of records of LSD sessions to study
specifically those statements that addressed themselves to fundamental cosmological and ontological questions—What is the
nature of the universe? What is the origin and purpose of life?
How is consciousness related to matter? Who am I and what is
my place in the overall scheme of things? While studying these
records, I was surprised to find that the seemingly disconnected
experiences of these LSD subjects could be integrated and organized into a comprehensive metaphysical system, a system that
I have called 'psychedelic cosmology and ontology.'

"The framework of this system is radically different from the ordinary framework of our everyday lives," Grof continued. "It is based on the concept of a Universal Mind, or Cosmic Consciousness, which is the creative force behind the cosmic design. All the phenomena we experience are understood as experiments in consciousness performed by the Universal Mind in an infinitely ingenious creative play. The problems and baffling paradoxes associated with human existence are seen as intricately contrived deceptions invented by the Universal Mind and built into the cosmic game; and the ultimate meaning of human existence is to experience fully all the states of mind associated with this fascinating adventure in consciousness; to be an intelligent actor and playmate in the cosmic game. In this framework, consciousness is not something that can be derived from or explained in terms of something else. It is a primal fact of existence out of which everything else arises. This, very briefly, would be my credo. It is a framework into which I can really integrate all my observations and experiences."

There was a long silence after Grof's inspired summary of the deepest aspects of his psychedelic research, and it was Laing who finally broke it with a powerful poetic statement: "Life, like a dome of many-colored glass, stains the white radiance of eternity." At that time, I did not know that Laing was quoting Shelley, and after another pause he addressed himself again to Grof: "That white radiance of eternity, as it were, from within itself, is that what you mean by pure consciousness? Of course we are taking our chances in using words to refer to these mysteries. There is not very much you really can say about what is ineffable."

Grof agreed: "When people were in these special states, their experience was always ineffable; there was no way they could describe it. Yet, they expressed again and again a feeling of having arrived, a sense that all questions had been answered. There was no need for them to ask anything and there was nothing to be explained."

Laing paused again and then slightly changed the subject: "Let me put to you the view of the skeptic," he said to Grof. "You said a while ago that people under LSD may have access to knowledge they would not normally possess; for example, knowledge about embryonic life gained from their memories or visions. Yet, these neo-Gnostic visions seem to have contributed nothing to scientific embryology. Similarly, psychedelic experiences of being drawn into a flower, of becoming a flower, seem to have contributed nothing whatsoever to the science of botany. Don't you think they ought to have contributed something if they were more than compelling, subtle illusions?"

"Not necessarily. According to my observations, experiencing oneself as an embryo can add an enormous amount to one's knowledge of the embryonic state. I have seen again and again that information was communicated about the embryonal physiology, anatomy, biochemistry, and so on, which was beyond what people knew. But in order to really contribute to embryology, the person having those experiences would have to be an embryologist."

"Well, there have certainly been a few doctors who have taken LSD," Laing pressed on. "I don't know whether there have been any distinguished embryologists. But anyway, when these professionally trained people, including myself, come back from their psychedelic experiences, there does not seem to be any translation into the objective, scientific terms that would appear in a paper on embryology."

"I think it is possible, though."

"Well, the formal pattern of correspondence between the forms of transformation in Gnostic visions and the forms of transformation in embryonic life is indeed very, very striking. Even the sequences are often exactly the same. The Orpheans, for instance, knew that the head of Orpheus floated down the river into the ocean, but, apparently, they did not ever dream that all of us, as spheres in our mothers' wombs, floated down the uterine canal into the ocean of the uterus. That connection was never made. The curious thing is that the descriptions of actual embryonic states, as given for example in Tibetan texts of embryology, are not nearly as close to what we now know as the description in the mystic visions. Once we had a microscope, we could actually see the correspondence between the embryonic forms and these cosmic visions. Until we had a microscope and actually saw it, looking *at* it from the outside, that match with visions from within was never made."

"You could also say that about Tantric models of cosmology," Grof added. "They are often extremely close to the models of modern astrophysicists. In fact, it was not until the last few decades that astrophysicists came up with similar concepts."

"In a way, there is no surprise," Laing mused, "that the

most profound structures in our consciousness correspond to the structures out there in the universe. And yet! Shamans may have been to the moon but they never brought back any moon rocks. Somehow, we don't know the limits of the possibilities of our own consciousness. We seem to be unable to say what are the heights and depths of our mind. Isn't that a strange thing?"

"Ronnie," Grof continued, "you mentioned before that until there were the appropriate tools, the inner visions could not be correlated with external, scientific facts. Would you agree that now that we have these tools, somehow we should be able to combine information that comes from inner states with knowledge gained through objective science and technology into a totally new vision of reality?"

"That's right," Laing agreed. "I think . . . that conjunction is the most exciting adventure of the contemporary mind. While everything is always there from the beginning and at the end, there is also a process of evolving, and the evolution of our time is exactly that possibility of the synthesis of what we see by looking at things from the outside with what we can know from within."

Understanding Laing

When I left Saragossa on the next day to return to the United States I could not leave Ronnie Laing behind. His voice kept ringing in my ears and for weeks I remembered every word of our conversations as if under a spell. The experience of our encounters was so intense that it took me several weeks to get Laing out of my system. My meetings with Bateson, Grof, and many other remarkable people were exciting, inspiring, and illuminating. My meetings with Laing were all of that, but more than anything else they were dramatic. Laing shook me up, attacked me, and challenged my thinking to its very core, but then he accepted me and embraced many of my tentative ideas. In the end we had formed a warm, personal relationship with a strong sense of camaraderie that has continued to the present day.

Since our conversations in Saragossa I have visited Ronnie several more times in London and we have also been together in other conferences, joint seminars, and panel discussions. These conversations have continued to enrich and inspire me and have also deepened my understanding of Laing's personality, ideas, and professional work. The question of how experience might be approached within a new scientific framework had been at the center of our discussions in Saragossa, and over the subsequent years I came to see experience as a key to understanding Laing. I think that his entire life may be viewed as a passionate exploration of the "many-colored dome" of human experience—through philosophy, religion, music, and poetry; through meditation and mind-altering drugs; through his writing, his intimate contacts with schizophrenics, and his struggles with the pathologies of our society. It is through experience, Laing insists, that we reveal ourselves to one another, and it is experience which gives meaning to our lives. "Experience weaves meaning and fact into one seamless robe," he argued in one of our conversations in Saragossa, and the book he was writing at that time is titled, characteristically, *The Voice of Experience*.

Experience, I believe, is also the key to understanding Laing's therapeutic work. The story he told me at our first meeting in London—of a patient bursting into tears after a seemingly ordinary conversation: "For the first time, I have felt like a human being"—stayed in my mind for many years. When Laing and I gave a joint seminar in San Francisco in January 1982, I finally understood that this story was a perfect illustration of the way Laing works. His therapy is largely nonverbal, goes far beyond technique, and, ultimately, has to be experienced in order to be understood.

"Psychotherapy," Laing explained during the seminar, "is a matter of communicating experience, not a matter of imparting objective information," and then he went on to illustrate his point by depicting a situation that seemed to encapsulate the very essence of his approach: "When someone comes into my room and stands there, making no movement and not saying anything, I don't think of this person as a mute catatonic schizophrenic. If I ask myself, 'Why is he not moving and not talking to me?' I don't need to enter into psychodynamic, speculative explanations. I see immediately that I've got a chap standing in front of me who is scared stiff! He's scared so stiff that he is frozen with terror. Why is he frozen with terror? Well, I don't know why. So, I'm going to make it clear to this chap through the way I conduct myself that he does not have anything to be scared about with me."

When asked how he would convey this message, Laing answered that he might do any number of things: "I might walk around the room; I might go to sleep; I might read a book. To be an effective therapist, so that such a person might 'thaw out,' as it were, I have to show that *I* am not frightened of *him*. That is a very important point. If you are frightened of your patients, you shouldn't bother to be a therapist."

As Laing spoke, I could imagine him falling asleep in front of a schizophrenic patient and I realized that he was probably the only psychiatrist in the world who would actually do such a thing. He would not be afraid of psychotics because their experience is not foreign to him. He has been to the farther reaches of the mind himself, has experienced their ecstasies as well as their terrors, and would be able to give an authentic response, based on his own experience, to virtually anything a patient could show him. Laing's response would be essentially nonverbal, while his conversation with the patient might seem most ordinary to an observer. He remarked that, indeed, it would be difficult to recognize his exchanges with schizophrenics as being any different from an ordinary conversation between two people. "Once a conversation has started up," he observed, "whatever was once called schizophrenia has evaporated completely."

In his therapy, then, Laing uses his rich reservoir of experience, great intuition, and ability to give people his undivided attention in order to allow the psychotic patient to breathe freely and feel comfortable in his presence. Paradoxically, the same Ronnie Laing often makes "normal" people feel very uncomfortable. I have long puzzled over this paradox without fully understanding it. Since Laing makes psychotics feel comfortable by showing that he is not frightened of them, does he make so-called normal people feel uncomfortable because they frighten him? "Normal" people, according to Laing, form our insane society, and he seems to use the same intuition and attention to disturb them and shake them up.

The two schools of Zen

My intensive conversations with Stanislav Grof and R. D. Laing now lie more than five years in the past. Looking back on them, I am tempted to compare the influence of these two extraordinary men on my thinking to the two schools of Zen that have coexisted in the Japanese Buddhist tradition with radically different methods of teaching. The Rinzai or "sudden" school creates long periods of intense concentration and sustained tension, leading up to sudden insights triggered occasionally by unexpected dramatic acts by the master, such as a blow with a stick or a loud yell. The Soto or "gradual" school avoids the shock methods of Rinzai and aims at the gradual maturing of the student through quiet sitting.

For several years I was most fortunate in receiving both kinds of instruction in alternating interchanges with two modern masters of the science of mind. My dramatic encounters with Laing and my quiet conversations with Grof gave me deep insights into the expressions of the new paradigm in psychology, and also had a tremendous impact on my own personal development. The teachings I received from them are well described by a classic summary of Zen Buddhism, "a special transmission outside the scriptures, pointing directly to the human mind."

5

The Search for Balance

CARL SIMONTON

When I planned to explore the change of paradigms in several fields beyond physics I first turned to the field of medicine. This was a natural choice for me because I had become interested in the parallels between the paradigm shifts in physics and those in medicine long before I planned to write *The Turning Point*. In fact, when I first became aware of the emergence of a new paradigm in medicine I had not even finished writing *The Tao of Physics*. I was introduced to new holistic approaches to health and healing in May 1974 at one of the most remarkable conferences I have ever been to. It was a weeklong residential retreat called the May Lectures, which took place in England at Brunel University near London, and was sponsored by several organizations from the British and American human potential movements. The subject of the conference was "New Approaches to

Health and Healing—Individual and Social." In addition to the residential program, to which about fifty participants from Europe and North America had been invited, public evening lectures were given in London by some participants.

At the May Lectures I met Carl Simonton, who would become one of my key advisers for *The Turning Point* a few years later, and I also had my first discussions with several other leaders of the budding holistic health movement with whom I would remain in contact for many years to come. In addition to Carl Simonton and his wife, Stephanie, who presented their revolutionary mind/body approach to cancer therapy, participants included Rick Carlson, a young lawyer who had just written *The End of Medicine*, a radical assessment of the health-care crisis; Moshe Feldenkrais, one of the most influential teachers of "bodywork" therapies; Elmer and Alyce Green, the pioneers of biofeedback research; Emil Zmenak, a Canadian chiropractor who demonstrated his intimate knowledge of the human muscular and nervous systems with impressive techniques of muscle testing; Norman Shealy, who later founded the American Holistic Medical Association; and a relatively large number of researchers in parapsychology and practitioners of psychic healing, reflecting the strong interest of the human potential movement in so-called paranormal phenomena.

The outstanding characteristic of this gathering was a tremendous sense of excitement among all the participants, generated by the collective awareness that a profound shift in concepts was about to happen in Western science and philosophy, which was bound to lead to a new medicine, based on different perceptions of human nature in health and illness. The assembled researchers, healers, and health professionals were all disenchanted with conventional medical care, had developed and tested new ideas and had pioneered new therapeutic approaches, but had for the most part never met before. Many of them, moreover, had been shunned or attacked by the medical establishment and were now discovering, for the first time, a large circle of peers who were not only intellectually stimulating but also gave one another moral and emotional support. The seminars, discussions, demonstrations, and informal meetings, which generally lasted until late at night, were infused with a captivating sense of adventure, cognitive expansion, and camaraderie that made a lasting impression on all of us.

The conceptual framework that emerged in outline at the end of the conference after one week of intensive discussions contained many elements of the framework I would research, develop, and synthesize in my work on *The Turning Point* several years later. The participants agreed that the paradigm shift in science was one from a mechanistic and reductionist view of human nature to a holistic and ecological vision. They clearly saw the mechanistic approach of conventional medicine, rooted in the Cartesian image of the human body as a clockwork, as the main source of the current crisis in health care. They were extremely critical of our system of acute, hospital-based, drug-oriented medical care, and many participants believed that modern scientific medicine had reached its limits and was no longer able to improve, or even maintain, public health.

The discussions made clear that future health care would have to go far beyond the scope of conventional medicine to deal with the large network of phenomena that influence health. It would not need to abandon the study of the biological aspects of illness, in which medical science excels, but would have to relate these aspects to the general physical and psychological conditions of human beings in their natural and social environments.

From the discussions emerged a set of new concepts that would form the basis of a future holistic system of health care. One of these basic new concepts was the recognition of the complex interdependence between mind and body in health and illness, suggesting a "psychosomatic" approach to all forms of therapy. The other was the realization of the fundamental interconnectedness between human beings and the surrounding environment and, accordingly, increased awareness of social and environmental aspects of health. Both kinds of interconnectedness—that between mind and body and that between organism and environment—were often discussed in terms of tentative notions of energy patterns. The Indian concept of *prana* and the Chinese concept of *ch'i* were mentioned as examples of traditional terms referring to these "subtle energies," or "life energies." In these traditional disciplines illness is seen as resulting from changes in the patterns of energy and therapeutic techniques have been developed to influence the body's energy system. Our exploration of these concepts led to long and fascinating discussions of yoga, psychic phenomena, and other esoteric subjects, which dominated major portions of the conference.

My most exciting and most moving experience at the May Lectures was my encounter with Carl and Stephanie Simonton. I remember sitting at the same table with them on the first day at lunch without knowing who they were, and trying very hard to start up a conversation with this young and very straight-looking couple from Texas, who seemed as far from my world of the sixties as I could imagine. But my impression of them changed dramatically as soon as they began to talk about their work. I realized that they had not been in touch with the counterculture simply because they had dedicated their lives totally to pioneering their new cancer therapy and had no time left for anything else. Their work involved extensive research of medical and psychological literature, continual testing and refining of new ideas and techniques, a frustrating struggle for recognition in the medical community, and, above all, constant intimate contact with a small group of highly motivated patients, all of whom had been considered medically incurable.

During their pilot study the Simontons formed strong emotional bonds with their patients, spending countless nights at their bedsides, laughing and crying with them, struggling with them to regain health, rejoicing with them about their successes, and supporting them with affectionate care through their dying. I felt that the Simontons' conceptual framework, even though still very tentative at that point, held tremendous promise for all of medicine, and they spoke of their patients with such dedication and depth of feeling that I was moved to tears.

In his lecture, Carl Simonton presented the main findings of his research as an oncologist trained in radiation therapy. "My subject matter is controversial," he began; "it is the role which the mind plays in the cause and cure of cancer." He told us that there was abundant evidence in the literature about the role of emotional stress in the onset and development of cancer, and he presented several dramatic case histories from his own practice which supported his thesis. "The question is not whether there *is* a relationship between emotional stress and cancer," he concluded, "but, rather, what is the precise link between the two?"

Simonton then described significant patterns in the life histories and emotional responses of cancer patients, which suggested to him the notion of a "cancer personality," that is, of a certain pattern of behavior in response to stress that contributes substantially to cancer, just as another type of behavior is known to contribute significantly to heart disease. "I have verified the existence of these personality factors in my own research," Simonton reported, "and my convictions are further reinforced by my own experience. I had cancer at the age of seventeen, and I can see how my personality then resembled the classical description."

In Simonton's cancer treatment, the main effort was directed toward changing the patient's belief system about cancer. He described the popular image of the disease as an external agent invading and attacking the body, and setting in motion a process over which the patient has little or no control. In contrast to this widespread image, Simonton's experience convinced him that the belief systems of the patient and the physician are crucial to the success of the therapy and can be used effectively to support the patient's potential for self-healing.

"The unconventional tool I use in the treatment of cancer, in addition to radiation," he explained, "is relaxation and mental imagery." He described how he provided his patients with full and detailed information about their cancer and the treatment, and then asked them to picture the entire process, in regular sessions, in whatever way seemed appropriate to them. Through this technique of guided visualization, he explained, patients begin to activate their motivation to get well and to develop the positive attitude that is crucial in the healing process.

Stephanie Matthews-Simonton, who is a trained psychotherapist, complemented her husband's lecture with detailed accounts of the psychological counseling and group therapy sessions they had developed together in order to help their patients identify and solve the emotional problems that are at the roots of their illnesses. Like her husband, Matthews-Simonton was systematic and concise in her presentation, and radiant as she spoke of their strong personal commitment.

At the end of the conference I felt so grateful to the Simontons for what they were doing that I offered to show them around London as a small token of my appreciation. They gladly accepted my offer, and we spent a very pleasant day together, sightseeing, shopping, and relaxing from the intense discussions of the week.

MARGARET LOCK

The May Lectures introduced me to the new and fascinating field of holistic medicine at a time when its originators were just beginning to pool their resources and form what would later become known as the holistic health movement. The discussions during that week also made it quite evident to me that the change of world view I was describing in *The Tao of Physics* was part of a much larger cultural transformation, and at the end of the week I felt with great excitement that I would actively participate in that transformation for many years to come.

For the time being, however, I was busy finishing my book, and I did not think of exploring the larger context of the paradigm shift until two years later when I began to lecture about the parallels between modern physics and Eastern mysticism in the United States. At my lectures I met people from various disciplines who pointed out to me that a shift from mechanistic to holistic concepts similar to the one in modern physics was also happening in their fields. The majority of these people were health professionals, and so my attention was directed once more toward medicine and health care.

My first impulse to study systematically the parallels between the paradigm shifts in physics and those in medicine came from Margaret Lock, a medical anthropologist whom I met at Berkeley while teaching a UC extension course on *The Tao of Physics*. After a lecture on Chew's bootstrap physics a woman with a marked English accent, a frequent participant in class discussions, made a rather surprising comment. "You know," she said with an ironic smile, "these diagrams of particle interactions, which you drew on the blackboard today, remind me very much of acupuncture diagrams. I wonder whether there is more to that than a superficial similarity." I was intrigued by this remark, and when I inquired further about her knowledge of acupuncture, she told me that she had written her thesis in medical anthropology on the use of classical Chinese medicine in modern Japan and was often reminded of the philosophy underlying the Chinese medical system during my course on *The Tao of Physics*.

These comments opened up a very exciting perspective for me. I remembered from the May Lectures that the paradigm shift in physics had some important implications for medicine. I also knew that the world view of the new physics was similar in many ways to that of classical Chinese philosophy. Finally, I was aware that Chinese culture, like many traditional cultures, was one in which knowledge of the human mind and body and the practice of healing were integral parts of natural philosophy and of spiritual discipline. Indeed, the *Tai Ji* master who instructed me in this ancient Chinese martial art—which is, more than anything else, a form of meditation—was also an accomplished herbalist and acupuncturist and would always emphasize the connections between the principles of *Tai Ji* and those of physical and mental health. It seemed that Lock was now providing an important link in this chain of reasoning by pointing out parallels between the philosophy of modern physics and that of Chinese medicine. I was naturally very eager to explore these ideas further with her and invited her for tea and a long chat.

I liked Margaret Lock right away, and when she came to visit we found that we had much in common. We belonged to the same generation, had both been strongly influenced by the social movements of the sixties, and shared a keen interest in Eastern culture. I immediately felt very comfortable with her, not only because she reminded me of some of my close friends in England, but also because our minds seemed to work in very similar ways. Like myself, Lock is a holistic and systemic thinker and a synthesizer of ideas while, at the same time, striving for intellectual rigor and clarity of expression.

Lock's professional field, medical anthropology, was quite new when I met her, and since then she has established herself as one of the leading scholars in that field. Her research on the practice of traditional East Asian medicine in modern urban Japan was a unique contribution. She spent two years in Kyoto with her husband and her two small children interviewing dozens of doctors, patients, and their families (she is fluent in Japanese) and visiting clinics, herbal pharmacies, traditional medical schools, and healing ceremonies at ancient temples and shrines in order to observe and experience the full range of the traditional East Asian medical system. Her work attracted great attention in the United States not only among her fellow anthropologists but also among the growing number of practitioners of holistic medicine, who recognized her careful and lucid account of the interactions between traditional East Asian and modern Western medicine in contemporary Japan as a rich and valuable source of information.

At our first conversation, I was most interested in finding out more about the parallels between the view of nature emerging from modern physics—especially from bootstrap physics, my own field of research—and the classical Chinese view of human nature and health.

"The Chinese idea of the body was always predominantly functional," Lock began. "The concern was not so much with anatomical accuracy but rather with the interrelationship of all the parts." She explained that the Chinese concept of a physical organ refers to a whole functional system, which has to be considered in its totality. For example, the idea of the lungs includes not only the lungs themselves but the entire respiratory tract, the nose, the skin, and the secretions associated with these organs.

I remembered from Joseph Needham's books that Chinese philosophy as a whole was more concerned with the interrelations between things than with their reduction to fundamental elements. Lock agreed, and she added that the Chinese attitude which Needham called "correlative thinking" also included their emphasis on synchronic patterning rather than causal relations. In the Chinese view, according to Needham, things behave in a certain way because their positions in the interrelated universe are such that they are endowed with intrinsic natures that make their behavior inevitable.

It was evident to me that such a view of nature came very close to that of the new physics, and I also knew that the similarity was reinforced by the fact that the Chinese saw the network of relationships they were studying as intrinsically dynamic. "This is also true for Chinese medicine," Lock observed. "The individual organism, like the cosmos as a whole, was seen as being in a state of continual flow and change, and the Chinese believed that all developments in nature—those in the physical world as well as those in the psychological and social realms—show cyclical patterns."

"These would be the fluctuations between *yin* and *yang*," I observed.

"Precisely, and it is important to realize that for the Chinese nothing is only *yin* or only *yang*. All natural phenomena are manifestations of continual oscillations between the two poles, and all transitions take place gradually and in unbroken progression. The natural order is one of dynamic balance between *yin* and *yang*."

At this point we engaged in a long discussion about the meanings of those ancient Chinese terms, and Lock told me that one of the best interpretations she knew was that given by Manfred Porkert in his comprehensive studies of Chinese medicine. She urged me to study Porkert's work. Together with Needham, she explained, he is one of the very few Western scholars who can actually read the Chinese classics in their original form. According to Porkert, *yin* corresponds to all that is contractive, responsive, and conservative; *yang* to all that is expansive, aggressive, and demanding.

"In addition to the *yin/yang* system," Lock continued, "the Chinese used a system called *Wu Hsing* to describe the great patterned order of the cosmos. This is usually translated as the 'five elements,' but Porkert has translated it as the 'five evolutive phases,' which conveys the Chinese idea of dynamic relationships much better." Lock explained that an intricate correspondence system was derived from the five phases, which extended to the entire universe. The seasons, atmospheric influences, colors, sounds, parts of the body, emotional states, social relations, and numerous other phenomena were all classified into five types related to the five phases. When the five-phase theory was fused with the *yin/yang* cycles, the result was an elaborate system in which every aspect of the universe was described as a well-defined part of a dynamically patterned whole. This system, Lock explained, formed the theoretical foundation for the diagnosis and treatment of illness.

"So what is illness in the Chinese view?" I asked her.

"Illness is an imbalance which occurs when the *ch'i* does not circulate properly. This is another important concept in Chinese natural philosophy, as you know. The word means literally 'vapor' and was used in ancient China to describe the vital breath, or energy, animating the cosmos. The flow and fluctuation of *ch'i* keep a person alive, and there are definite pathways of *ch'i*, the well-known meridians, along which lie the acupuncture points." Lock told me that, from the Western scientific point of view, there is now considerable documentation to show that the acupuncture points have distinct electrical resistance and thermosensitivity, unlike other areas at the body surface, but that no scientific demonstration of the existence of meridians has been given.

"A key concept in the Chinese view of health," she continued, "is that of balance. The classics state that diseases become manifest when the body gets out of balance and the *ch'i* does not circulate naturally."

"So they do not see disease as an outside entity that invades the body, as we tend to do?"

"No, they don't. Although this aspect of disease causation is acknowledged, sickness, in their view, is due to a pattern of causes leading to disharmony and imbalance. However, they also say that the nature of all things, including the human body, is one of homeostasis. In other words, there is a natural striving to return to equilibrium. Going in and out of balance is seen as a natural process that happens constantly throughout the life cycle, and the traditional texts draw no sharp line between health and illness. Both are seen as natural and as being part of a continuum, as aspects of the same fluctuating process in which the individual organism changes continually in relation to a changing environment."

I was very impressed by this concept of health and, as always when I studied Chinese philosophy, I felt deeply moved by the beauty of its ecological wisdom. Margaret Lock agreed when I observed that Chinese medical philosophy seemed inspired by ecological awareness.

"Oh, yes, absolutely," she said. "The human organism is always seen as part of nature and constantly subject to the influences of natural forces. In the classics, seasonal changes are given special attention and their influences on the body are described in great detail. Both doctors and lay people are extremely sensitive to climatic changes, and they use this sensitivity to apply some preventive medicine. You know, I have observed in Japan how even small children are taught that they must pay careful attention to the changes of the weather and the seasons, and to observe the reactions of the body to those changes."

Lock's outline of the principles of Chinese medicine made it clear to me why the Chinese, as I had often heard, strongly emphasize the prevention of illness. A system of medicine which regards balance and harmony with the environment as the basis of health will naturally emphasize preventive measures.

"Yes, indeed," Lock agreed. "And it must be added that, according to Chinese beliefs, it is one's personal responsibility to try to keep healthy by looking after one's body, by observing the rules of society, and by living in accordance with the laws of the universe. Illness is seen as signaling a lack of care on the part of the individual."

"What, then, is the role of the doctor?"

"It is quite different from that in the West. In Western medicine, the doctor with the highest reputation is a specialist who has detailed knowledge about a specific part of the body. In Chinese medicine, the ideal doctor is a sage who knows how all the patterns of the universe work together, who treats each patient on an individual basis and records as fully as possible the individual's total state of mind and body and its relation to the natural and social environment. As far as treatment is concerned, only a small portion of it is expected to be initiated by the doctor and to take place in the doctor's presence. Therapeutic techniques are viewed by both doctors and patients as a kind of catalyst for the natural healing process."

The Chinese picture of health and medicine, which Lock had outlined for me in this first conversation, seemed to be fully consistent with the new paradigm emerging from modern physics, and it also seemed to be in harmony with many ideas I remembered from the discussions at the May Lectures. The fact that her framework came from a different culture did not worry me. I knew that Lock, being an anthropologist and having carefully studied the use of classical Chinese medicine in modern urban settings in Japan, would be able to show me how its basic principles could be applied to holistic health care in our culture. In fact, I planned to explore this question in detail with her in future conversations.

Exploring ch'i with Manfred Porkert

Among the Chinese concepts Lock and I had discussed in our first conversation, the concept of *ch'i* held a special fascination for me. I had often encountered it in my studies of Chinese philosophy and was also familiar with its use in the martial arts. I knew that it is generally translated as "energy" or "vital energy," but I sensed that these terms did not convey the Chinese concept adequately. As with the Jungian term "psychic energy," I was most interested in finding out how *ch'i* was related to the concept of energy in physics, where it is a quantitative measure of activity.

Following Lock's advice, I studied some of Porkert's writings but found them rather difficult to penetrate because of the very special, mostly Latin, terminology he had created to translate the Chinese medical terms. It was only several years later, after my studies of systems theory and my conversations with Bateson and Jantsch, that I began to understand the Chinese concept of *ch'i*. Like Chinese natural philosophy and medicine, the modern systems theory of life views a living organism in terms of multiple, interdependent fluctuations, and it seemed to me that the concept of *ch'i* is used by the Chinese to describe the total pattern of these multiple processes of fluctuation.

When I finally wrote the chapter "Wholeness and Health" in *The Turning Point*, I included an interpretation of *ch'i* that reflected my tentative understanding of both ancient Chinese medical science and the modern systems view of life:

> *Ch'i* is not a substance, nor does it have the purely quantitative meaning of our scientific concept of energy. It is used in Chinese medicine in a very subtle way to describe the various patterns of flow and fluctuation in the human organism, as well as the continual exchanges between organism and environment. *Ch'i* does not refer to the flow of any particular substance but rather seems to represent the principle of flow as such, which, in the Chinese view, is always cyclical.

Three years after writing this passage I was invited to speak at a conference sponsored by the Traditional Acupuncture Foundation, at which, to my great delight, Manfred Porkert was also among the speakers. When I met Porkert at the conference I was very surprised that he was only a few years older than I; his great erudition and extensive publications had led me to assume that he would be at least in his seventies—a venerable scholar like Joseph Needham. Instead I met a youthful, dynamic, charming man, who immediately engaged me in an animated conversation.

Naturally, I was very eager to discuss the fundamental concepts of Chinese medicine with Porkert, and especially the concept of *ch'i*, which had intrigued me for many years. I told him about my wish, and, following the bold approach I had so often used successfully in the past, I asked Porkert whether he would agree to a public discussion during the conference. He immediately agreed, and on the following day the organizers staged a dialogue between the two of us on "the new vision of reality and the nature of *ch'i*."

When I sat down face to face with Manfred Porkert in front of an audience of several hundred people, I realized how foolhardy it had been of me to put myself in this situation. My knowledge of Chinese medicine and philosophy was, after all, very limited, and here I would be discussing these subjects with one of the greatest Western scholars in the field. Moreover, this discussion would not take place in private over a cup of coffee but in public in front of a large group of professional acupuncturists. Nevertheless, I was not intimidated. In contrast to my conversations with many other remarkable people, which represent the fabric of my story, this one took place two years after I had completed *The Turning Point*. I had assimilated the systems view of life, had fully integrated it into my world view, and had made it the core of my presentation of the new paradigm; I was ready and eager to use this new framework for exploring a wide range of concepts. What better opportunity to increase my understanding than by probing Porkert's extensive knowledge!

To begin the discussion, I gave a brief summary of the systems view of life, emphasizing in particular the focus on patterns of organization, the importance of process thinking, and the central role of fluctuations in the dynamics of living systems. Porkert confirmed my understanding that, in the Chinese view of life, fluctuation is also seen as the basic dynamic phenomenon, and, having thus prepared the ground, I went straight to the heart of the matter—the nature of *ch'i:*

"It seems, then, that fluctuation is the fundamental dynamic the Chinese sages observed in nature, and in order to systematize their observations, they used the concept of *ch'i*, which is a rather complex concept. What is *ch'i?* I believe it is a common word in Chinese."

"Of course it is," Porkert replied. "It's an ancient word."

"What does it mean?"

"It means a directed and structured expression of movement; it is *not* a haphazard expression of movement."

Porkert's explanation seemed rather sophisticated, and I tried to find a simpler, more concrete meaning of the term: "Is there an everyday context in which *ch'i* can be easily translated?"

Porkert shook his head: "There is no direct translation. This is why we avoid it. Even scholars who are not very particular about using Western equivalents do not translate *ch'i.*"

"Can you at least talk around it and tell us some of the meanings?" I persisted.

"That is all I can do. *Ch'i* comes close to what our term 'energy' conveys. It comes close, but it is not equivalent. The term *ch'i* always implies a qualification, and this qualification is the definition of direction. *Ch'i* implies directionality, movement in a particular direction. This direction may also be explicit; for example, when the Chinese say *tsang ch'i* they refer to the *ch'i* moving within the functional orbs, which are called *tsang.*"

I remembered that Porkert uses the term "functional orb" instead of the conventional "organ" to translate the Chinese *tsang* in order to convey the idea that *tsang* refers to a set of functional relations rather than an isolated physical part of the body. I also knew that these functional orbs are associated in the Chinese system with a set of conduits, commonly called "meridians," for which Porkert has chosen the term "sinarteries." Since I had often heard that the meridians were the pathways of *ch'i*, I was curious to hear Porkert's view.

"When you talk about the conduits," I inquired, "the idea seems to be that something flows in these conduits, and that this something is the *ch'i.*"

"Among other things."

"Is *ch'i* then some kind of substance that flows?"

"No, it is certainly not a substance."

So far, Porkert had not contradicted any of the tentative ideas about *ch'i* I had developed, and I was now ready to present the interpretation I had derived from modern systems theory to him.

"From the systems point of view," I began carefully, "I would say that a living system is characterized by multiple fluctuations. These fluctuations have certain relative intensities, and there are also directions and many other patterns one can describe. It seems to me that *ch'i* has something of our scientific concept of energy in the sense that it is associated with process. But it is not quantitative; it seems to be a qualitative description of a dynamic pattern, of a pattern of processes."

"Exactly. In fact, *ch'i* transmits patterns. In Taoist texts, which in a way are parallel to the medical tradition, and which I studied at the very beginning of my research, the term *ch'i* expresses this transmission and conservation of patterns."

"Now, since it is used as a device for describing dynamic patterns, would you say that *ch'i* is a theoretical concept? Or is there really something out there, which is *ch'i*?"

"In this sense, it is a theoretical concept," Porkert agreed. "It is an evolved and rational concept in Chinese medicine, science, and philosophy. But in everyday language, of course, it is not."

I was thrilled that Porkert had largely confirmed my interpretation of *ch'i*, and I also realized that he had given it greater precision by adding the notion of directionality. This was completely new to me and I wanted to return to it for further clarification.

"You mentioned before," I continued, "that the qualitative aspect of *ch'i* lies in its directionality. This seems to be a somewhat narrow use of the notion of quality. Generally, of course, quality can mean all kinds of things."

"Yes. I have used quality for almost two decades in a restrictive sense, as a complement to quantity. Quality, in that sense, corresponds to defined, or definable, directionality, the direction of movement. You see, we are dealing here with two aspects of reality: mass, which is static and fixed, which has extension and is accumulated; and movement, which is dynamic and has no extension. Quality, for me, refers to movement, to processes, to functions, or to change, and especially to the vital changes that are of importance in medicine."

"So direction is the key aspect of quality. Is it the only one?"

"Yes, it's the only one."

At this point, as the notion of *ch'i* came more and more into focus, I thought about another fundamental concept in Chinese philosophy, that of the pair of polar opposites, *yin* and *yang*. I knew that this concept is used throughout Chinese culture to give the idea of cyclical patterns a definite structure by creating two poles, which set the limits for all cycles of change. Porkert's comments about the qualitative aspect of *ch'i* made me realize that directionality seems to be crucial also to the notions of *yin* and *yang*.

"By all means," Porkert agreed. "The terminology implies directionality even in the original, archaic sense. The original meaning of *yin* and *yang* was that of two aspects of a mountain, the shady side and the sunny side. That implies the direction of movement of the sun. It's the same mountain, but the aspects change because of the movement of the sun. And when you talk about *yin* and *yang* in medicine, it's the same person, the same individual, but the functional aspects change with the passage of time."

"So the quality of direction is implicit when the terms *yin* and *yang* are used to describe cyclical movement; and when you have many movements forming an interrelated dynamic system, you get a dynamic pattern, and that is *ch'i?*"

"Yes."

"But when you describe such a dynamic pattern, it is not enough to specify the directions; you also have to describe the interrelations to get the entire pattern."

"Oh, yes. Without relationship there would be no *ch'i*, because *ch'i* is not empty air. It is the structured pattern of relationships, which are defined in a directional way."

I felt that this was the closest we could come to a definition of *ch'i* in Western terms, and Porkert agreed. During the rest of our conversation we touched on several other parallels between the systems view of life and Chinese medical theory, but none of them was as exciting to me as our joint endeavor to clarify the concept of *ch'i*. It had been an intellectual encounter of great precision and beauty; a dance of two minds in search of understanding, which both of us enjoyed tremendously.

Lessons from East Asian medicine

Between my first conversation with Margaret Lock and my discussion with Manfred Porkert lay seven years of intensive research. With the help of many friends and colleagues I was able to gradually bring together the various pieces of a new conceptual framework for a holistic approach to health and healing. The need for such a new approach had been evident to me ever since the May Lectures, and after meeting Lock I began to see the outlines of the framework that would slowly emerge over the years. In its final formulation it would represent a systems view of health corresponding to the systems view of life, but, in the early days, in 1976, I was still very far from such a formulation.

The philosophy of classical Chinese medicine seemed extremely attractive to me, since it was fully consistent with the world view I had explored in *The Tao of Physics*. The big question, of course, was how much of the Chinese system could be adapted to our modern Western culture. I was very eager to discuss this with Lock, and several weeks after our first conversation I invited her again for tea, with the purpose of talking specifically about this problem. In the meantime, Margaret and I had got to know each other much better. She had been a guest lecturer at my seminar "Beyond the Mechanistic World View" at UC Berkeley. I had met her husband and her children, and had spent many hours listening to delightful stories about their experience of Japanese culture.

Lock warned me right away about the pitfalls of comparing medical systems from different cultures. "Any medical system," she insisted, "including modern Western medicine, is a product of its history and exists within a certain environmental and cultural context. As this context keeps changing, the medical system will also change. It will be modified by new economic, political, and philosophical influences. Any health-care system, therefore, is unique at a certain time and within a certain context."

Given this situation, I wondered whether it was at all helpful to study medical systems from other cultures.

"I would strongly question the usefulness of any medical system as a model for another society," Lock replied; "and, in fact, we have witnessed Western medicine fall flat on its face again and again in developing countries."

"Maybe," I ventured, "the purpose of cross-cultural comparisons would be not so much to use other systems as models for our culture, but rather as mirrors, so that we can better recognize the advantages and shortcomings of our own approach."

"That can certainly be very helpful," Lock agreed. "And you know, you will find in particular that not all traditional cultures have approached health care in a holistic way."

I found this remark very intriguing. "Even if the approaches of these traditional cultures are not holistic," I observed, "their fragmented, or reductionistic, approaches may be different from the one that dominates our current scientific medicine. And to see that difference might be very instructive."

Lock agreed, and to illustrate the point she told me a story of a traditional healing ceremony in Africa in which someone was afflicted by witchcraft. The healer assembled the entire village for a long political debate, during which the population split into several lineages which brought forth a series of accusations and grievances. During all that time, the sick person lay on the side of the road rather neglected. "The entire procedure was primarily a social event," Lock commented. "The patient was merely a symbol of conflict within the society; and the healing, in that case, was certainly not holistic."

This story led us to a long and fascinating discussion of shamanism, a field that Lock had studied in some detail but which was completely foreign to me. "A shaman," she told me, "is a man or woman who is able, at will, to enter into a nonordinary state of consciousness in order to make contact with the spirit world *on behalf of members of his or her community*." Lock insisted on the crucial importance of the last part of this definition, and she also emphasized the close link of the patient's social and cultural environment to shamanistic ideas about disease causation. Whereas the focus of Western scientific medicine has been on the biological mechanisms and physiological processes that produce evidence of illness, the principal concern of shamanism is the sociocultural context in which the illness occurs. The disease process is either ignored altogether or is relegated to secondary significance. "When a Western doctor is asked about the causes of illness," Lock explained, "he will talk about bacteria or physiological disorders; a shaman is likely to mention competition, jealousy and greed, witches and sorcerers, wrongdoing by a member of the patient's family, or some other way in which the patient or his kin failed to keep the moral order."

This comment stayed in my mind for a long time and helped me greatly to realize, several years later, that the conceptual problem at the center of our contemporary health care is the confusion between disease processes and disease origins. Instead of asking why an illness occurs and trying to modify the conditions that led to it, medical researchers focus their attention on the mechanisms through which the disease operates, so that they can then interfere with them. These mechanisms, rather than the true origins, are often seen as the causes of disease in current medical thinking.

While Lock was speaking of shamanism, she often referred to the "medical models" of traditional cultures, as she had done before when we discussed classical Chinese medicine. I found this somewhat confusing, especially since I remembered that people at the May Lectures had often referred to "the medical model" when they meant Western scientific medicine. I therefore asked Lock to clarify the terminology for me.

She suggested that I should use the term "biomedical model" when referring to the conceptual foundation of modern scientific medicine, since it expresses the emphasis on biological mechanisms, which distinguishes the modern Western approach from medical models in other cultures and from models coexisting with it in our own culture.

"Most societies show a pluralism of medical systems and beliefs," Lock explained. "Even today shamanism is still the most important medical system in most countries with large rural areas. Besides, shamanism is also very much alive in the major cities of the world, especially in those with large populations of recent migrants." She also told me that she preferred to speak of "cosmopolitan" rather than "Western" medicine because of the global extension of the biomedical system, and of "East Asian" rather than "classical Chinese" medicine for similar reasons.

We had now reached the point where I could ask Lock the question I was most curious about: How can we use the lessons learned from a study of East Asian medicine to develop a system of holistic health care in our culture?

"You are really asking two questions that need to be examined," she replied. "To what extent is the East Asian model holistic, and which of its aspects, if any, can be adapted to our cultural context?" Once more I was impressed by Lock's clear and systematic approach, and I asked her to comment on the first aspect of the problem—holism in East Asian medicine.

"It might be useful to distinguish two kinds of holism here," she observed. "In a more narrow sense, holism means to consider all aspects of the human organism as being interconnected and interdependent. In a broader sense, it means to recognize, in addition, that the organism is in constant interplay with its natural and social environment.

"In the first, narrow sense, the East Asian medical system is certainly holistic," Lock continued. "Its practitioners believe that their treatments will not just remove the principal symptoms of the patient's illness but will affect the entire organism, which they treat as a dynamic whole. In the broader sense, however, the Chinese system is holistic only in theory. The interdependence of organism and environment is acknowledged in the diagnosis of illness and is discussed extensively in the medical classics, but as far as therapy is concerned, it is usually neglected. You see, most contemporary practitioners have not read the classical texts; these are studied mainly by scholars who never practice medicine."

"So East Asian doctors would be holistic in the broader, environmental sense in their diagnosis but not in their therapies?"

"That's right. When they make their diagnosis, they spend considerable time talking to the patients about their work situations, their families, and their emotional states, but when it comes to therapy they concentrate on dietary counseling, herbal medicine, and acupuncture. In other words, they restrict themselves to techniques that manipulate processes inside the body. I have observed this again and again in Japan."

"Was this also the attitude of Chinese doctors in the past?"

"Yes, as far as we can tell. In practice the Chinese system was probably never holistic, as far as the psychological and social aspects of illness are concerned."

"What do you think was the reason?"

"Well, part of it was certainly the strong influence of Confucianism on all aspects of Chinese life. The Confucian system, as you know, was mainly concerned with maintaining the social order. Illness, in the Confucian view, could arise from inadequate adjustment to the rules and customs of society, but the only way for an individual to get well was to change, so that one would fit the given social order. My observations in Japan have shown me that this attitude is still deeply ingrained in East Asian culture. It underlies modern medical therapy in both China and Japan."

It was clear to me that this would be a major difference between the East Asian medical system and the holistic approach we were now trying to develop in the West. Our framework would certainly have to include psychologically oriented therapies and social activism as important aspects if it were to be truly holistic. Margaret and I, both being strongly motivated by our political experience of the sixties, agreed completely on this point.

Throughout my conversations with Margaret Lock I had the strong feeling that the philosophy underlying East Asian medicine is very much in agreement with the new paradigm that is now emerging from modern Western science. Moreover, it was evident to me that many of its characteristics should be important aspects of our new holistic medicine as well—for example, the view of health as a process of dynamic balance, the attention given to the continual interplay between the human organism and its natural environment, and the importance of preventive medicine. But how would we begin to incorporate these aspects into our system of health care?

I realized that Lock's detailed study of medical practice in contemporary Japan would be extremely helpful to answer this question. She had told me that modern Japanese doctors use traditional East Asian medical concepts and practices to deal with diseases that are not too different from those in our society, and I was very eager to hear what her observations had taught her.

"Do modern Japanese doctors actually combine Eastern and Western approaches?" I asked.

"Not all of them do," Lock explained. "The Japanese adopted the Western medical system about a hundred years ago and most Japanese doctors today practice cosmopolitan medicine. But, as in the West, there has been growing dissatisfaction with that system. You know, the kind of criticism you heard during your May Lectures—that has been expressed also in Japan. And in response the Japanese are now increasingly revaluating their own traditional practices. They believe that traditional East Asian medicine can fulfill many functions beyond the capacities of the biomedical model. The doctors who are part of this movement do combine Eastern and Western techniques. They are known as *kanpō* doctors, by the way. *Kanpō* literally means the 'Chinese method.' "

I asked Lock what we in the West could learn from the Japanese model.

"I believe that one factor is especially important," Lock began after a moment of reflection. "In Japanese society, as all over East Asia, subjective knowledge is highly valued. In spite of their extensive training in the scientific approach to medicine, Japanese doctors are able to accept subjective judgments—both their own and their patients'—without feeling that this is a threat to their medical practice or their personal integrity."

"What kind of subjective judgments would these be?"

"For example, *kanpō* doctors would not measure temperatures but would note their patients' subjective feelings about having a fever; nor do they measure the duration of an acupuncture treatment—they simply determine it by asking the patient how it feels.

"The value of subjective knowledge is surely something we could learn from the East," Lock continued. "We have become so obsessed with rational knowledge, objectivity, and quantification that we are very insecure in dealing with human values and human experience."

"And you feel that human experience is an important aspect of health?"

"Of course! It is the central aspect. Health itself is a subjective experience. Intuition and subjective knowledge are also used by every good physician in the West, but this is not acknowledged in the professional literature and is not taught in medical schools."

Lock maintained that several key aspects of East Asian medicine could be incorporated into a Western holistic medical system if we adopted a more balanced attitude toward rational and intuitive knowledge, toward the science and the art of medicine. In addition to the aspects we had already discussed, she emphasized especially that the responsibility for health and healing would not rest so heavily with the medical profession in such a new approach. "In traditional East Asian medicine," she explained, "the doctor never took on complete responsibility; it was always shared with the family and with the government."

"How would this work in our society?" I asked.

"At the level of day-to-day primary health care, the patients themselves, their families, and the government should have the lion's share of the responsibility for health and healing. At the level of hospital-based secondary care, in emergency cases, and so on, most of the responsibility would lie with the doctor, but even there doctors would respect the ability of the body to heal itself and would not try to dominate the healing process."

"How long do you think it will take to develop such a new medicine?" I asked in conclusion of our long conversation.

Margaret gave me one of her ironic smiles: "The holistic health movement is certainly moving in this direction, but a truly holistic medicine will require very fundamental changes in our attitudes, our socialization practices, our education, and our basic values. This will only happen very gradually, if ever."

The paradigm shift in medicine

In all my conversations with Margaret Lock I was very impressed by her clear and concise descriptions, her sharp analytic mind, and, at the same time, her broad perspective. At the end of several meetings I felt that she had given me a clear framework for studying the paradigm shift in medicine and the confidence to undertake such a study in a systematic way.

At that time I still saw the change of paradigms in physics as the model for the other sciences, and so I naturally began by comparing the conceptual frameworks of physics and medicine. I had realized at the May Lectures that the mechanistic approach of the biomedical model was rooted in the Cartesian imagery of the body as a machine, just as classical physics was based on the Newtonian view of the universe as a mechanical system. From the very beginning it was clear to me that there was no reason to abandon the biomedical model. It could still play a useful role for a limited range of health problems within a large, holistic framework, as Newtonian mechanics was never abandoned but remains useful for a limited range of phenomena within the larger framework of quantum-relativistic physics.

The task, then, was to develop that larger framework, an

approach to health and healing that would enable one to deal with the entire network of phenomena that influence health. The new holistic approach would have to take into account, in particular, the interdependence of mind and body in health and illness. I remembered Carl Simonton's emphasis on the crucial role of emotional stress in the onset and development of cancer, but at that time I did not know of any psychosomatic model that would picture the interplay of mind and body in some detail.

Another important aspect of the new framework would have to be the ecological view of the human organism as being in continual interaction with its natural and social environment. Accordingly, special attention would have to be given to environmental and social influences on health, and social policies would have to play an important role in the new system of health care.

It was clear to me that in such a holistic approach to health and healing the concept of health itself would have to be much more subtle than in the biomedical model, where health is defined as the absence of disease and disease is seen as a malfunctioning of biological mechanisms. The holistic concept would picture health as reflecting the state of the whole organism, mind and body, and would also see it in relation to the organism's environment. I also realized that the new concept of health should be a dynamic concept, seeing health as a process of dynamic balance and acknowledging, somehow, the healing forces inherent in living organisms.

But at that time I did not know how to formulate these concepts in a precise way. It was only several years later that the systems view of life would provide me with the scientific language for a precise formulation of the holistic model of health and illness.

As far as therapy was concerned, I recognized that preventive medicine would have to play a much larger role and that the responsibility for health and healing would have to be shared with the physician by the patient and by society. At the May Lectures I had also heard about a great variety of alternative therapies based on widely differing views of health, and it was not clear to me which of these could be integrated into a coherent system of health care. However, the idea of facing a wide variety of approaches which could deal successfully with different aspects of health was not a problem for me. I quite naturally adopted a "bootstrap" attitude and decided to embark on a detailed investigation of these different therapeutic models and techniques, looking forward to the intellectual adventure of such a task and hoping that, eventually, a mosaic of mutually consistent approaches would emerge.

In September 1976 I was invited to speak at a conference on "The State of American Medicine" sponsored by the UC extension program at Santa Cruz. The conference was designed to explore alternatives to the present health-care system and offered me a unique opportunity to present the outlines of the conceptual framework I was developing. My talk, "The New Physics as a Model for a New Medicine," generated lively discussions among the doctors, nurses, psychotherapists, and other health professionals in the audience, and as a result I got several invitations to speak at similar gatherings, which the rapidly growing holistic health movement was now organizing with increasing frequency. These conferences and seminars led to a long series of discussions with numerous health professionals, which helped me enormously in gradually developing and refining my conceptual framework.

Mind-body approach to cancer

One of these early "holistic health conferences" was held in Toronto in March 1977, which not only gave me the opportunity to hear the first extensive presentation by Stan Grof but also brought me together once more with Carl and Stephanie Simonton. Both of them greeted me warmly and reminisced about the exciting days we had spent together during the May Lectures and the fun we had had afterward roaming around London.

At the Toronto conference the Simontons presented new insights and results from their work with cancer patients, and once again I was deeply impressed by their intellectual openness, their courage, and their strong sense of commitment. When Carl presented the theoretical ideas underlying their treatment, I also realized that he had made considerable progress in the four years since the May Lectures. He was not only convinced of the crucial link between cancer and emotional stress but had also developed the outlines of a psychosomatic model to describe the complex interdependence between mind and body in the development of the disease and in the healing process.

"One of my main aims," Simonton began, "is to reverse the popular image of cancer, which does not correspond to the findings of biological research. Our image of cancer is that of a powerful invader that strikes the body from outside. In reality, the cancer cell is not a powerful cell; it is a weak cell. It does not invade; it pushes out of the way—and it is not capable of attacking. Cancer cells are big, but they are sluggish and confused.

"My work has convinced me," Simonton continued, "that cancer has to be understood as a systemic disorder; a disease that has a localized appearance but has the ability to spread, and that really involves the entire organism—the mind as well as the body. The original tumor is merely the tip of the iceberg."

Simonton's psychosomatic model is based on the so-called surveillance theory of cancer, according to which every organism occasionally produces abnormal, cancerous cells. In a healthy organism the immune system will recognize abnormal cells and destroy them, but if, for some reason, the immune system is not strong enough, the cancerous cells will reproduce and the result will be a tumor composed of a mass of imperfect cells.

"According to this theory," Simonton pointed out, "cancer is not an attack from without but a breakdown within. And the crucial question is: What inhibits a person's immune system, at a particular time, from recognizing and destroying abnormal cells and thus allows them to grow into a life-threatening tumor?"

Simonton then outlined his tentative model of how psychological and physical states can work together in the onset of the disease. He emphasized in particular that emotional stress has two principal effects. It suppresses the body's immune system and, at the same time, leads to hormonal imbalances that result in an increased production of abnormal cells. Thus optimal conditions for cancer growth are created. The production of malignant cells is enhanced precisely at a time when the body is least capable of destroying them.

The basic philosophy of the Simonton approach affirms that the development of cancer involves a number of interdependent psychological and biological processes, that these processes can be recognized and understood, and that the sequence of events which leads to illness can be reversed to lead the organism back into a healthy state. To do so, the Simontons help their patients to become aware of the wider context of their illness, identify the major stresses in their lives, and develop a positive attitude about the effectiveness of the treatment and the potency of the body's defenses.

"Once feelings of hope and anticipation are generated," Simonton explained, "the organism translates them into biological processes that begin to restore balance and to revitalize the immune system, using the same pathways that were used in the development of illness. The production of cancerous cells decreases, and at the same time the immune system becomes stronger and more efficient in dealing with them. While this strengthening takes place, we use physical therapy in conjunction with our psychological approach to help the organism destroy the malignant cells."

As I listened to Carl Simonton, I realized with great excitement that he and Stephanie were developing a therapeutic approach which could become exemplary for the entire holistic health movement. They see illness as a problem of the whole person and their therapy does not focus on the disease alone but deals with the total human being. It is a multidimensional approach involving various treatment strategies—conventional medical treatment, visualization, psychological counseling, and others—all of which are designed to initiate and support the organism's innate psychosomatic process of healing. Their psychotherapy, which usually takes place in group sessions, concentrates on the patients' emotional problems but does not separate these from the larger patterns of their lives, and thus generally includes social, cultural, philosophical, and spiritual aspects.

After the Simontons' lectures it was clear to me that both of them would be ideal guides for my further explorations of health and healing, and I resolved to remain in contact with them as much as possible. I realized, however, that this might prove quite difficult, knowing that their lives were filled with research, lectures within the medical community, and constant attention to the welfare of their patients to such an extent that they had very little time for anything else.

After the conference, Carl Simonton and I visited our friend Emil Zmenak, the chiropractor whom we had both met at the May Lectures, and the three of us spent a long, relaxed evening together, catching up with one another's lives and sharing insights and experiences. During the evening I told Carl that I had embarked on a detailed study of the paradigm shift in medicine and on a search for a new conceptual framework of health and healing. I expressed my great excitement about the progress he had made in the formulation of his model, and said that I would love to continue exchanging ideas with him in the future. He responded that he would be very interested in working with me on this project and added that he had believed ever since the May Lectures that all of us were destined to remain in contact and collaborate in one way or another in the future. He also told me that his working schedule was extremely overloaded, but he encouraged me to get in touch with him when I had more concrete ideas about our collaboration.

Piecing together the holistic health framework

My meeting with Carl Simonton in Toronto inspired me tremendously and encouraged me further in my endeavor of assembling the pieces of the conceptual mosaic that would provide a new framework for health care. I saw parallels to the East Asian approach in many of Simonton's attitudes and techniques—especially in his emphasis on restoring balance and enhancing the organism's potential for self-healing—and, at the same time, he left me with the conviction that it was indeed possible to formulate the new holistic framework in Western scientific language.

During the next two years, from March 1977 to May 1979, I carried out my detailed investigation of the paradigm shift in medicine and of the emerging holistic approaches to health and healing. While pursuing this research I also studied the changes in basic ideas in psychology and economics, and I discovered many fascinating relationships among the paradigm shifts in these three fields.

My initial task was to identify and synthesize the critique of the mechanistic biomedical model and the current practice of medical care as clearly and comprehensively as possible, and I began with a systematic search of the relevant literature. Margaret Lock recommended six authors to me, all of whom I found very inspiring and enlightening: Victor Fuchs, Thomas McKeown, Ivan Illich, Vicente Navarro, René Dubos, and Lewis Thomas.

Fuchs's clear analysis of the economics of health care in his challenging book *Who Shall Live?*, McKeown's detailed account of the history of infections in his classic *The Role of Medicine: Dream, Mirage, or Nemesis?*, Illich's vigorous indictment of the "medicalization of life" in his provocative *Medical Nemesis*, and Navarro's trenchant Marxist critique *Medicine Under Capitalism* made me see the relationship between medicine and health care in a new light. These books showed me convincingly that, since the biomedical approach limits itself to a relatively small portion of factors that influence health, progress in medicine does not necessarily mean progress in health care. They also showed me that biomedical interventions, although extremely helpful in individual emergencies, have very little effect on general public health.

What, then, are the main factors influencing health? This question was answered for me in the clearest and most beautiful way in the books and articles by René Dubos, who rephrases in modern scientific language many ideas I first encountered in my conversations with Lock about East Asian medical philosophy—that our health is determined above all by our behavior, our food, and the nature of our natural and social environment; that the origin of disease is to be found in a pattern of several causative factors; that complete freedom from illness is incompatible with the process of living.

The author whose writings I found most intriguing was Lewis Thomas. Many of his essays, especially those in the collection *Lives of a Cell*, reflect deep ecological awareness. They are full of beautiful, highly poetic passages depicting the mutual interdependence of all living creatures, the symbiotic relationships between animals, plants, and microorganisms, and the cooperative principles according to which life organizes itself at all levels. In other essays Thomas clearly expresses his belief in the mechanistic approach of the biomedical model, for example when he writes: "For every disease there is a single key mechanism that dominates all others. If one can find it, and then think one's way around it, one can control the disorder. . . . In short, I believe that the major diseases of human beings have become approachable biological puzzles, ultimately solvable."

Among the six authors recommended to me by Lock, René Dubos was the one who impressed and inspired me most, and I contacted him during one of my visits to New York in the hope of meeting him personally. Unfortunately, this meeting never took place, but Dubos very kindly introduced me to David Sobel, a young M.D. in San Francisco who was just putting together an anthology on holistic approaches to ancient and contemporary medicine, entitled *Ways of Health*. This book, which Sobel published a couple of years later, contains twenty essays by eminent authorities on holistic medicine, including one essay by Manfred Porkert and three by Dubos, and is, in my view, still one of the very best books on this subject.

When I visited David Sobel in his study I found it filled with stacks of books and articles, which Sobel had carefully collected over many years. He gave me a guided tour through this immensely valuable collection and very generously allowed me to photocopy the articles I was most interested in. I left David Sobel with a great sense of gratitude and a heavy bag filled with invaluable reading material. I now had a rich reservoir of exciting ideas from which I would compose, several years later, my own conceptual synthesis.

While I was studying the material Sobel had given me over the following months, I also continued to lecture on the paradigm shifts in physics and medicine and discussed the subject with numerous health professionals at several conferences. These discussions continually introduced me to new ideas, among which I especially remember two areas that had been quite foreign to me. One was the feminist critique of medical practice, advanced forcefully in two well-documented books, *The Hidden Malpractice* by Gena Corea and *For Her Own Good* by Barbara Ehrenreich and Deirdre English. The other new area was the powerful critique of medical attitudes toward death and dying expressed by Elisabeth Kübler-Ross, whose eloquent books and lectures generated an enormous amount of interest in the existential and spiritual dimensions of illness. At the same time, my discussions with Stan Grof and R. D. Laing helped me to extend the critique of the biomedical approach to psychiatry and to gain a deeper understanding of mental illness and the multiple levels of human consciousness.

My interest in new approaches to psychiatry was also greatly stimulated by my encounter with Antonio Dimalanta, a young and very ingenious family therapist whom I met in a psychiatric hospital in Chicago, where I had been invited to lecture on *The Tao of Physics*. In a long conversation after my lecture, Dimalanta told me that he saw many parallels to my ideas in his psychiatric practice. He emphasized in particular the limitations of ordinary language, the role of paradox, and the importance of intuitive, nonrational methods.

I was especially fascinated by Dimalanta because he seemed to combine his bold, intuitive approaches to psychotherapy with a strong desire to understand them in terms of scientific models. He was one of the first to direct my attention to the potential role of systems theory as a common language for understanding physical, mental, and social aspects of health, and he told me that, even though he was just beginning to synthesize his thoughts on this subject, he had been able to incorporate explicitly some of the new systems concepts into his practice of family therapy. After our meeting Dimalanta and I continued our discussion in several exchanges of letters, which provided many challenges and fresh insights in my search for holistic approaches to health and healing.

At one of my lectures at UC Berkeley I met Leonard Shlain, a San Francisco surgeon with a deep interest in philosophy, science, and art, whose friendship and interest in my work would become invaluable in my exploration of the medical field. During the lecture Shlain involved me in a prolonged discussion of some subtle aspects of quantum physics, and when we went out for a beer afterward we soon found ourselves in the midst of a fascinating comparison between ancient Taoism and modern surgery.

At that time, I had a rather strong prejudice against surgeons, having just read a critical survey of American surgery in Victor Fuchs's book, according to which the current "surplus" of surgeons not only does not seem to drive down their fees but also, according to many critics, results in considerable overuse of surgical procedures. In Shlain I encountered a surgeon of a very different kind, a compassionate physician with deep respect for the mystery of life, who brings not only tremendous skills but also a broad philosophical perspective to the art and science of his profession. Over the following months and years he and I became good friends and had many long discussions, which clarified numerous questions for me and helped me enormously in understanding the complex field of modern medicine.

Social and political dimensions of health

In the spring of 1978 I spent seven weeks at Macalester College in St. Paul, Minnesota, as a Hubert Humphrey Visiting Professor, giving regular seminars to undergraduate students and delivering a series of public lectures. This was an excellent opportunity for me to summarize what I had learned about the paradigm shift in medicine and health care from numerous discussions and from the extensive literature I had collected. The college provided me with a large and comfortable apartment, in which I could work without any disturbance and spread out my books, articles, and notes over many empty shelves and tables. I remember noticing a couple of small African wood sculptures when I moved in, and I regarded it as a good omen when my hosts told me that they had been left behind by Alex Haley, who had spent several weeks in the same apartment working on his celebrated epic *Roots*. It was in this apartment that I actually began to lay out the chapters of *The Turning Point* and to order my notes and references accordingly.

These seven weeks at Macalester were very satisfying and enriching for me. They were a time of concentrated study and writing, which I enjoyed enormously, and they gave me an opportunity to meet many interesting and very kind people, not only at the college but also in the twin cities of St. Paul and Minneapolis. In particular, I was fortunate to be introduced to a large network of artists and social activists through whom I experienced the cooperative spirit and community feeling that is a valued tradition in Minnesota.

As I mapped out the conceptual framework for a holistic approach to health and healing, my discussions with numerous social activists and community organizers brought about a significant change in my perspective. In my discussions with

Simonton and with many other health professionals in California I had explored primarily the psychological dimensions of health and the psychosomatic nature of the healing process. In the very different social and cultural climate of Minnesota my attention shifted to the environmental, social, and political dimensions of health. I began with a survey of environmental health hazards—air pollution, acid rain, toxic chemical wastes, radiation hazards, and many others—and realized very soon that these manifold health hazards are not just incidental by-products of technological progress but integral features of an economic system obsessed with growth and expansion.

Thus I was led to investigate the economic, social, and political environment in which today's health care operates, and in doing so I realized more and more that our social and economic system itself has become a fundamental threat to our health.

In Minnesota I became especially interested in agriculture and its impact on health at multiple levels. I read frightening accounts of the disastrous effects of the modern system of mechanized, chemical, and energy-intensive farming. Having grown up on a farm myself, I was very interested in hearing about the pros and cons of the so-called Green Revolution from farmers themselves, and I spent many hours with farmers of all ages discussing their problems. I even attended a two-day conference on organic, ecological agriculture to learn about this new grassroots movement in farming.

These discussions revealed to me a fascinating parallel between medicine and agriculture, which helped me greatly in understanding the entire dynamics of our crisis and cultural transformation. Farmers, like doctors, deal with living organisms that are severely affected by the mechanistic approaches of our science and technology. Like the human organism, the soil is a living system that has to remain in a state of dynamic balance to be healthy. When the balance is disturbed there will be pathological growth of certain components—bacteria or cancer cells in the human body, weeds or pests in the fields. Disease will occur, and eventually the whole organism may die and turn into inorganic matter. These effects have become major problems in modern agriculture because of the farming methods promoted by the petrochemical companies. As the pharmaceutical industry has conditioned doctors and patients to believe that the human body needs continual medical supervision and drug treatment to stay healthy, so the petrochemical industry has made farmers believe that soil needs massive infusions of chemicals, supervised by agricultural scientists and technicians, to remain productive. In both cases these practices have seriously disrupted the natural balance of the living system and thus generated numerous diseases. Moreover, the two systems are directly connected, since any imbalance in the soil will affect the food that grows in it and thus the health of the people who eat that food.

As I spent a long weekend visiting farmers on their land, traveling from one farm to another on cross-country skis, I found that many of these men and women have preserved their ecological wisdom, passed down from generation to generation. In spite of massive indoctrination by the petrochemical corporations, they know that the chemical way of farming is harmful to people and to the land. But they are often forced to adopt it because the whole economy of farming—the tax structure, credit system, real estate system, and so on—has been set up in a way that gives them no choice.

My close look at the tragedy of American farming taught me an important lesson, perhaps the most important of my entire stay in Minnesota. The pharmaceutical and petrochemical industries have been extremely successful in achieving extensive control over the consumers of their products, because the same mechanistic world view and associated value system that underlie their technologies also form the basis of their economic and political motives. And although their methods are generally anti-ecological and unhealthy, they are firmly supported by the scientific establishment, which also subscribes to the same outdated world view. To change this situation is now absolutely vital for our well-being and survival, and change will only be possible if we are able, as a society, to shift to a new holistic and ecological vision of reality.

A mosaic of therapies

When I returned to Berkeley from my seven-week visit to Macalester College, I had worked through my collection of medical literature, compiled a set of systematic notes on the critique of the biomedical model, and gathered a lot of new material on the environmental and social dimensions of health. I was now ready to explore the alternatives to conventional health care.

To do so, I threw myself into an intensive exploration of a wide range of therapeutic models and techniques, which took over a year and brought a variety of new and unusual experiences. While I experimented with numerous unorthodox approaches, I also continued to discuss them and to integrate them into the theoretical framework that slowly began to take shape in my mind. As the concept of dynamic balance emerged more and more as the key to that framework, I began to see that the aim of restoring and maintaining the organism's balance was common to all the therapeutic techniques I investigated. Different schools would address different aspects of balance— physical, biochemical, mental, or emotional balance; or balance at the more esoteric level of "subtle energy patterns." In the bootstrap spirit, I regarded all these approaches as different parts of the same therapeutic mosaic, but I accepted only those schools in my holistic framework which recognized the fundamental interdependence of the biological, mental, and emotional manifestations of health.

A large group of therapeutic techniques that were quite new to me were those approaching psychosomatic balance through physical methods, collectively known as bodywork. As I lay down on the massage tables of practitioners of Rolfing, the Feldenkrais method, the Trager technique, and many others, I began a fascinating journey into the subtle realms of relationships between muscle tissues, nerve fibers, breath, and emotions. I experienced the amazing connections—first pointed out in the pioneering work of Wilhelm Reich—between emotional experiences and muscular patterns, and I also recognized that many Eastern disciplines—yoga, *Tai Ji*, Aikido, and others—can be seen as "bodywork techniques" integrating multiple levels of body and mind.

As I became more familiar with the theory and practice of bodywork, I learned to pay attention to the subtle signs of "body language," and gradually began to see the body as a whole as a reflection, or manifestation, of the psyche. I vividly remember spending an evening in New York in animated discussions with Irmgard Bartenieff and several of her students, who showed me with astonishing accuracy how we express something about ourselves with every movement we make, even in such seemingly trivial gestures as reaching for a spoon or holding a glass of wine. Bartenieff, then in her late seventies, was the founder of a school of movement therapy based on the work of Rudolf Laban, who developed a precise method and terminology for analyzing human movement. During the evening Bartenieff and her students carefully watched my movements and gestures, often commenting about them to one another in a technical language I could not understand, and during the entire discussion they kept surprising me with astonishing knowledge of many fine details of my personality and varying emotional patterns to an extent that was almost embarrassing.

One of the women who was especially lively and expressive, verbally as well as in her gestures, was Bartenieff's assistant, Virginia Reed. She and I became good friends later on, and I had many inspiring conversations with her every time I went to New York. Reed introduced me to Wilhelm Reich's work, showed me the influence of the modern dance movement on several bodywork schools, and made me recognize rhythm as an important aspect of health, closely related to the notion of dynamic balance. She demonstrated how our interaction and communication with our environment consist of complex rhythmic patterns, flowing in and out of one another in various ways, and she emphasized the idea of illness as lack of synchrony and integration.

While I experienced the fascinating world of bodywork I also explored the nature of mental health and the multiple realms of the unconscious with Stan Grof and R. D. Laing. Shifting my attention back and forth between physical and mental phenomena, I was able to go beyond the Cartesian split in a tentative, intuitive way before I found a scientific formulation of the psychosomatic approach to health.

The culminating synthesis of my experiential explorations of body and mind came in the fall of 1978, when I had several sessions of "Grof breathing" with Stan and Christina Grof at Esalen. The Grofs had developed this technique during the previous years, and Stan had often expressed his enthusiasm about its potential as a powerful tool for psychotherapy and self-exploration. After relatively short periods of fast, deep

breathing, surprisingly intense sensations, related to unconscious emotions and memories, will emerge and may trigger a
wide range of revealing experiences.

The Grofs encourage their clients to suspend intellectual
analysis as much as possible while surrendering to the emerging sensations and emotions, and they assist in the resolution
of encountered problems with skillful, focused bodywork. Years
of experience have taught them how to sense the physical manifestations of experiential patterns, and they are able to facilitate experiences by physically amplifying the manifest symptoms and sensations and helping to find appropriate modes of
expressing them—through sounds, movements, postures, and
many other nonverbal ways. To make the experience available
to large numbers of people, the Grofs hold workshops in which
up to thirty participants work in the same room in teams of
two—one "breather" lying on a comfortable carpet or mattress,
and one "sitter" facilitating the breather's experience and pro-
tecting him or her from potential injuries.

My first experience of Grof breathing as a sitter was quite
unsettling. For two hours I felt as if I were in a madhouse. The
powerful music in the dimly lit room began with a slowly
intensifying Indian raga, which changed at its height into a
wild Brazilian samba, followed by passages from a Wagner
opera and a Beethoven symphony, and ending in majestic
Gregorian chants. The people around me who went through
the breathing experience joined the music with forceful sounds
of their own—moaning, screaming, crying, laughing—and
through this pandemonium of expressive sounds and writhing
bodies Stan and Christina Grof slowly and calmly made their
rounds, applying pressure to somebody's head here, massaging
a muscle there, carefully watching the entire scene without
being in the least disturbed by its chaotic appearance.

After this initiation I hesitated for a while to experience
the breathing myself, but when I finally did the whole setting
appeared in a totally different light. To begin with, I was
amazed to experience the entire session simultaneously at two
levels. At one level my legs, for example, would feel paralyzed
and I would be unable to move from the hips down. But at
another level I remained fully aware of the fact that this was
a voluntarily induced experience and knew that I could always
break it off, get up, and leave the room. This gave me a sense

of great security and helped me to remain in the experiential, nonanalyzing mode for long periods of time.

One of the most powerful and moving experiences in that self-exploratory state of consciousness was that of the music and other sounds in the room. I was able to associate different kinds of music—classical, Indian, jazz—with sensations in different parts of my body, and at the height of a Baroque concerto I suddenly noticed how the screams and groans of my fellow breathers blended harmoniously with the violins, oboes, and bassoons into a vast symphony of human experience.

Death, life, and medicine

Throughout my explorations of alternative therapeutic techniques I kept the Simonton approach to cancer in my mind, and I often found it very helpful to use it as a measure in judging the various therapeutic models I was studying. By the spring of 1978 I was sure that I wanted Carl Simonton to be my adviser for medicine and health care and sent him a specific proposal of the collaboration I had in mind. To my great disappointment, however, Simonton did not answer my letter, nor did he respond to a follow-up note a couple of months later. After several more months had gone by I began, with great reluctance, to look for another adviser when Carl suddenly called me and told me that he was on his way to California and wanted to discuss our collaboration.

I was overjoyed by this good news and when Simonton arrived I visited him at a retreat near San Francisco where he spent a long weekend with a group of patients. This visit was a very moving experience for me. Simonton asked me to give an informal seminar about the paradigm shift in science to this group, which I did very gladly as it gave me the opportunity to experience Carl's unique interactions with his patients. I was somewhat nervous at the idea of speaking to a group of people who were ill with cancer, but when I met them it was impossible for me to distinguish between the patients and their spouses or other family members, who always participate in the Simonton group sessions. I immediately noticed the warm relationships and the strong bond among the entire group. There was a lot of humor and there was great excitement. The spirit of the group, in fact, was quite similar to that in the groups Stan and Christina Grof lead at Esalen in their monthlong explorations of consciousness.

I also spent some time with Carl alone, and I particularly remember a long discussion of spiritual aspects of healing while relaxing in a sauna. Finally we made concrete plans about our collaboration. Carl told me that the past year had been so packed with research, therapeutic work, and speaking engagements that he had not even had time to read his mail. Just before coming to California he attended an international cancer congress in Argentina and upon leaving his office he took a small selection of letters with him to read on the plane. "That was the first time I sat down to read my mail this year," he added, "and your letter was among the very few I had taken with me." I felt very fortunate, but at the same time it was clear to me that Simonton would never have the time to write background papers for me like my other advisers. Instead he very generously proposed that he would visit me for several days at my home in Berkeley for extensive discussions.

Simonton's visit took place in December 1978 and marked the culmination of my theoretical explorations of health and healing. We spent three days together in intensive discussions that covered a broad range of issues and went on virtually around the clock. We talked through breakfast, lunch, and dinner; we went for long walks in the afternoons; and we stayed up late every night, usually going out for a snack and a glass of wine around midnight. We were both extremely excited by the intensity of our interchanges, which brought many new insights for both of us.

As before, I was deeply impressed by Carl's honesty and personal commitment. Although our discussions were of a theoretical nature, he always spoke in the personal tone I had noticed in his lectures. When it came to psychological issues, he would usually take himself as an example, and when we discussed various therapeutic tools he made it clear to me that he would never expect his patients to accept anything he had not tried out himself. Simonton's reply to my question about the role of nutrition in cancer therapy was typical of his personal touch. "I have much stronger feelings about it now than I did a year ago," he told me. "I am experimenting myself with different diets, and there's no doubt in my mind that over the next few years diet is going to become more and more important in our approach. It is just that I am very reluctant to do things without feeling strongly about them." Simonton's strong personal involvement in all our conversations encouraged me to become personally involved to the same degree, and consequently these three days brought me not only many intellectual insights and clarifications but were also of tremendous help in my personal growth.

On the first day I presented my critique of the biomedical approach to Simonton and asked him for comments and clarifications. Simonton agreed with my assertion that the contemporary theory and practice of medicine is firmly grounded in Cartesian thought, but he also urged me to acknowledge the great variety of attitudes within the medical community. "There are family physicians who are very caring, and there are specialists who are very uncaring," he remarked. "There are very human experiences in hospitals and there are others that are very inhuman. Medicine is practiced by men and women with different personalities, attitudes, and beliefs."

Nevertheless, Simonton agreed that there was a common belief system, a shared paradigm underlying modern medical practice, and when I asked him to identify some of its characteristics he especially emphasized the lack of respect for self-healing. "Medicine in America is allopathic," he explained, "which means that it basically relies on medication and other outside forces to do the healing. There is virtually no emphasis on the healing potential within the patient. This allopathic philosophy is so widespread that it is never even discussed."

This brought us to a long discussion of what is and what is not discussed in medical schools. To my great surprise Simonton told me that many of the issues I considered to be of crucial importance to medicine were hardly ever mentioned during his medical training. "The question of what is health was never addressed," he said. "It was considered to be a philosophical question. You see, when you go to medical school, you never deal with general concepts. A question like 'What is disease?' is never discussed. What is good nutrition, or what is a good sex life, will not be discussed. Similarly, medicine would not address itself to relaxation because relaxation is too subjective. You can talk about muscular relaxation with an EMG, but that's about it."

It was easy for me to see that this was another consequence of the Cartesian split between mind and matter, which led medical scientists to concentrate exclusively on the physical aspects of health and to leave out anything belonging to the mental or spiritual realm.

"That's right," Simonton agreed. "You see, medicine is supposed to be an objective science. It avoids making moral judgments, and it avoids dealing with philosophical and existential issues. But by not addressing itself to such issues, medicine implies that they are not important."

Simonton's mention of existential issues reminded me of Kübler-Ross's critique of medical attitudes toward death and dying, which Carl fully shared. "It is important to talk about death in connection with medicine," he asserted emphatically. "Until very recently we, as a society, have been death-denying; and within the medical profession we still are death-denying. Bodies are carried out of the hospital secretly at night. We see death as failure. We have been looking at death as an absolute phenomenon without qualifying it."

Again the relation to the Cartesian division was obvious to me. "If you separate the mind from the body," I submitted, "it doesn't make sense to qualify death. Death then simply becomes the total standstill of the body-machine."

"Yes, that's how we tend to deal with it in medicine. We don't distinguish a good death from a poor death."

Since I knew that Simonton had to deal with death continually in his practice I was very interested to hear how he himself would qualify death.

"One of the big problems with cancer," he explained, "is that we assume people who die of cancer don't want to die that way, that they are dying against their will. Many cancer patients feel that way."

I was not quite sure what Simonton was driving at. "I thought that people generally just don't want to die, period," I interjected.

"That's what we've been taught to believe," Simonton continued, "but I don't believe that. My own belief is that we all want to live and to die to varying degrees on various days. At the moment, the part of me that wants to live is fairly dominant and the part of me that wants to die is fairly small."

"But there is always a part of us that wants to die?"

"Yes, I believe that. Now, to say that I want to die doesn't really make sense to me, but what does make sense is to say that I want to escape; escape from certain responsibilities, and so on. And when there is no other escape left, then death—or at least illness—becomes a lot more acceptable."

"So death as an escape would be a poor way of dying?"

"Yes, I don't think it's a healthy way to die. Another part that may want to die," Simonton continued, "is the part that wants to punish. Many people punish themselves and others through illness and through death."

Now I began to understand. "Eventually," I wondered, "there might be a part that says: I have lived my life and it's time to go. That would be the spiritual part."

"Yes," Simonton concluded, "and I would say that that's the healthy way to die. I believe that it is possible to die in such a context without illness. But we don't study that very much. We don't look at people who live a full life and then die a beautiful, healthy death."

Once again I was deeply impressed by Carl's profoundly spiritual attitude, an awareness that must have matured gradually in his daily practice of his healing art.

To conclude our discussion of the biomedical approach I asked Simonton about his views on the future of biomedical therapy. He answered by referring to his own practice.

"Let me say, first of all, that I don't administer medical treatment myself to my patients," he began. "I merely make sure that they get it. And what I observe is that my patients tend to take less medication as they get better. Since they are declared incurable by the medical system, their doctors do not object if they take the lead and phase out medical treatment."

"What if you left out medical treatment altogether?" I asked. "What would happen with your patients?"

"It would be very difficult," Simonton said thoughtfully. "It is important to appreciate that we grow up expecting medicine to get us well. Giving medication is a very powerful symbol in our culture. I think it would be a bad thing to eliminate it before the culture has developed to the point where we are ready to let it fall by the wayside."

"Will this ever happen?"

Simonton paused for reflection before he gave a careful answer to my question.

"I think that medical therapy will still be used for a long

time, maybe even forever, for people who operate in that mode. But as society changes, there will be less and less demand for medical therapy. As we understand more and more about the psyche, we will depend less and less on physical treatment, and under the influence of the cultural changes medicine will evolve into much more subtle forms."

At the end of our first day of conversations I had gained many important clarifications in my conceptual framework, new insights, and lively illustrations. On the second and third days I tried to deepen and substantiate my newly gained knowledge by focusing the discussion on Simonton's approach to cancer. I began by asking him what his practice had taught him about the general nature of illness.

Simonton told me that the role of illness as a "problem solver" had been a major insight for him. Because of social and cultural conditioning, he explained, people often find it impossible to resolve stressful problems in a healthy way and therefore choose—consciously or unconsciously—to get sick as a way out.

"Does this include depression or other forms of mental illness?" I asked.

"Absolutely," Simonton replied. "What intrigues me about mental illness is that most mental illnesses tend to exclude malignancy. For instance, it is essentially unheard of for a catatonic schizophrenic to develop cancer."

This observation was indeed very intriguing. "It seems to suggest," I speculated, "that, when I'm faced with a stressful life situation or a crisis in my life, I will have several options. Among other things I may develop cancer, or I may develop catatonic schizophrenia; but I won't do both."

"That's right," Simonton confirmed. "They are almost mutually exclusive decisions. And it makes sense if we look at the psychological dynamics of the two cases. Catatonic schizophrenia is a tremendous withdrawal from reality. Catatonic schizophrenics almost shut off their own thinking as well as shutting off the outside world. In this way they do not experience the frustration, sense of loss, or various other experiences that lead to the development of cancer."

"So these would be two different unhealthy ways to escape from a stressful life situation," I summarized, "one leading to physical illness, the other to mental illness."

"Exactly; and we should also acknowledge a third kind of

escape route," Simonton continued, "the one into social pathologies—violent and reckless behavior, crime, drug abuse, and so on."

"But you wouldn't call that illness?"

"Yes, I would. I think it would be proper to call it social illness. Antisocial behavior is a common reaction to stressful life situations that has to be taken into account when we talk about health. If there is a reduction in illness but at the same time it is offset by an increasing crime rate, we haven't done anything to improve the health of the society."

I was most impressed and extremely excited by this broad, multidimensional view of illness. If I understood Simonton correctly, he was suggesting that individuals have the choice of several pathological escape routes when they are confronted with stressful life situations. If the escape into physical illness is blocked by successful medical intervention, the person might choose to escape into crime or into insanity.

"That's right," Simonton concluded, "and that is a much more meaningful way of looking at health than from the narrow medical point of view. The question of whether medicine has been successful then really becomes very interesting. I don't think it is fair to talk about strides made in medicine if you don't look at the other global aspects of health. If you are able to reduce physical illness, but at the same time this increases mental illness or crime, what the hell have you done?"

I told Carl that this was a completely new and fascinating idea for me, and he added with his characteristic candor: "It is really new for me, too. I had never verbalized it before."

After this general discussion of the nature of illness we spent many hours reviewing the theory and practice of Simonton's cancer therapy. In our previous conversations I had come to recognize cancer as an exemplary illness, characteristic of our age, which forcefully illustrates many key aspects of the holistic conception of health and illness. I planned to conclude my chapter on holistic health care with the Simonton approach and was eager to clarify many details.

When I asked Carl what changes he would like to see occurring in the public image of cancer, he returned to the view of illness we had discussed before.

"I would like to see people realize that illnesses are problem solvers," he said, "and that cancer is a major problem solver. I would like people to recognize a big part of cancer as a breakdown of host resistance and a big part of regaining health as rebuilding basic body resistance. So there would not be so much emphasis on intervention but rather on supporting the person who is ill. Also, I would like to see people appreciate that the cancer cell is not a powerful but a weak cell."

When I asked for clarification of this last point, Simonton explained, as he had done in his Toronto lecture, that even though cancer cells tend to be larger than normal cells, they are sluggish and confused. He emphasized that, contrary to the popular image of cancer, these abnormal cells are incapable of invading or attacking; they simply overproduce.

"The image of cancer as a very powerful disease involves a lot of people's preconceived ideas," Simonton continued. "You see, people would say: 'My grandmother died of cancer and she fought very valiantly, so it must be a strong disease. If it is a weak disease, how could it kill my grandmother?' If you insist that cancer is a weak disease people will have to rethink their grandmother's death, and that is too painful. It is much easier for them to say that I'm crazy. I have had very bright people get extremely upset over the issue of cancer cells being weak cells. But that is a solid biological fact."

As Simonton was speaking, I could see the enormity of changes in people's belief systems that would be necessary for his approach to be accepted, and I could well imagine the resistance he was experiencing, both from his patients and from his colleagues. "What else would you like to see changing?" I pressed on, and Carl was quick to reply:

"The idea that people who get cancer die, that cancer is absolutely lethal, that it is only a matter of time."

That, too, would be very difficult to change, I thought, and I wondered what evidence Simonton had to offer to change people's beliefs that cancer was lethal. One always seemed to hear that everybody dies of cancer.

"But everybody doesn't," Carl insisted. "Even with our crude ways of treating cancer now, between thirty and forty percent of people who develop it get over their illness and never have any further problems with it.

"That percentage, by the way, has not changed in the last forty years," he added, "which shows you that we have had no impact on the cure rate of cancer."

Simonton's comments triggered a profusion of thoughts in me as I tried to interpret the statistics he gave me in terms of his theory. "In your model," I finally ventured, "would that mean that for those thirty to forty percent the incidence of cancer is a disruption of their lives that is severe enough for them to make some significant changes?"

Simonton hesitated: "I don't know. That is a very interesting question."

"It has to be something like that," I insisted. "Otherwise the cancer would recur, according to your theory."

"Well, not necessarily. The person might replace it with a different illness. They would not necessarily develop cancer the next time."

"Of course, it might also be that the problem was temporary anyway," I added.

"That's right," Simonton agreed. "You see, I believe that lesser cancers are related to lesser traumas."

"So, by the time the cancer clears up, the problem has gone away."

"Yes, I think that is a valid possibility and I have considered it. Conversely, I think that some people go ahead and die after the problem has cleared up because of the problem the cancer creates. People have problems, then develop cancer, and then get caught up in the viciousness of the cancer. The problems in their lives clear up considerably and yet they go ahead and die. I think both sides of that coin have significant validity."

I was impressed by the great ease in Simonton's way of speaking as he continually shifted back and forth between the physical and psychological aspects of cancer, and I could not help wondering how our conversation would sound to the ears of his medical colleagues. "What is the opinion in medical circles today on the role of emotions in the development of cancer?" I asked.

"I would say that people are becoming more open to the concept," Simonton replied. "I think there has been a steady progression. The reason for this is that more and more diseases are shown to have an emotional component. Take the case of heart disease, for example. All the major work about heart disease in the last seven or eight years points to the role of the psyche and of personality factors in heart disease. Our society as a whole is changing its attitude toward heart disease very rapidly, and we are seeing a big change in the medical community. In view of all that work it is now much easier to accept that there is also an emotional component in the development of cancer. So, I would say there is much more openness to that concept now."

"Openness but not yet acceptance?"

"Oh, no, there is no acceptance yet. You see, physicians have a big vested interest in maintaining the same way of thinking. If the psyche is significant, that means they will have to address the psyche in working with the patient. They are not equipped to do that, and therefore it is easier for them to deny the psychological component than to change their role."

At this point I was curious as to whether the systemic nature of cancer was recognized in medical circles—the fact that cancer is a disease with a localized appearance but one that must really be understood as a disorder of the system as a whole. Simonton remarked that it was not fair to put all physicians in one category. Cancer specialists see the disease in a much wider context, he explained, whereas surgeons would tend to see it much more as an isolated problem. "By and large," he concluded, "I would say that physicians are moving in the direction of a systemic outlook. Certainly cancer specialists are seeing the tumor more as a systemic disease."

"Including psychological aspects?"

"No, no. They do not include the psyche."

"So, what is the current medical view of cancer?" I wondered.

Simonton answered my question without any hesitation. "Confusion is the order of the day," he said. "At the recent World Cancer Congress in Argentina it was obvious that there is tremendous confusion. Among the cancer specialists around the world the agreement is tiny, and there is a tremendous amount of discord and arguing. In fact, cancer management today almost looks like the disease itself—fragmented and confused."

Our conversation now moved to a careful review of Simonton's ideas on the psychosomatic processes leading to the onset and development of cancer, beginning with the psychological patterns typical of cancer patients. Simonton told me that the big problems in the development of cancer have to do with early childhood experiences. "Those experiences are fragmented," he pointed out; "they are not integrated into the person's life."

I found it interesting that integration seemed to play a crucial role both at the psychological and at the biological level.

"That's right," Simonton agreed. "In the biological development of cancer, the situation is the opposite of integration; it is fragmentation." He then went on to describe how a cancer patient becomes his perception of himself as a child. "For example," he illustrated, "the person might think he's not lovable and will carry this fragmented childhood experience through his life as his identity. And then tremendous energy is used to make that identity come true. People often create a whole reality around that fragmented image of themselves."

"And they would develop cancer twenty or forty years later when that reality doesn't work any longer?"

"Yes, it develops when they can't put enough energy into it to make it work any longer.

"Of course," Simonton added after a pause, "the tendency to isolate painful experiences rather than integrate them is not just a problem for cancer patients but for all of us."

"In psychotherapy you are supposed to reintegrate these experiences by reliving them," I interjected. "The idea seems to be that reliving the trauma will resolve it."

"I don't believe that," Simonton declared. "The key to me is not the reliving of past experiences, although that is certainly very helpful, but the reconstruction of reality. Integrating the experience intellectually is one thing, but putting it into practice is something else. Changing the way I live my life is the real statement of my changing beliefs. That, to me, is the hard part of psychotherapy: putting our insights into action."

"So, for you the key to successful psychotherapy is that insights are followed by action?"

"Yes, and it applies to meditation as well. If I get an insight in my meditation about something that seems very important for me to do, the best thing I can do is to act on it. Now, I may not be able to act on it immediately, and I would not stop my meditation in order to act, but I should act on it as soon as it is reasonable. If I don't, I believe very strongly that I will stop getting such insights."

"Because the unconscious will give up?"

"Right. It will say: 'No good telling him; he doesn't listen anyway.' I believe that the same thing happens not only in meditation but also in everyday life. If, all of a sudden, I get a deep insight into what's going on in my life and see a way of changing it, and if I don't change it, then I will stop getting those insights."

"So this applies to all kinds of insights, whether they come in meditation, through therapy, or through other channels?"

"Yes. If you don't act on them you will stop getting these insights, no matter how much therapy you do."

As our conversation proceeded I was delighted to see more and more interconnections between the various elements of my new conceptual framework. We continued to discuss Simonton's approach to cancer, but we continually touched upon issues essential to any holistic approach to health and healing. The question of emotional stress was one we discussed at great length, and Simonton told me that the holding back of emotions is a crucial factor in the development of cancer in general, and of lung cancer in particular. I still remembered R. D. Laing's impressive demonstration, a few months earlier, of the connection between holding back one's emotions and developing asthma, as a consequence of holding back one's breath as well, and I asked Simonton whether he thought that these emotional patterns were linked to one's breath.

"Yes, I think they are connected with breath," he replied, "although I don't how they are connected. That's why breathing is so important in many meditative practices."

I told Simonton about my conversations with Virginia Reed and the idea of rhythm as an important aspect of health. If one looked at manifestations of rhythmic patterns, breath would be an obvious one. Personality characteristics would be reflected in an individual's breath, I speculated, and if one could make a corresponding profile of breath, that might be a very useful tool.

"I think so, too," Simonton said thoughtfully, "especially if you stress the person and then see what the breathing pattern looks like under stress. I would certainly agree with that, and you could probably do the same thing with pulse."

"That, of course, is what the Chinese do," I observed. "In their pulse diagnosis, they relate pulse to various flow patterns of energy that reflect the state of the entire organism."

Simonton nodded in agreement: "That also makes sense. If I am receiving, for example, alarming stimuli and I don't express anything, then I am blocking the flow of energy. And that, it seems to me, would be reflected in all of my system."

In the last part of our conversations we discussed multiple aspects of the cancer therapy that grew out of the Simontons' scientific model, their philosophy, and their experience with patients. At the very core of the Simonton approach lies the thesis that people participate, consciously or unconsciously, in the onset of their disease and that the sequence of psychosomatic processes that leads to illness can be reversed to lead the patient back to health. I had heard from several physicians that the notion of the patient participating in the development of cancer was extremely problematic, as it tended to evoke a lot of guilt, which was countertherapeutic. I was therefore especially interested in hearing from Carl how he dealt with this problem.

"As I understand it, the problem is the following," I began. "You want to convince your patients that they can participate in the healing process—that's the main thing—but that implies that they have also participated in getting sick, which they don't want to accept."

"Right."

"So if you are forceful in one direction you may create psychological problems in the other."

"That's true," Simonton agreed, "but if they are going to restructure their lives it is important for patients to look at what has been going on and how they got themselves sick. It is important for them to go back and analyze the unhealthy aspects of their lives. So it becomes important in the therapeutic process that they take on a stance of responsibility in order to better see what changes will be necessary. You see, the concept of patient participation has lots of implications."

"But how do you deal with feelings of guilt?"

"It's a matter of not stripping down a person's defense mechanisms," Simonton continued. "With new patients we don't push the concept of patient participation very hard. We put it to them in a much more hypothetical way. You see, it is very easy to build a case for it by looking at stressful events and trying to find new ways of dealing with them. That makes sense to practically everyone."

"And that implies the concept of patient participation."

"Yes, and if people then are further interested and ask questions, you can show them the role of the immune system, you can mention the experimental evidence, and you can do all that without confronting them strongly. We always attempt to avoid strong confrontation with a patient who is not psychologically equipped for it. That would be very detrimental because patients would lose the tools they have developed to live their lives without being able to replace them with any other tools. Gradually, as they grow and develop, they will be able to modify their defense system and take care of themselves in new ways."

I found the entire question of patient participation very intriguing from a theoretical point of view as well. I suggested to Simonton that one could perhaps say that the person's unconscious psyche participates in the development of cancer but that the conscious ego does not, because the patient does not make a conscious decision to get sick.

Simonton disagreed. "I don't think the ego is central," he argued, "but I do think that it is involved. The more I talk to patients, the more I find that they had little inklings. However, the ego is not centrally involved."

"In the healing process, on the other hand, the ego does become centrally involved," I said, continuing the train of thought. "That seems to be your approach, to work with the conscious part of the psyche in the healing process."

At that point I commented on the methods of spiritual teachers, Zen masters for example, who use a variety of ingenious methods to address themselves directly to the student's unconscious. "You don't do that, do you?" I asked Simonton. "Or do you also have ways of tricking patients into these situations?"

Carl smiled: "Yes, I have some."

"What would those be?" I pressed on.

"I would work through metaphor. For example, I would tell patients metaphorically over and over that we are not going to take their disease away before they are ready to let go of it, that their disease serves a lot of useful purposes. Now, a conversation like this really doesn't register much with the conscious ego. It is really addressed to the unconscious and this is very important for quieting a lot of anxieties."

Indeed, it seemed strange to me that a physician would have to assure his patients that he would not take the disease away from them prematurely. But it made more sense to me as Simonton elaborated the point.

"Something that happens very often with my patients," he explained, "is that they are terrified when they are told after successful medical treatment and visualization sessions that they have no evidence of disease. This is very common. They are terrified! As we explored this with our patients we found that they had recognized that they had indeed developed the tumor for a reason and were using it as a crutch to live their lives. Now, all of a sudden, they are told that they have no more tumor and they haven't replaced it with another tool. That's a big loss."

"So now they have to face their stressful life situation again."

"Yes, and without the tumor. They are not ready to be well; they are not ready to act in a healthy way; their family and the society they live in are not prepared to treat them any differently, and so on."

"In that case," I observed, "you have only eliminated the symptom without dealing with the basic problem. It's almost like taking a medicine to get rid of a sore throat."

"Yes."

"So what happens then?"

"They get a recurrence," Simonton continued, "and that is an extremely upsetting episode. You see, they had been saying to themselves: If I get rid of my cancer I will be okay. Now they got rid of it and they feel worse than before, so there is no hope. They were unhappy with the cancer and they are even unhappier without it. They didn't like living with cancer; they like living even less without it."

As Simonton described this situation, it became clear to me that his cancer therapy is much more than the visualization technique that is usually associated with his name. In Simonton's view, the physical disease is a manifestation of underlying psychosomatic processes that may be generated by various psychological and social problems. As long as these problems are not solved the patient will not get well, even though the cancer may temporarily disappear. Although visualization is a central part of the Simonton therapy, the very essence of the approach is to deal with the underlying psychological patterns through psychological counseling and psychotherapy.

When I asked Carl whether he saw psychological counseling as an important therapeutic tool for other illnesses as well, he was quick to respond.

"Yes, absolutely," he said. "It is important to point out that we don't give people permission to seek counseling. Psychotherapy is still considered unacceptable in most segments of our society. It is more acceptable than a few years ago but still not enough. I was taught that bias in medical school, but since then I've come to see counseling as an essential part of the future holistic health-care system. Until we have adopted new, healthier ways of living, psychological counseling is going to be vital over the next generation."

"Does this mean that there will be more psychotherapists?" I wondered.

"Not necessarily. Counselors do not need to be at the Ph.D. level; they simply need to be skilled in counseling."

"It seems that this was the function of the churches and the extended family in the past."

"That's right. You see, basic counseling skills are not difficult to acquire. Teaching people basic assertiveness, for example, is an important skill that is easily taught. How to deal with resentment is fairly easy to learn; or how to deal with guilt. There are pretty standard techniques for these situations. And, most important, just to be able to talk to somebody about one's problems is of tremendous help. It leads one out of the sense of helplessness that is so devastating."

At the end of our three days of intensive discussions I was deeply impressed by the truly holistic nature of Simonton's theoretical model and the many facets of his therapy. I realized that the Simonton approach to cancer will have far-reaching implications for many areas of health and healing. At the same time I also realized how radical it was and how long it would take for it to be embraced by cancer patients, the medical establishment, and by society as a whole.

When I reflected on the contrasts between Simonton's thinking and the views commonly held in the medical community, the statement I had come across in the writings of Lewis Thomas came to my mind—that every disease is dominated by a central biological mechanism, and that a cure would be found once that mechanism was discovered. Carl told me that this was a widely shared belief among cancer specialists. I asked him whether *he* thought that a central biological mechanism of cancer would be discovered. I assumed I knew what Simonton would say, but his answer surprised me. "I believe that this is a distinct possibility," he said, "but I don't think that it would be particularly healthy for our culture."

"Because we would then just find something else?"

"Exactly. The psyche would replace cancer with some other disease. If we look at the history of disease patterns, we see that we have done that throughout our history. Whether it was the plague, or TB, or polio—whatever the illness was— as soon as it was handled we moved on to something else."

Like many of Simonton's assertions during these three days, this was certainly a radical view, but one that made perfect sense to me in the light of our conversations. "So, the discovery of a biological mechanism for cancer would not invalidate your work at all?" I continued.

"No, it wouldn't," Simonton affirmed calmly. "My basic model would still be valid. And if we develop and apply that model now, regardless of whether or not a biological mechanism is found, we have the chance of really changing people's consciousness. We can make a major evolutionary change in health around this disease."

Wholeness and health

My discussions with Carl Simonton had given me so many important new insights and clarifications that I felt ready, during the following weeks, to synthesize the notes I had gathered in three years of exploring health and healing into a coherent conceptual framework. While exploring the multiple aspects of holistic health care I had become very interested in systems theory as a common language for describing the biological, psychological, and social dimensions of health, and as I went through my notes I naturally began to formulate a systems view of health corresponding to the systems view of living organisms. My first formulation was based on the view of living organisms as cybernetic systems, characterized by multiple, interdependent fluctuations. In that model the healthy organism is seen as being in a state of homeostasis, or dynamic balance; health is associated with flexibility, and stress with imbalance and loss of flexibility.

This first cybernetic model allowed me to integrate many important aspects of health I had come to recognize over the years. However, I could also see that it had several serious shortcomings. For example, I found it impossible to introduce the concept of change into the model. The cybernetic system would return to its homeostatic state after a disturbance, but there was no room for development, growth, or evolution. Moreover, it was clear to me that the psychological dimensions of the organism's interactions with its environment had to be taken into account, but I saw no way of integrating them into the model. Although the cybernetic model was much more subtle than the conventional biomedical model it was, ultimately, still mechanistic and did not allow me to really transcend the Cartesian division.

At that time, in January 1979, I saw no solution to these serious problems. I continued with the synthesis of my conceptual framework, acknowledging its inconsistencies and hoping that eventually I would be able to develop some kind of cybernetic model of health that would include the psychological and social dimensions. Indeed, this rather unsatisfactory situation changed dramatically one year later when I studied Prigogine's theory of self-organizing systems and connected it with Bateson's concept of mind. After extensive discussions with Erich Jantsch, Gregory Bateson, and Bob Livingston I was finally able to formulate a systems view of life which included all the advantages of my previous cybernetic model while incorporating Bateson's revolutionary synthesis of mind, matter, and life.

Now everything fell into place. I had learned from Prigogine and Jantsch that living, self-organizing systems not only have the tendency to maintain themselves in their state of dynamic balance but also show the opposite, yet complementary, tendency to transcend themselves, to reach out creatively beyond their boundaries and generate new structures and new forms of organization. The application of this view to the phenomenon of healing showed me that the healing forces inherent in every living organism can work in two different directions. After a disturbance the organism may return, more or less, to its previous state through various processes of self-maintenance.

Examples of this phenomenon would be the minor illnesses that are part of our everyday life and usually cure themselves. On the other hand, the organism may also undergo a process of self-transformation and self-transcendence, involving stages of crisis and transition and resulting in an entirely new state of balance.

I was very excited by this new insight, and my excitement increased even further when I realized the profound implications of Bateson's concept of mind for my systems view of health. Following Jantsch I had epitomized Bateson's definition of mental process as the dynamics of self-organization, which means that, according to Bateson, the organizing activity of a living system is mental activity and all of its interactions with its environment are mental interactions. I had realized that this revolutionary new concept of mind was the first that truly transcended the Cartesian division. Mind and life had become inseparably connected, with mind—or, more accurately, mental process—being immanent in matter at all levels of life.

Bateson's concept of mind gave my systems view of health the depth and comprehensive scope it had lacked before. It had been obvious to me that getting sick and healing are both integral parts of an organism's self-organization. Now I realized with tremendous excitement that, since all self-organizing activity is mental activity, the processes of getting sick and of healing are essentially mental processes. Because mental activity is a multileveled pattern of processes, most of them taking place in the unconscious realm, we are not always fully aware of how we move in and out of illness, but this does not alter the fact that illness is a mental phenomenon in its very essence. Hence it became clear to me that all disorders are psychosomatic in the sense that they involve the continual interplay of mind and body in their origin, development, and cure.

The new systems view of health and illness provided me with a solid framework for presenting a truly holistic approach to health care. As I had hoped, I was now able to integrate my notes on Simonton's cancer therapy, Chinese medicine, stress, the relation between medicine and health, social and political aspects of health care, preventive medicine, mental illness and psychiatry, family therapy, numerous therapeutic techniques, and many other subjects into a coherent and comprehensive presentation. When I wrote the corresponding chapter of *The Turning Point*, "Wholeness and Health," in the fall of 1980 it became the longest chapter of the book and my most detailed and concrete account of a specific part of the emerging new paradigm.

My long search for the new holistic approach to health was inspired early on during the May Lectures in 1974 and took four years of intensive explorations, from 1976 to 1980. Those years were not only full of stimulating encounters with many remarkable women and men and full of exciting intellectual insights; they were also years during which my own attitudes toward health, my belief system, and my life-style changed significantly. Like Carl Simonton, I realized from the beginning that I could not restrict myself to exploring new approaches to health and healing at a purely theoretical level but had to apply my insights to my own life. The deeper I went into my exploration, the more extensive were the changes in the ways I took care of my own health. For many years I did not take a single medical drug, although I was prepared to do so in emergencies. I adopted a regular discipline of relaxation and physical exercise, changed my diet and cleansed my body twice a year with fruit-juice fasts, practiced preventive health care through chiropractic and other bodywork techniques, worked with my dreams, and experienced the broad range of therapeutic techniques I was investigating.

These changes had a profound effect on my health. Throughout my adolescence and young adulthood I had always been too thin; now I gained about twelve pounds, in spite of years of intensive and stressful intellectual work, and then maintained my weight. I became exquisitely sensitive to bodily changes and was able to prevent any excessive stress from turning into illness by changing my patterns of diet, physical exercise, relaxation, and sleep. Indeed, during these years I was virtually never ill and did not even experience the minor episodes of colds and flu I had been used to before.

Today I no longer practice all these methods of preventive health care, but I have continued the most important ones and they have become natural parts of my life. Thus my long exploration of health not only expanded my knowledge and world view but also brought me tremendous personal gains for which I shall always be grateful to all the health professionals with whom I interacted. My long search for balance was rewarded with a new and exciting conceptual framework and, at the same time, with increased balance within my own body and mind.

6

Alternative Futures

E. F. SCHUMACHER

In the summer of 1973, when I had just begun to write *The Tao of Physics*, I sat in the London Underground one morning reading *The Guardian* and as my train rattled through the dusty tunnels of the Northern Line the phrase "Buddhist economics" caught my eye. It was in a review of a book by a British economist, former adviser to the National Coal Board and now, as the review put it, "a sort of economist-guru preaching what he calls 'Buddhist economics.'" The newly published book was entitled *Small Is Beautiful*; the author's name was E. F. Schumacher. I was intrigued enough to read on. While I was writing about "Buddhist physics" somebody else had apparently made another connection between Western science and Eastern philosophy.

The review was skeptical but summarized Schumacher's main points well enough. "How can one argue that the American economy is efficient," Schumacher was paraphrased, "if it uses forty percent of the world's primary resources to support six percent of the world's population, without any observable improvement in the level of human happiness, well-being, peace, or culture?" These words had a very familiar ring to me. I had become interested in economics in the sixties during my two years in California, as I recognized the unhealthy and unpleasant effect of economic policies and practices on my life. When I left California in 1970 I wrote an essay on the hippie movement, which contains the following passages.

To understand the hippies one has to understand the society from which they have dropped out and against which their protest is directed. For most Americans the American Way of Life is their true religion. Their god is money, their liturgy profit maximizing. The American flag has become the symbol for that way of life and is worshipped with religious fervor. . . .

American society is totally oriented toward work, profits, and material consumption. People's dominant goal is to make as much money as possible to buy the gadgets they associate with a high standard of living. At the same time, they feel that they are good Americans because they contribute to the expansion of their economy. They don't realize that their profit maximizing leads to continual deterioration of the goods they buy. For example, the optical appearance of food produce is considered highly important to increase profits, while the quality of the food keeps deteriorating because of all kinds of manipulations. Artificially colored oranges and artificially raised bread are offered in the supermarkets; yogurt contains chemicals for coloring and flavoring; tomatoes are sprayed with wax to make them shiny. Similar effects can be observed in clothing, housing, cars, and other goods. While Americans keep making more and more money they don't get any richer; on the contrary, they keep getting poorer.

The expanding economy destroys the beauty of the natural scenery with ugly buildings, pollutes the air, and poisons the rivers and lakes. Through relentless psychological conditioning it robs people of their sense of beauty, while it gradually destroys the beauty of their environment.

I wrote these observations in the angry tone of the sixties, but they expressed many of the ideas I would encounter several years later in Schumacher's *Small Is Beautiful*. In the sixties, my critique of our modern economic system was based entirely on personal experience and I knew of no alternatives. Like many of my friends I simply felt that an economy based on unlimited material consumption, on excessive competition, and on the reduction of all quality to quantity was not viable in the long run and bound to collapse sooner or later. I remember a long conversation with my father when he visited me in California in 1969, during which he maintained that the present economic system, in spite of some shortcomings, was the only one available, and that my criticism was gratuitous because I could not offer any alternatives. At that time I had no answer to his argument, but ever since that conversation I felt that someday I would be involved, somehow, in helping to create an alternative economic system.

So when I read about Schumacher's work that summer morning in the London Underground, I immediately recognized its relevance and its potential for revolutionizing economic thinking. However, I was too involved in writing *The Tao of Physics* at that time to read books on any other subject, and it took several more years for me to finally read *Small Is Beautiful*. By that time Schumacher had become very well known in the United States, and especially in California, where Governor Jerry Brown had embraced his economic philosophy.

Small Is Beautiful is based on a series of papers and essays written mostly during the fifties and sixties. Influenced partly by Gandhi and partly by his experience of Buddhism during an extended visit to Burma, Schumacher promoted a nonviolent economics, one that would cooperate with nature rather than exploiting it. He advocated the use of renewable resources as early as the mid-fifties, at a time when technological optimism was at its height, when the emphasis everywhere was on growth and expansion, and natural resources seemed unlimited. Against this powerful cultural current Fritz Schumacher, prophet of the ecology movement that was to emerge two decades later, patiently raised his voice of wisdom, emphasizing the importance of human scale, quality, "good work," an economics of permanence based on sound ecological principles, and a "technology with a human face."

The key idea of Schumacher's economic philosophy is to introduce values explicitly into economic thinking. He criticizes his fellow economists for failing to recognize that all economic theory is based on a certain value system and a certain view of human nature. If that view changes, Schumacher points out, nearly all economic theories have to change, and he illustrates his point very eloquently by comparing two economic systems embodying entirely different values and goals. One is our present materialist system, in which the standard of living is measured by the amount of annual consumption, and which therefore tries to achieve maximum consumption along with an optimal pattern of production. The other is a system of Buddhist economics, based on the notions of "right livelihood" and the "Middle Way," in which the aim is to achieve a maximum of human well-being with an optimal pattern of consumption.

When I read *Small Is Beautiful* three years after its publication, as I was embarking on my investigation of the paradigm shift in various fields, I found in Schumacher's book not only an eloquent and detailed confirmation of my intuitive critique of the American economic system, but also, to my even greater delight, a clear formulation of the basic premise I had adopted for my research project. Present-day economics, Schumacher states emphatically, is a remnant of nineteenth-century thinking and is totally incapable of solving any of the real problems of today. It is fragmentary and reductionistic, restricting itself to purely quantitative analysis and refusing to look into the real nature of things. Schumacher extends his accusation of fragmentation and lack of values to modern technology, which, as he pointedly observes, deprives people of the creative and useful work they enjoy most, while giving them plenty of fragmented and alienating work they do not enjoy at all.

Current economic thinking, according to Schumacher, is obsessed with unqualified growth. Economic expansion has become the abiding interest of all modern societies and any growth of GNP is believed to be a good thing. "The idea that there could be pathological growth, unhealthy growth, disruptive or destructive growth, is to [the modern economist] a perverse idea which must not be allowed to surface," Schumacher continues in his scathing critique. He acknowledges that growth is an essential feature of life, but he emphasizes that all economic growth must be qualified. While some things ought to be growing, others ought to be diminishing, he points out, and he observes that "it does not require more than a simple act of insight to realise that infinite growth of material consumption in a finite world is an impossibility."

Finally, Schumacher maintains that it is inherent in the methodology of modern economics and in the value system underlying modern technology to ignore our dependence on the natural world. "Ecology ought to be a compulsory subject for all economists," Schumacher insists, and he observes that, contrary to all natural systems, which are self-balancing, self-adjusting, and self-cleansing, our economic and technological thinking recognizes no self-limiting principle. "In the subtle system of nature," Schumacher concludes, "technology, and in particular the super-technology of the modern world, acts like a foreign body, and there are now numerous signs of rejection."

Schumacher's book contains not only his articulate and eloquent critique but also an outline of his alternative vision. It is a radical alternative. An entirely new system of thought is needed, Schumacher maintains, based on attention to people, an economics "as if people mattered." But people, he notes, can be themselves only in small, comprehensible groups, and he concludes that we must learn to think in terms of small-scale, manageable units—thus, "Small is beautiful."

Such a shift, according to Schumacher, will require a profound reorientation of science and technology. He demands nothing less than to incorporate wisdom into the very structure of our scientific methodology and our technological approaches. "Wisdom," he writes, "demands a new orientation of science and technology towards the organic, the gentle, the non-violent, the elegant and beautiful."

Conversations in Caterham

When I finished reading *Small Is Beautiful* I was enthusiastic. I had found a clear confirmation of my basic thesis in economics, a field of which I had no detailed knowledge. More than that, Schumacher had also provided me with a first outline of an alternative approach, which, at least to the extent that it incorporated an ecological perspective, seemed to be consistent with the holistic world view I saw emerging from the new physics. So when I planned to assemble a group of advisers for my project, I naturally decided to approach Fritz Schumacher, and when I went to London for a three-week visit in May 1977 I wrote to him and asked him whether he would allow me to visit him to discuss my project.

This was the same visit to London during which I also had my first meeting with R. D. Laing, and looking back on these two meetings I cannot help being struck by some curious similarities. Both men received me very kindly, but both disagreed with me—Schumacher right away, Laing three years later in Saragossa—on fundamental issues connected with the role of physics in the paradigm shift. In both cases the disagreement seemed at first insurmountable but was resolved in subsequent discussions that contributed enormously to the expansion of my world view.

Schumacher replied to my letter very kindly and suggested that I should call him from London to arrange a visit to Caterham, the small town in Surrey where he lived. When I did so he invited me for tea and said that he would pick me up at the railway station. Several days later I took the train to Caterham in the early afternoon of a glorious spring day, and as I rode through the lush, green countryside, I felt excited and yet calm and peaceful.

My relaxed mood was further enhanced when I met Fritz Schumacher at the Caterham station. He was easygoing and very charming—a tall gentleman in his sixties with longish white hair, a kind, open face, and gentle eyes twinkling under bushy white brows. He welcomed me warmly and told me that we could walk to his house, and as we fell into a leisurely stroll I could not help thinking that the phrase "economist-guru" described Schumacher's appearance perfectly.

Schumacher was born in Germany but had become a British citizen at the end of World War II. He spoke with a rather elegant German/English accent, and although he knew that I was Austrian he conducted our entire conversation in English. Later on, when we spoke about Germany, we would naturally switch to German for many expressions and short phrases, but after these brief excursions into our native language he would always continue the conversation in English. This subtle use of language created a very pleasant sense of camaraderie between us. We both shared a certain Germanic style of expression and, at the same time, we spoke as world citizens, having long transcended our native culture.

Schumacher's home was idyllic. The rambling Edwardian house was comfortable and open to the outdoors, and as we sat down to tea we were surrounded by an abundance of nature. The vast garden was luxuriant and overgrown. The flowering trees were alive with the activity of insects and birds, a whole ecosystem basking in the warm spring sun. It was a peaceful oasis where the world still seemed whole. Schumacher spoke with great enthusiasm about his garden. He had spent many years making compost and experimenting with a variety of organic gardening techniques, and I realized that this had been his approach to ecology—a practical approach, grounded in experience, which he was able to integrate with his theoretical analyses into a comprehensive philosophy of life.

After tea we moved to Schumacher's study to begin our discussion in earnest. I opened it by presenting the basic theme of my new book, much in the way I would present it a few days later to R. D. Laing. I began with the observation that our social institutions are unable to solve the major problems of our time because they adhere to the concepts of an outdated world view, the mechanistic world view of seventeenth-century science. The natural sciences, as well as the humanities and social sciences, have all modeled themselves after classical Newtonian physics, and the limitations of the Newtonian world view are now manifest in the multiple aspects of global crisis. While the Newtonian model is still the dominant paradigm in our academic institutions and in society at large, I continued, physicists have gone far beyond it. I described the world view I saw emerging from the new physics—its emphasis on interconnectedness, relationship, dynamic patterns, and continual change and transformation—and I expressed my belief that the other sciences would have to change their underlying philosophies accordingly in order to be consistent with this new vision of reality. Such radical change, I maintained, would also be the only way to really solve our urgent economic, social, and environmental problems.

I presented my thesis carefully and concisely, and when I paused at the end I expected Schumacher to agree with me on the essential points. He had expressed very similar ideas in his book and I was confident that he would help me formulate my thesis more concretely.

Schumacher looked at me with his friendly eyes and said slowly: "We have to be very careful to avoid head-on confrontation." I was stunned by this remark, and when he saw my puzzled look, he smiled. "I agree with your call for a cultural transformation," he said. "This is something I have often said myself. An epoch is drawing to a close; a fundamental change is necessary. But I don't think physics can give us any guidance in this matter."

Schumacher went on to point out the difference between what he called "science for understanding" and "science for manipulation." The former, he explained, has often been called wisdom. Its purpose is the enlightenment and liberation of the person, while the purpose of the latter is power. During the Scientific Revolution in the seventeenth century, Schumacher continued, the purpose of science shifted from wisdom to power. "Knowledge itself is power," he said, quoting Francis Bacon, and he observed that since that time the name "science" remained reserved for manipulative science.

"The progressive elimination of wisdom has turned the rapid accumulation of knowledge into a most serious threat," Schumacher declared emphatically. "Western civilization is based on the philosophical error that manipulative science is the truth, and physics has caused and perpetuated this error. Physics got us into the mess we are in today. The great cosmos is nothing but a chaos of particles without purpose or meaning, and the consequences of this materialistic view are felt everywhere. Science is concerned primarily with knowledge that is useful for manipulation, and the manipulation of nature almost invariably leads to the manipulation of people.

"No," Schumacher concluded with a sad smile, "I don't believe at all that physics can help us in solving our problems today."

I was deeply impressed by Schumacher's passionate plea. This was the first I had heard of Bacon's role in shifting the purpose of science from wisdom to manipulation. Several months later I would come upon a detailed feminist analysis of that crucial development, and the obsession of scientists with domination and control would also be one of the main themes in my discussions with Laing. At that moment, however, as I faced Fritz Schumacher in his study in Caterham, I had not given much thought to these issues. I only felt very deeply that science could be practiced in a very different way, that physics, in particular, could be "a path with a heart," as I had suggested in the opening chapter of *The Tao of Physics*.

In defending my point of view I pointed out to Schumacher that physicists today no longer believe they are dealing with absolute truth. "Our attitude has become much more modest," I explained. "We know that whatever we say about nature will be expressed in terms of limited and approximate models, and part of this new understanding is the recognition that the new physics is merely one part of a new vision of reality that is now emerging in many fields."

I concluded that physics, nevertheless, may still be helpful for other scientists who are often reluctant to adopt a holistic, ecological framework for fear of being unscientific. The recent developments in physics can show these scientists, I maintained, that such a framework is not at all unscientific. On the contrary, it is in agreement with the most advanced scientific theories of physical reality.

Schumacher replied that even though he recognized the usefulness of the emphasis on interrelatedness and process thinking in the new physics, he could not see any room for quality in a science based on mathematical models. "The whole notion of a mathematical model has to be questioned," he insisted. "The price of this kind of model building is the loss of quality, the very thing that matters most."

A very similar argument formed the cornerstone of Laing's passionate attack in Saragossa three years later. By that time I had absorbed the thoughts of Bateson, Grof, and other scientists who had reflected deeply on the role of quality, experience, and consciousness in modern science. Consequently I was able to present a credible answer to Laing's critique. In my conversation with Schumacher I had only some elements of that answer.

I pointed out that quantification, control, and manipulation represent only one aspect of modern science. The other, equally important aspect, I insisted, has to do with the recognition of patterns. The new physics, in particular, implies a shift from isolated building blocks, or structures, to patterns of relationships. "That notion of a pattern of relationships," I speculated, "seems to be closer, somehow, to the idea of quality. And I feel that a science concerned primarily with networks of interdependent dynamic patterns will be closer to what you call 'science for understanding.' "

Schumacher did not respond immediately. He seemed lost in his thoughts for a while, and finally he looked at me with a warm smile. "You know," he said, "we had a physicist in the family, and I had many discussions of this kind with him." I expected to hear of some nephew or cousin who had studied physics, but before I could make a polite comment Schumacher surprised me with the name of my own hero: "Werner Heisenberg. He was married to my sister." I had been completely unaware of the close family tie between these two revolutionary and influential thinkers. I told Schumacher how much I had been influenced by Heisenberg and recounted my meetings and discussions with him during the preceding years.

Schumacher then proceeded to explain the crux of his discussions with Heisenberg and of his disagreement with my position. "The guidance we need for solving the problems of our time cannot be found in science," he began. "Physics cannot have any philosophical impact because it cannot entertain the qualitative notion of higher and lower levels of being. With Einstein's statement that everything is relative the vertical dimension disappeared from science and with it the need for any absolute standards of good and evil."

In the long discussion that followed Schumacher expressed his belief in a fundamental hierarchical order consisting of four levels of being—mineral, plant, animal, and human—with four characteristic elements—matter, life, consciousness, and self-awareness—which are manifest in such a way that each level possesses not only its own characteristic element but also those of all lower levels. This, of course, was the ancient idea of the Great Chain of Being, which Schumacher presented in modern language and with considerable subtlety. However, he maintained that the four elements are irreducible mysteries that cannot be explained, and that the differences between them represent fundamental jumps in the vertical dimension, "ontological discontinuities," as he put it. "This is why physics cannot have any philosophical impact," he repeated. "It cannot deal with the whole; it deals only with the lowest level."

This was indeed a fundamental difference in our views of reality. Although I agreed that physics was limited to a particular level of phenomena, I did not see the differences between various levels as absolute. I argued that these levels are essentially levels of complexity which are not separate but are all interconnected and interdependent. Moreover, I observed, following my mentors Heisenberg and Chew, the way in which we divide reality into objects, levels, or any other entities depends largely on our methods of observation. What we see depends on how we look; patterns of matter reflect the patterns of our mind.

To conclude my argument I expressed my belief that the science of the future would be able to deal with the entire range of natural phenomena in a unified way, using different but mutually consistent concepts to describe different aspects and levels of reality. But during that discussion, in May 1977, I could not justify my belief with concrete examples. In particular, I was unaware of the emerging theory of living, self-organizing systems that goes a long way toward a unified description of life, mind, and matter. However, I explained my view well enough for Schumacher to leave the matter without further argument. We agreed on the basic differences between our philosophical approaches, each of us respecting the other's position.

Economics, ecology, and politics

From that point on the nature of our dialogue changed from a rather intense discussion to an animated but much more relaxed conversation, in which Schumacher's role became increasingly that of a teacher and storyteller, while I listened attentively and kept the conversation flowing by interjecting brief questions and comments. During the whole time several of Schumacher's children kept coming into the study, in particular a little boy who could not have been more than three or four and for whom Schumacher showed great tenderness. I remember being quite confused by all these sons and daughters, some of whom seemed a generation apart. Somehow it seemed incongruous to me that the author of *Small Is Beautiful* should have such a large family. Later on I learned that Schumacher had married twice and had had four children in each marriage.

During our discussion about the role of physics and the nature of science it had become clear to me that the difference in our approaches was too substantial to permit asking Schumacher to be an adviser to my book project. However, I did want to learn from him as much as I could during that afternoon, and so I engaged him in a long conversation about economics, ecology, and politics.

I asked him whether he saw a new conceptual framework that would allow us to solve our economic problems. "No," he replied without hesitation. "We do need an entirely new system of thought, but there are no appropriate economic models today. At the Coal Board we had this experience again and again. We had to rely on experiment far more than on understanding.

"Because of the smallness and patchiness of our knowledge," Schumacher continued animatedly, "we have to go in small steps. We have to leave room for non-knowledge*: Take a small step, wait for feedback, and then proceed further. There is wisdom in smallness, you see." Schumacher affirmed that, in his view, the greatest danger arises from ruthless application of partial knowledge on a vast scale, and he cited nuclear energy as the most dangerous example of such an unwise application. He emphasized the importance of appropriate technologies that would *serve* people rather than destroy them. This was especially important in Third World countries, Schumacher insisted, where "intermediate technology," as he called it, would often be the most appropriate form.

"What exactly is intermediate technology?" I asked.

"Intermediate technology is simply the finger pointing at the moon," Schumacher said with a smile, using the well-known Buddhist expression. "The moon itself can't be fully described, but it can be pointed out in terms of specific situations."

To give me an example, Schumacher told me the story of how he helped an Indian village produce steel rims for its oxcarts. "In order to have efficient oxcarts, the wheels ought to have steel rims," he began. "Our forefathers could bend steel accurately on a small scale, but we have forgotten how to do it, except with big machines in Sheffield. How did our forefathers do it?

"They had a most ingenious tool," Schumacher continued excitedly. "We found one of those tools in a French village. It was brilliantly conceived but awkwardly manufactured. We took it to our College of Agricultural Engineering in England and said, 'Come on, chaps, show us what you can do!' The result was a tool of the same design but upgraded to our level of know-how. It costs five pounds, can be made by the village blacksmith, doesn't require any electricity, and anyone can use it. That's intermediate technology."

* *This was Schumacher's own word for "ignorance," a direct translation from the German* Nichtwissen.

The more I listened to Schumacher, the more clearly I recognized that he was not so much a man of grand conceptual designs as a man of wisdom and action. He had arrived at a clear set of values and principles and was able to apply these in most ingenious ways to the solution of a great variety of economic and technological problems. The secret of his immense popularity lay in his message of optimism and hope. He asserted that anything people really needed could be produced very simply and very efficiently, on a small scale, with very little initial capital, and without doing violence to the environment. With hundreds of examples and little success stories he kept affirming that his "economics as if people mattered" and his "technology with a human face" could be realized by ordinary people, that action could and should begin right away.

In our conversation Schumacher often returned to the awareness of the interdependence of all phenomena and the immense complexity of the natural pathways and processes in which we are embedded. We found ourselves in complete agreement on this basic ecological awareness, and we also shared the belief that the notion of complementarity—the dynamic unity of opposites—is crucial to the understanding of life. As Schumacher put it: "The whole crux of economic life, and indeed of life in general, is that it constantly requires the living reconciliation of opposites." He illustrated this insight with the universal pair of opposite processes manifest in all ecological cycles, growth and decay, "the very hallmark of life," as he put it.

Similarly, Schumacher pointed out, there are many problems of opposites in social and economic life that cannot be solved but can be transcended by wisdom. "Societies need stability *and* change," he observed, "order *and* freedom, tradition *and* innovation, planning *and* laissez-faire. Our health and happiness continually depend on the simultaneous pursuit of mutually opposed activities or aims."

To conclude our conversation I asked Schumacher whether he had met any politicians who appreciated his views. He told me that the ignorance of European politicians was appalling and I sensed that he especially resented the lack of appreciation in his native Germany. "Even politicians in high positions are very ignorant," he complained. "It is a case of the blind leading the blind."

"How about the United States?" I inquired.

There the situation seemed more hopeful, Schumacher felt. He had recently been on a six-week lecture tour through the United States and had been received enthusiastically by huge crowds everywhere he went. During that tour, he told me, he also met with several politicians and found more understanding than in Europe. These meetings culminated in a reception at the White House by Jimmy Carter, whom Schumacher spoke of with great admiration. President Carter seemed to be genuinely interested in Schumacher's ideas and ready to learn from him. Moreover, it seemed to me from the way Schumacher spoke about Carter that the two had had an excellent rapport and had communicated sincerely at many levels.

When I mentioned that, in my experience, Jerry Brown was the American politician most open to ecological awareness and to holistic thinking in general, Schumacher agreed. He told me how much he appreciated Brown's lively and creative mind, and I had the impression that he had become quite fond of Brown. "Indeed," Schumacher acknowledged when I told him of my impression. "You see, Jerry Brown is the same age as my oldest son. I have a very fatherly feeling for him."

Before seeing me off at the train station Schumacher took me on a tour through his beautiful untamed garden, returning to what seemed to be one of his favorite subjects, organic horticulture. With great passion he spoke about planting trees as the most effective action one could take to solve the problem of world hunger. "Trees are much easier to grow than crops, you see," he explained. "They sustain the habitats of countless species, they produce vital oxygen, and they nourish animals and people.

"Did you know that trees can produce high-protein beans and nuts?" Schumacher asked excitedly. He told me that he had recently planted several dozen of these protein-producing trees and was working on promoting the idea throughout Britain.

My visit was now coming to a close and I thanked Schumacher for making this such an inspiring and challenging afternoon. "It was a great pleasure," he graciously replied, and after a pensive moment he added with a warm smile: "You know, we differ in our approach, but we don't differ in basic ideas."

As we walked back to the station, I mentioned that I had lived in London for four years and still had many friends in England. I told Schumacher that, after having been away for over two years, what impressed me most during this visit was the striking difference between the bleak reports on the British economy I had read in the newspapers and the cheerful and joyous mood of my friends in London and other parts of the country. "You are right," Schumacher agreed. "People in England live according to new values. They work less and live better, but our industrial leaders haven't caught on to that yet."

"Work less and live better!" were the last words I remember Schumacher saying to me at the Caterham train station. He placed great emphasis on this phrase, as if it were something very important that I should remember. Four months later I was shocked to learn that Schumacher had died, apparently of a heart attack, while on a lecture tour in Switzerland. His admonition—"Work less and live better!"—took on an ominous meaning. Perhaps, I thought, he meant it more for himself than for me. However, when my own lecture schedule became quite hectic a couple of years later I often thought back to the last words of the gentle sage at Caterham. This memory helped me considerably in my struggle to keep my professional engagements from taking away the simple pleasures of life.

Reflections on Schumacher

On the train journey back to London I tried to evaluate my conversations with Fritz Schumacher. As I had expected from reading his book, I found him to be a brilliant thinker with a global perspective and a creative, questioning mind. More important, however, I was deeply impressed by his great wisdom and kindness, his relaxed spontaneity, his quiet optimism, and his gentle humor. Two months before my visit to Caterham I had had an important insight in a conversation with Stan Grof. I had recognized the fundamental connection between ecological awareness and spirituality. After spending several hours with Schumacher I felt that he personified that connection. In our conversations we did not talk much about religion, yet I felt very strongly that Schumacher's outlook on life was that of a deeply spiritual person.

But notwithstanding my great admiration for Schumacher I also realized there were substantial differences in our views. Thinking back to our discussion about the nature of science I came to the conclusion that these differences were rooted in Schumacher's belief in a fundamental hierarchical order, the "vertical dimension," as he called it. My own philosophy of nature had been formed by Chew's "network thinking" and, later on, was further shaped by Bateson's scientific monism. It had also been strongly influenced by the nonhierarchical perspectives of Buddhist and Taoist philosophy. Schumacher, on the other hand, had developed a rather rigid, almost scholastic, philosophical framework. This was quite a surprise for me. I had gone to Caterham to meet a Buddhist economist. Instead, I found myself engaged in debate with a traditional Christian humanist.

Germaine Greer—the feminist perspective

During the following months I thought a lot about Schumacher's philosophy of life. Shortly after his death his second book, *A Guide for the Perplexed*, was published. It is a brilliant compendium of Schumacher's world view—his "summa," as it were. Schumacher had, in fact, mentioned to me that he had recently completed a philosophical work that meant a great deal to him, and when I read the book I was not surprised to find in it articulate and concise treatments of many issues he had touched upon in our conversation. The *Guide* confirmed many of the impressions I had gathered during my visit to Caterham, and I finally concluded that Schumacher's firm belief in fundamental hierarchical levels was strongly connected with his tacit acceptance of the patriarchal order. In our conversation we never discussed this issue, but I noticed that Schumacher often used patriarchal language—the mind of "man," the potential of all "men," and so on—and I also sensed that his status and demeanor in his large family were those of a traditional patriarch.

By the time I met Schumacher I had become very sensitive to sexist language and behavior. I had come to embrace the feminist perspective, which, over the subsequent years, would have the most powerful impact both on my explorations of the new paradigm and on my personal growth.

I first encountered feminism—or, rather, "women's liberation" as it was called in those days—in London in 1974

when I read Germaine Greer's classic, *The Female Eunuch*.
Three years after its original publication the book had become
a best-seller and was widely hailed as the most articulate and
subversive manifesto of a new, radical, and exciting movement—
the "second wave" of feminism.

Indeed, Greer opened my eyes to a world of issues I had
been totally unaware of. I was familiar with the cause of wom-
en's liberation and its main accusations: the widespread dis-
crimination against women, the daily injustices and casual in-
sults, the continual exploitation in a society dominated by men.
But Greer went further than that. In eloquent and incisive
prose, with language that is both forceful and literate, she questioned the basic assumptions about female nature in our male-
oriented culture. In chapter after chapter she analyzed and
illustrated how women have been conditioned to accept patriarchal stereotypes of themselves; to view themselves—their
bodies, their sexuality, their intellects, their emotions, their
entire womanhood—through the eyes of men. This thorough
and relentless conditioning, Greer declared, distorted women's
bodies and souls. Woman had been castrated by patriarchal
power; she had become a female eunuch.

Greer's book provoked both anger and exhilaration. She
proclaimed that woman's first duty was not to her husband or
her children but to herself, and she urged her sisters to liberate
themselves by embarking on the feminist path of self-discovery,
a challenge so radical that its strategies had yet to be designed.
Even as a man I was inspired by these exhortations, which
made me realize that women's liberation was also men's liberation. I sensed the joy and excitement of a new expansion of
consciousness and, indeed, Greer herself wrote about that joy
at the very beginning of her book. "Liberty is terrifying but it
is also exhilarating," she affirmed. "The struggle which is not
joyous is the wrong struggle."

My first feminist friend was an English documentary film-
maker, Lyn Gambles, whom I met around the time I read
Germaine Greer. I remember many discussions with Lyn in
the numerous alternative restaurants and coffeehouses that had
sprung up all over London in those days. Lyn was familiar with
most of the feminist literature and was active in the women's
movement, but our discussions were never antagonistic. She
joyfully shared her insights with me, and together we explored

new modes of thinking, new values, and new ways of relating to each other. We were both extremely excited by the liberating power of feminist awareness.

Carolyn Merchant—feminism and ecology

After returning to California in 1975 I continued to explore feminist issues as my plans to investigate the paradigm shift slowly matured and I began my first round of discussions with my advisers. It was easy to find feminist literature and to engage in discussions with feminist activists in Berkeley, which was and continues to be a major intellectual center of the American women's movement. Among the many discussions I had in those years I particularly remember those with Carolyn Merchant, historian of science at UC Berkeley. I had met Merchant several years before in Europe at a conference on the history of quantum physics.

At that time her work had been concerned mainly with Leibniz and at the conference we had several conversations about the similarities and differences between Chew's bootstrap physics and the view of matter presented by Leibniz in his *Monadology*. When I saw Carolyn Merchant again in Berkeley five years later she was very excited about her new research, which not only added a fascinating new perspective to the history of the Scientific Revolution in seventeenth-century England but also had far-reaching implications for feminism, ecology, and our entire cultural transformation.

Merchant's research, which she later published in her book *The Death of Nature*, concerned Francis Bacon's crucial role in shifting the goal of science from wisdom to manipulation. When she told me about her work I immediately recognized its importance. I had visited Schumacher just a few months earlier, and his passionate condemnation of the manipulative nature of modern science was still vivid in my memory.

In the papers she gave me to read, Merchant showed how Francis Bacon personified a very important connection between two principal strands of the old paradigm: the mechanistic conception of reality and the male obsession with domination and control in patriarchal culture. Bacon was the first to formulate a clear theory of the empirical approach of science, and he advocated his new method of investigation in passionate and often downright vicious terms. I was shocked by the extremely violent language, which Merchant exposed in her papers in quotation after quotation. Nature has to be "hounded in her wanderings," wrote Bacon, "bound into service" and made a "slave." She was to be "put in constraint" and the aim of the scientist was to "torture nature's secrets from her."

In her analysis of these statements Merchant pointed out that Bacon used the traditional image of nature as a female and that his advocacy of torturing nature's secrets from her with the help of mechanical devices is strongly suggestive of the widespread torture of women in the witch trials of the early seventeenth century. Indeed, Merchant showed that Francis Bacon, as attorney general of King James I, was intimately familiar with the prosecution of witches, and she suggested that he must have carried over the metaphors used in the courtroom into his scientific writings.

I was very impressed by this analysis, which exposes a crucial and frightening connection between mechanistic science and patriarchal values, and I became aware of the tremendous impact of the "Baconian spirit" on the entire development of modern science and technology. From the time of the ancients the goals of science had been wisdom, understanding the natural order, and living in harmony with it. In the seventeenth century this attitude changed radically into its opposite. Ever since Bacon the goal of science has been knowledge that can be used to dominate and control nature, and today both science and technology are used predominantly for purposes that are dangerous, harmful, and profoundly anti-ecological.

In our conversations Carolyn Merchant and I spent many hours discussing the broad implications of her work. She showed me that the connection between the mechanistic world view and the patriarchal ideal of "man" dominating nature is apparent not only in the works of Bacon but also, to lesser degrees, in those of René Descartes, Isaac Newton, Thomas Hobbes, and other founding "fathers" of modern science. Since the rise of mechanistic science, Merchant explained, the exploitation of nature has gone hand in hand with that of women. Thus the ancient association of woman and nature links women's history and the history of the environment and is the source of a natural kinship between feminism and ecology. I realized that Carolyn Merchant had made me aware of an extremely important aspect of our cultural transformation. She was the first to direct my attention to that natural kinship between feminism and ecology, which I have continued to explore ever since.

Adrienne Rich—the radical feminist critique

The next important phase in the sharpening of my feminist awareness began in the spring of 1978 during my seven-week visit to Minnesota. In Minneapolis I became friends with Miriam Monasch, a stage actress, playwright, and social activist, who introduced me to a large network of artists and activists. Miriam was also the first radical feminist I had met. She found my interest in feminist issues highly commendable but also pointed out that many of my attitudes and behavior patterns were still very sexist. To remedy the situation she urged me to read *Of Woman Born* by Adrienne Rich and gave me a copy of the book.

This book transformed my entire perception of social and cultural change. Over the following months I carefully read it several times, compiled a systematic compendium of its key passages, and bought numerous copies of the book for friends and acquaintances. *Of Woman Born* became my feminist bible, and ever since that time the struggle of manifesting and promoting feminist awareness has been an integral part of my work and my life.

Germaine Greer had shown me how our perception of female nature has been conditioned by patriarchal stereotypes. Adrienne Rich provided further confirmation and, at the same time, radically extended the feminist critique to the perception of the entire human condition. As she takes her reader through a comprehensive and scholarly yet passionate discussion of female biology and psychology, childbirth and motherhood, family dynamics, social organization, cultural history, ethics, art, and religion, the full force of patriarchy unfolds. "Patriarchy is the power of the fathers," Rich begins her analysis, "a familial-social, ideological, political system in which men—by force, direct pressure, or through ritual, tradition, law, language, customs, etiquette, education, and the division of labor—determine what part women shall or shall not play, and in which the female is everywhere subsumed under the male."

As I worked through Adrienne Rich's extensive material I

experienced a radical change of perception, which threw me into an intellectual and emotional turmoil. I realized that the full power of patriarchy is extremely difficult to grasp because it is omnipresent. It has influenced our most basic ideas about human nature and about our relation to the universe—"man's" nature and "his" relation to the universe in patriarchal language. It is the one system which, until recently, had never been openly challenged, and whose doctrines were so universally accepted that they seemed to be laws of nature; indeed, they were usually presented as such.

My experience of that crisis of perception was not unlike the experience of the physicists who developed quantum theory in the 1920s, which Heisenberg had described to me so vividly. Like those physicists, I found myself questioning my very basic assumptions about reality. These were not assumptions about physical reality but about human nature, society, and culture. This process of questioning and exploration had direct personal relevance. Whereas the subject of Germaine Greer's book had been perceptions of female nature, I now felt that Adrienne Rich forced me to critically examine my own human nature, my role in society and in my cultural tradition. I remember those months as a time of great insecurity and frequent anger. I became very aware of some of my own patriarchal values and behavior patterns and had heated arguments with my friends when I accused them of similar sexist behavior.

At the same time, the radical feminist critique held a strong intellectual fascination for me, which has persisted to the present day. It is the fascination one experiences on those rare occasions when one encounters an entirely new mode of inquiry. It has been said that students of philosophy discover such a new mode when reading Plato, students of the social sciences when reading Marx. For me the discovery of the feminist perspective was an experience of comparable depth, disturbance, and attraction. It was a challenge to redefine what it means to be human.

As an intellectual, I was especially excited by the impact of feminist awareness on our mode of thinking. According to Adrienne Rich, our intellectual systems are inadequate because, having been created by men, they lack the wholeness that female consciousness could provide. "Truly to liberate women," Rich insisted, "means to change thinking itself: to reintegrate what has been named the unconscious, the subjective, the emotional with the structural, the rational, the intellectual." These words resonated very strongly with me, as one of my main aims in writing *The Tao of Physics* had been to reintegrate rational and intuitive modes of consciousness.

The connection between Adrienne Rich's discussion of female consciousness and my explorations of mystical traditions went even further. I had learned that bodily experience is seen in many traditions as a key to the mystical experience of reality and that numerous spiritual practices train the body specifically for that purpose. This is exactly what Rich exhorted women to do in one of the most radical and visionary passages of her book:

> In arguing that we have by no means yet explored or understood our biological grounding, the miracle and paradox of the female body and its spiritual and political meanings, I am really asking whether women cannot begin, at last, to think through the body, to connect what has been so cruelly disorganized.

Childhood memories of matriarchy

I have often been asked why I have found it easier than other men to embrace feminism. It is a question I pondered myself during those months of intense exploration in the spring of 1978. In searching for an answer my mind went back to the sixties. I remembered the deep experience of being allowed to show my feminine side by wearing long hair, jewelry, and colorful clothes. I thought of the female folk and rock stars of that period—Joan Baez, Joni Mitchell, Grace Slick, and many others—who projected a newly found independence; and I realized that the hippie movement definitely undermined patriarchal stereotypes of male and female nature. However, this did not fully answer the question of why I was quite open, personally, to the feminist awareness that emerged during the seventies.

Eventually I found an answer because of my discussions of psychology and psychoanalysis in conversations with Stan Grof and R. D. Laing. These conversations naturally led me to examine influences from my own childhood, and I discovered that the structure of the family I grew up in between the ages of four and twelve may have had a decisive impact on my attitude toward feminism as an adult. During those eight years my parents, my brother, and I lived in my grandmother's home in southern Austria. We had moved to her estate, which functioned as a fully self-sufficient farm, from our home in Vienna to escape the ravages of World War II. Our household consisted of the extended family—my grandmother, my parents, two aunts and uncles, and seven children—plus several other children and adults who were refugees from the war and had become part of the household.

This large family was run by three women. My grandmother was the head of the household and spiritual authority. The estate and the whole family was known under her name. So whenever anybody in town asked me who I was, I would respond with "Teuffenbach," my grandmother's and my mother's name. My mother's elder sister worked in the fields and provided material security. My mother, a poet and writer, was responsible for the education of us children, keeping an eye on our intellectual growth and teaching us the rules of social etiquette.

The collaboration of these three women was harmonious and efficient. Between them they made most of the decisions concerning our lives. The men played secondary roles, partly because of their long absence during the war but also because of the women's strong natures. I still remember very vividly how my aunt stepped out on the dining room balcony every day after lunch and gave strong and clear instructions to the farm hands and other employees assembled in the courtyard below. From that time on I have never had a problem with the idea of women in positions of power. I had experienced during most of my childhood a matriarchal system that worked extremely well. I have come to believe that this experience prepared the ground for my acceptance of the feminist perspective that was to emerge twenty-five years later.

*Charlene Spretnak—the coalescence of
feminism, spirituality, and ecology*

During the years 1978 and 1979 I slowly absorbed the comprehensive framework of radical feminist critique laid out by

Adrienne Rich in her powerful book *Of Woman Born*. Through discussions with feminist authors and activists and through the gradual maturing of my own feminist awareness many ideas from that framework were refined and further developed in my mind and became integral parts of my world view. In particular, I became increasingly aware of the important connections between the feminist perspective and other aspects of the emerging new paradigm. I came to recognize the role of feminism as a major force of cultural transformation and of the women's movement as a catalyst for the coalescence of various social movements.

Over the last seven years this realization, and my thinking on feminist issues in general, has been influenced enormously by my professional associations and my friendship with one of today's leading feminist theorists, Charlene Spretnak. Her work exemplifies the coalescence of three major currents in our culture: feminism, spirituality, and ecology. Spretnak's main focus is on spirituality. Drawing on her studies of a variety of religious traditions, her experience of many years of Buddhist meditation, and on female experiential knowledge, she has explored multiple facets of what she calls "women's spirituality."

According to Spretnak, the failures of patriarchal religion are now becoming ever more apparent, and as patriarchy declines our culture will evolve toward very different, post-patriarchal forms of spirituality. She sees women's spirituality with its emphasis on the unity of all forms of being and on cyclical rhythms of renewal as leading the way to such a new direction. Women's spirituality, as described by Spretnak, is securely grounded in the experience of connectedness with the essential life processes. It is thus profoundly ecological and is close to Native American spirituality, Taoism, and other life-affirming, Earth-oriented spiritual traditions.

In her early work as a "cultural feminist" Spretnak explored the pre-patriarchal myths and rituals of Greek antiquity and their implications for today's feminist movement. She published her findings in a scholarly treatise, *Lost Goddesses of Early Greece*. This remarkable book contains a concise discussion together with beautiful, poetic renderings of pre-Hellenic goddess myths that Spretnak had carefully reconstructed in their original forms from various sources.

In the scholarly part Spretnak argues convincingly, supporting her argument with numerous references to archeological and anthropological literature, that there is nothing "natural" about patriarchal religion. On the scale of the entire evolution of human culture it is a relatively recent invention, preceded by more than twenty millennia of goddess religions in "matrifocal" cultures. Spretnak shows how the classical Greek myths, as recorded by Hesiod and Homer in the seventh century B.C., reflect the struggle between the early matrifocal culture and the new patriarchal religion and social order, and how the pre-Hellenic goddess mythology was distorted and co-opted into the new system. She also points out that the various goddesses worshiped in different parts of Greece must themselves be seen as derivative forms of the Great Goddess, the supreme deity for millennia in most parts of the world.

When I met Charlene Spretnak in early 1979 I was impressed by the clarity of her thinking and the force of her arguments. At that time I was just beginning to write *The Turning Point* and she was busy putting together her anthology, *The Politics of Women's Spirituality*, which has since become a feminist classic. We both recognized the many similarities in our approaches and were very excited to find confirmation and mutual stimulation in each other's work. Over the years Charlene and I became close friends, co-authored a book and collaborated on several other projects, and gave each other encouragement and support as we shared the joys and frustrations of writing.

When Spretnak described the experience of women's spirituality to me, I realized that it was grounded in what I had come to call deep ecological awareness—the intuitive awareness of the oneness of all life, the interdependence of its multiple manifestations and its cycles of change and transformation. Indeed, Spretnak sees women's spirituality as the crucial link between feminism and ecology. She uses the term "eco-feminism" to describe the merging of the two movements and to highlight the profound implications of feminist awareness for the new ecological paradigm.

Spretnak has responded to the challenge posed by Adrienne Rich and has explored in some detail the "spiritual and political meanings" of women's ability "to think through the body." In *The Politics of Women's Spirituality* she speaks of the experiences inherent in women's sexuality, pregnancy, childbirth, and motherhood as "body parables" of the essential connectedness of all life and the embeddedness of all existence in the cyclical processes of nature. She also discusses patriarchal perceptions and interpretations of differences between the sexes and cites recent research on the real psychological differences between women and men; for example, the predominance of contextual perception and integrative skills in women and of analytic skills in men. The most important insight I gained from my numerous discussions with Charlene Spretnak has been to recognize female thinking as a manifestation of holistic thinking and female experiential knowledge as a major source for the emerging ecological paradigm.

HAZEL HENDERSON

When I visited Fritz Schumacher in 1977 I was still unaware of the full depth and far-reaching implications of the feminist perspective. Nevertheless I sensed that my principal disagreement with Schumacher's approach—his belief in fundamental hierarchical levels of natural phenomena—was connected, somehow, with his tacit acceptance of the patriarchal order. During the following months I continued to wonder who would be my adviser for the field of economics and began to envision the attributes of the person I needed. It would have to be somebody who, like Schumacher, was able to cut through the academic jargon, expose the basic fallacies of current economic thinking, and outline alternatives based on sound ecological principles. In addition to all that, I felt that it would have to be somebody who understood the feminist perspective and could apply it to the analysis of economic, technological, and political problems. Naturally, this radical economist/ecologist would have to be a woman. I had little hope of ever finding that "adviser of my dreams" but, having learned to trust my intuition and "flow with the Tao," I did not undertake any systematic search; I merely kept my eyes and ears open. And, sure enough, the miracle occurred.

During the late fall of that year, while I gave many lectures around the country and my mind was focused on exploring the paradigm shift in medicine and psychology, I heard repeated rumors of a self-educated futurist, environmentalist, and economic iconoclast by the name of Hazel Henderson. This extraordinary woman, then living in Princeton, was challenging economists, politicians, and corporate leaders with her well-founded and radical critique of their fundamental concepts and values. "You *have* to meet Hazel Henderson," I was told several times, "you two have a lot in common." It sounded almost too good to be true and I resolved that I would try to find out more about Henderson as soon as I had time to concentrate again on the field of economics.

In the spring of 1978 I bought Henderson's book *Creating Alternative Futures*, a collection of her essays which had just been published. As I sat down to look through the book I felt immediately that I had found exactly the person I was looking for. The book includes an enthusiastic foreword by E. F. Schumacher, whom Henderson knew well, as I learned later, and considers her mentor. Her opening chapter left no doubt in my mind that our thinking was indeed very close. Henderson forcefully asserts that "the Cartesian paradigm [is] bankrupt" and that our economic, political, and technological problems result, ultimately, from the "inadequacy of the Cartesian world view" and the "masculine-oriented style" of our social organizations. I could not have asked for more agreement with my views, but I was even more surprised and delighted when I read on. Henderson suggests in her opening essay that the multiple paradoxes indicating the limits of current economic concepts play the same role as the paradoxes discovered by Heisenberg in quantum physics, and she even refers to my own work in this connection. Naturally, I took this as an excellent omen and decided right away to write to Hazel Henderson and ask her whether she would consider being my adviser for economics.

In another chapter of *Creating Alternative Futures* I came across a passage which beautifully summarized the intuition that had led me to my systematic investigation of the paradigm shift in various fields. Speaking of our current series of crises, Henderson affirms: "Whether we designate them as 'energy crises,' 'environmental crises,' 'urban crises,' or 'population crises,' we should recognize the extent to which they all are rooted in the larger crisis of our inadequate, narrow perceptions of reality." It was this passage that inspired me three years later to state in the preface to *The Turning Point*: "The basic thesis of this book is that [the major problems of our time] are all different facets of one and the same crisis, and that this crisis is essentially a crisis of perception."

As I glanced through several chapters of Henderson's book, I saw immediately that the main points of her critique are completely consistent with Schumacher's and, indeed, were inspired by his work. Like Schumacher, Henderson criticizes the fragmentation in current economic thinking, the absence of values, the obsession of economists with unqualified economic growth, and their failure to take into account our dependence on the natural world. Like Schumacher, she extends her critique to modern technology and advocates a profound reorientation of our economic and technological systems, based on the use of renewable resources and the attention to human scale.

But Henderson goes considerably beyond Schumacher both in her critique and in her outline of alternatives. Her essays offer a rich mixture of theory and activism. Each point of her critique is substantiated by numerous illustrations and statistical data, each suggestion for "alternative futures" accompanied by countless concrete examples and references to books, articles, manifestos, projects, and activities of grass-roots organizations. Her focus is not limited to economics and technology but deliberately includes politics. In fact, she asserts: "Economics is not a science; it is merely politics in disguise."

The more I read of her book, the more I admired Henderson's trenchant analysis of the shortcomings of conventional economics, her deep ecological awareness, and her broad, global perspective. At the same time, I was somewhat overwhelmed by her unique style of writing. Her sentences are long and packed with information, her paragraphs collages of striking insights and powerful metaphors. In her efforts to create new maps of economic, social, and ecological interdependence, Henderson constantly seeks to break out of the linear mode of thinking. She does so with great verbal virtuosity, showing a distinct flair for catchy phrases and deliberately outrageous statements. Academic economics, for Henderson, is "a form of brain damage," Wall Street is chasing "funny money," and Washington is engaged in "the politics of the Last Hurrah," while her own efforts are directed toward "defrocking the economic priesthood," "autopsying the Golden Goose" invoked by the business community, and promoting a "politics of reconceptualization."

On my first reading of *Creating Alternative Futures* I was quite dazzled by Henderson's verbal brilliance and by the rich complexity of her thought patterns. I felt that I would have to spend considerable time working through her book with full concentration to really comprehend the breadth and depth of her thinking. Fortunately, an ideal opportunity to do so soon presented itself. In June 1978 Stan Grof invited me to spend several weeks in his beautiful home at Big Sur while he and his wife were away on a lecture tour, and I used this retreat to systematically go through Henderson's book chapter by chapter, excerpt its key passages, and use these to construct the framework for my discussion of the paradigm shift in economics. In a previous chapter I described the joy and beauty of these solitary weeks of work and meditation at the edge of a cliff high above the Pacific Ocean. As I carefully mapped out the multiple interconnections between economics, ecology, values, technology, and politics, new dimensions of understanding opened themselves and I became aware to my great delight that my writing project was acquiring new substance and depth.

Henderson opens her book with the clear and forceful statement that the current mismanagement of our economy calls into question the basic concepts of contemporary economic thought. She cites a wealth of evidence to support her claim, including statements from several leading economists who acknowledge that their discipline has reached an impasse. More important, perhaps, Henderson observes that the anomalies economists can no longer address are now painfully visible to every citizen. Ten years later, in the face of widespread deficits and indebtedness, continuing destruction of the natural environment, and the persistence of poverty with progress even in the richest countries, this statement has lost none of its pertinence.

The reason for the impasse in economics, according to Henderson, lies in the fact that it is rooted in a system of thought that is now outdated and in need of radical revision. Henderson shows in great detail how today's economists speak in "heroic abstractions," monitor the wrong variables, and use obsolete conceptual models to map a vanished reality. The key point of her critique is the striking inability of most economists to adopt an ecological perspective. The economy, she explains, is merely one aspect of a whole ecological and social fabric. Economists tend to divide this fabric into fragments, ignoring social and ecological interdependence. All goods and services are reduced to their monetary values and the social and environmental costs generated by all economic activity are ignored. They are "external variables" that do not fit into the economists' theoretical models. Corporate economists, Henderson points out, not only treat the air, water, and various reservoirs of the ecosystem as free commodities, but also the delicate web of social relations, which is severely affected by continuing economic expansion. Private profits are being made increasingly at public cost in the deterioration of the natural environment and the general quality of life. "They tell us about the sparkling dishes and clothes," she observes with wry humor, "but forget to mention the loss of those sparkling rivers and lakes."

To provide economics with a sound ecological basis, Henderson insists, economists will need to revise their basic concepts in a drastic way. She illustrates with many examples how these concepts were narrowly defined and have been used without their social and ecological context. The gross national product, for example, which is supposed to measure a nation's wealth, is determined by adding up indiscriminately all economic activities associated with monetary values, while all nonmonetary aspects of the economy are ignored. Social costs, like those of accidents, litigation, and health care, are added as positive contributions to the GNP, rather than being subtracted. Henderson quotes Ralph Nader's incisive comment, "Every time there is an automobile accident the GNP goes up," and she speculates that those social costs may be the only fraction of the GNP that is still growing.

In the same vein she insists that the concept of wealth "must shed some of its present connotations of capital and material accumulation and give way to a redefinition as human enrichment," and that profit must be redefined "to mean only the creation of *real* wealth, rather than private or public gain won at the expense of social or environmental exploitation." Henderson also shows with numerous examples how the concepts of efficiency and productivity have been similarly distorted. "Efficient for whom?" she asks with her characteristic breadth of vision. When corporate economists talk about efficiency, do they refer to the level of the individual, the corporation, the society, or the ecosystem? Henderson concludes from her critical analysis of these basic economic concepts that a new ecological framework is urgently needed, in which the concepts and variables of economic theories are related to those used to describe the embedding ecosystems. She predicts that energy, so essential to all industrial processes, will become one of the most important variables for measuring economic activities, and she cites examples of such energy modeling that have already been used successfully.

In outlining her new ecological framework Henderson does not limit herself to its conceptual aspects. She emphasizes throughout her book that the reexamination of economic concepts and models needs to deal, at the deepest level, with the underlying value system. Many of the current social and economic problems, she submits, will then be seen to have their roots in the painful adjustments of individuals and institutions to the changing values of our time.

Contemporary economists, in a misguided attempt to provide their discipline with scientific rigor, have consistently avoided acknowledging the value system on which their models are based. In doing so, Henderson points out, they tacitly accept the grossly imbalanced set of values which dominates our culture and is embodied in our social institutions. "Economics," she contends, "has enthroned some of our most unattractive predispositions: material acquisitiveness, competition, gluttony, pride, selfishness, shortsightedness, and just plain greed."

A fundamental economic problem that has resulted from the imbalance in our values, according to Henderson, is our obsession with unlimited growth. Continuing economic growth is accepted as a dogma by virtually all economists and politicians, who assume that it is the only way to ensure that material wealth will trickle down to the poor. Henderson shows, however, by citing abundant evidence, that this "trickle-down" model of growth is totally unrealistic. High rates of growth not only do little to ease urgent social and human problems but in many countries have been accompanied by increasing unemployment and a general deterioration of social conditions. Henderson also points out that the global obsession with growth has resulted in a remarkable similarity between capitalist and Communist economies. "The fruitless dialectic between capitalism and communism will be exposed as irrelevant," she argues, "since both systems are based on materialism, . . . both are dedicated to industrial growth and technologies with increasing centralism and bureaucratic control."

Henderson realizes, of course, that growth is essential to life, in an economy as well as in any other living system, but she urges that economic growth has to be qualified. In a finite environment, she explains, there has to be a dynamic balance between growth and decline. While some things need to grow, others have to diminish so that their constituent elements can be released and recycled. With a beautiful organic analogy she applies this basic ecological insight also to the growth of institutions: "Just as the decay of last year's leaves provides humus for new growth the following spring, some institutions must decline and decay so that their components of capital, land, and human talents can be used to create new organizations."

Throughout *Creating Alternative Futures* Henderson makes it clear that economic and institutional growth are inextricably linked to technological growth. She points out that the masculine consciousness that dominates our culture has found its fulfillment in a certain "macho" technology—a technology bent on manipulation and control rather than cooperation, self-assertive rather than integrative, suitable for central management rather than regional and local application by individuals and small groups. As a result, Henderson observes, most technologies today have become profoundly anti-ecological, unhealthy, and inhuman. They need to be replaced by new forms of technology, she affirms, technologies that incorporate ecological principles and correspond to a new set of values. She shows with abundant examples how many of these alternative technologies—small scale and decentralized, responsive to local conditions and designed to increase self-sufficiency—are already being developed. They are often called "soft" technologies because their impact on the environment is greatly reduced by the use of renewable resources and constant recycling of materials.

Solar energy production in its multiple forms—wind-generated electricity, biogas, passive solar architecture, solar collectors, photovoltaic cells—is Henderson's soft technology par excellence. She contends that a central aspect of the current cultural transformation is the shift from the Petroleum Age and the industrial era to a new Solar Age. Henderson extends the term "Solar Age" beyond its technological meaning and uses it metaphorically for the new culture she sees emerging. This culture of the Solar Age, she explains, includes the ecology movement, the women's movement, and the peace movement; the many citizen movements formed around social and environmental issues; the emerging counter-economies based on decentralized, cooperative, and ecologically harmonious life-styles; "and all those for whom the old corporate economy is not working."

Eventually, she predicts, these various groups will form new coalitions and develop new forms of politics. Since the publication of *Creating Alternative Futures* Hazel Henderson has continued to advocate the alternative economies, technologies, values, and life-styles that she sees as the foundation of the new politics. Her numerous lectures and articles on these issues are published in a second collection of essays entitled *The Politics of the Solar Age*.

The end of economics?

A few weeks before I went to Big Sur to work through Henderson's book I received a very friendly letter from her. She said that she was interested in my book project and was looking forward to meeting me. She told me that she would be in California in June and suggested that we meet during her visit. Her arrival in San Francisco coincided with the end of my stay in Stan Grof's house, so I drove directly from there to the airport to pick her up. I remember being very excited during that four-hour drive and curious to meet the woman behind the revolutionary ideas I had just encountered.

As she stepped off the plane, Hazel Henderson was a radiant contrast to the drab businessmen who were her fellow passengers—a buoyant woman, tall and slim with a mass of blond hair, dressed in jeans and a brilliant yellow sweater, a small bag casually slung over her shoulder. She walked through the arrival gate with brisk long steps and greeted me with a big, warm smile. No, she assured me, she did not have any other luggage, just this small bag. "I always travel light," she added with a distinct British accent. "You know, just my toothbrush and my books and papers. I just can't be bothered by all that unnecessary stuff."

On our way across the Bay Bridge to Berkeley we had a lively chat about our experience as Europeans living in America, mixing personal accounts with shared perceptions of many signs of cultural transformation, both in Europe and in the United States. During this first relaxed conversation I immediately noticed Henderson's unique use of language. She speaks the way she writes, in long sentences filled with vivid images and metaphors. "This is the only way for me to break through the constraints of the linear mode," she explained, and then she added with a smile: "It's like your bootstrap model, you know. Each part of what I write contains all the other parts." The other thing that impressed me right away was her imaginative use of organic, ecological metaphors. Expressions like "recycling our culture," "composting ideas," or "sharing a newly baked economic pie" constantly crop up in her sentences. I remember that she even described to me a method of "composting my mail," by which she meant distributing the many ideas she receives in letters and articles among her extensive network of friends and associates.

When we arrived at my home and sat down for tea, I was most curious to hear from Henderson how she had become the radical economist she was. "I am not an economist," she corrected me. "You see, I don't *believe* in economics. I call myself an independent, self-employed futurist. Although I have co-founded a fair number of organizations, I try to put institutions at as much distance as possible, so that I can look at the future from many angles without the interest of a particular organization in mind."

So how did she become an independent futurist?

"Through activism. That's who I *really* am: a social activist. I get impatient with people who only talk about social change. I keep telling them that we must walk our talk. Don't you think so? I think it's very important for all of us to walk our talk. Politics, for me, has always meant organizing around social and environmental issues. When I come across a new idea, the first thing I ask is, 'Could you organize a bake sale around it?' "

Henderson began her activist career in the early sixties, she told me. She had dropped out of school in England at sixteen, arrived in New York at twenty-four, married an IBM executive, and had a baby. "I was the perfect corporate wife," she said with a mischievous smile, "as happy as you were supposed to be."

Things began to change for Henderson when she got worried about air pollution in New York: "Here I was sitting in the play park and watching my baby daughter getting covered with soot." Her first reaction was to start a one-woman letter-writing campaign to the television networks; her second was to organize a group called "Citizens for Clean Air." Both endeavors were wildly successful. She got ABC and CBS to establish an air pollution index and received hundreds of letters from concerned citizens who wanted to join her group.

"And what about economics?" I inquired.

"Well, I *had* to teach myself economics, because every time I wanted to organize something there was always some economist telling me it would be uneconomic." I asked Henderson whether that did not deter her. "No," she said with a broad smile. "I knew I was right in my activism; I felt it in my body. So there had to be something wrong with economics, and I decided that I had better find out just what it was that all those economists had got wrong."

To find out Henderson plunged into intensive and prolonged reading, beginning with economics but soon branching out into philosophy, history, sociology, political science, and many other fields. At the same time she continued her activist career. Because of a special talent for presenting her radical ideas in a disarming, nonthreatening manner her voice was soon heard and respected in government and corporate circles. At the time of our meeting in 1978 she had lined up an impressive string of advisory positions: member of the Advisory Council of the U.S. Congress Office of Technology Assessment, member of President Carter's economic task force, adviser to the Cousteau Society, adviser to the Environmental Action Foundation. In addition, she was directing several of the organizations she had helped found, including the Council on Economic Priorities, Environmentalists for Full Employment, and the Worldwatch Institute. After going through this impressive list, Henderson leaned over to me and said in a mock conspiratorial tone: "You know, there comes a time when you don't want to mention all the organizations you have founded, because it shows your age."

Another thing I was curious to learn was Henderson's view of the women's movement. I told her how deeply moved and disturbed I had been by Adrienne Rich's book *Of Woman Born*, and how exciting I found the feminist perspective. Henderson nodded with a smile. "I don't know that particular book," she said. "In fact, I haven't read much of the feminist literature at all. I just didn't have time for it. I had to get up to speed in economics to do my organizing." However, she fully agreed with the feminist critique of our patriarchal culture. "For me, all this came together when I read Betty Friedan's book. I remember reading *The Feminine Mystique* and thinking, 'My God!' Because, you see, like so many women I had the same perceptions. But they were private, isolated perceptions. Reading Betty Friedan, they all came together and I was ready to turn them into politics."

When I asked Henderson to describe the kind of feminist politics she had in mind, she turned to the issue of values. She reminded me that in our society the values and attitudes that are favored and invested with political power are the typical masculine values—competition, domination, expansion, etc.—while those neglected and often despised—cooperation, nurturing, humility, peacefulness—are designated as female. "Now notice that these values are essential for the male-dominated industrial system to work," she observed, "but they are most difficult to operationalize and have always been thrust upon women and minority groups."

I thought of all the secretaries, receptionists, and hostesses whose work is so crucial to the business world. I thought of the women in all the physics departments I had been to, who make the tea and serve the cookies over which the men discuss their theories. I also thought of the dishwashers, hotel maids, and gardeners who are usually recruited from minority groups. "It is usually women and minorities," Henderson continued, "who perform the services that make life more comfortable and create the atmosphere in which the competitors can succeed."

Henderson concluded that a new synthesis was now needed that would allow us to express a healthier balance of the so-called masculine and feminine values. When I asked her whether she saw any signs of such a new synthesis, she pointed to the women who are the new leaders in many of the alternative movements—the ecology movement, the peace movement, the citizen movements. "All those women and minorities, whose ideas and whose consciousness have been suppressed, are now emerging as leaders. We know that we are now called upon to do that; it's almost a body wisdom.

"Look at me," she added with a laugh. "I act as a one-woman truth squad for the economics profession."

That remark brought our conversation back to the subject of economics, and I was very eager to check my understanding of Henderson's basic framework with her. During the next hour or so I reviewed with her what I had learned from studying her book and asked many detailed questions. I realized that my new knowledge was still very fresh and that the many thoughts that had arisen during the past weeks of concentrated work needed further clarification. However, I was very happy to see that I had grasped the main points of Henderson's critique of economics and technology as well as the basic outlines of her vision of "alternative futures."

One question that puzzled me particularly was that of the future role of economics. I had noticed that Henderson had subtitled her book *The End of Economics*, and I remembered that she claimed in several passages that economics was no longer viable as a social science. What, then, would replace it?

"Economics is likely to remain an appropriate discipline for accounting purposes and various analyses of micro-areas," Henderson explained, "but its methods are no longer adequate to examine macroeconomic processes." Macroeconomic patterns, she continued, would have to be studied in multidisciplinary teams within a broad ecological framework. I told Henderson that this reminded me of the health field, where a similar approach was needed to deal with the multiple aspects of health in a holistic way. "I'm not surprised," she responded. "We are talking about the health of the economy, you know. At the moment our economy and our whole society are very ill."

"So for micro-areas, like the management of a business, economics will still be all right?" I repeated.

"Yes, and there it will have an important new role: to estimate as accurately as possible the social and environmental costs of economic activities—you know, the health costs, costs of environmental damage, social disruption, and so on—and to internalize these costs within the accounts of private and public enterprises."

"Can you give me an example?"

"Sure. For example, one could assign to tobacco companies a reasonable portion of the medical costs caused by cigarette smoking and to distillers a corresponding portion of the social costs of alcoholism."

When I asked Henderson whether this was a realistic proposal that would be politically feasible, she told me that she had no doubt that such a new kind of accounting would be required by law in the future, once the various citizen and alternative movements were sufficiently powerful. In fact, she mentioned that work on new economic models of this kind was already in progress, for example, in Japan.

We had spent several hours together in this first conversation, and as it got dark outside Henderson told me she was very sorry that she did not have more time for me during this visit. However, she added that she would be very happy to act as an adviser for my book project and invited me to visit her at her home in Princeton for more extensive discussions. I was overjoyed and thanked her warmly for her visit and for all her help. As she left, she said good-bye with an affectionate hug that made me feel we had always been friends.

The ecological perspective

The intensive work on Henderson's book and the subsequent conversation with her opened up a whole new field for me that I was very eager to explore. My intuitive feeling that there was something profoundly wrong with our economic system had been confirmed by Fritz Schumacher, but before meeting Hazel Henderson I had found the technical jargon of economics too difficult to penetrate. During that month of June it gradually became transparent, as I acquired a clear framework for understanding the basic economic problems. To my great surprise I found myself turning to the economics sections of newspapers and magazines and actually enjoying the reports and analyses I found there. I was amazed how easy it had become to see through the arguments of government and corporate economists, to recognize where they were glossing over unwarranted assumptions or failed to understand a problem because of their narrow point of view.

As I consolidated my understanding of economics, a host of new questions arose, and over the following months I made countless phone calls to Princeton to ask Henderson for help: "Hazel, the prime rate has gone up again; what does that signify?"—"Hazel, what is a mixed economy?"—"Hazel, did you see Galbraith's article in the *Washington Post*?"—"Hazel, what do you think of deregulation?" Henderson patiently responded to all my questions, and I was amazed at her ability to answer every one of them with clear and succinct explanations, approaching each issue from her broad ecological and global perspective.

These conversations with Hazel Henderson not only helped me enormously in understanding economic problems but also made me fully appreciate the social and political dimensions of ecology. I had spoken and written of the emerging new paradigm as an ecological world view for many years. In fact, I had used the term "ecological" in that sense already in *The Tao of Physics*. During 1977 I discovered the profound connection between ecology and spirituality. I realized that deep ecological awareness is spiritual in its very essence and came to believe that ecology, grounded in such spiritual awareness, may well become our Western equivalent to the Eastern mystical traditions. Subsequently I learned about the important links between ecology and feminism and became aware of the emerging eco-feminist movement; and finally Hazel Henderson expanded my appreciation of ecology further by opening my eyes to its social and political dimensions. I became aware of numerous examples of economic, social, and ecological interdependence. I became convinced that the design of a sound ecological framework for our economies, our technologies, and our politics is one of the most urgent tasks of our time.

All this confirmed me in my earlier intuitive choice of the term "ecological" to characterize the emerging new paradigm. Moreover, I began to see important differences between "ecological" and "holistic," the other term that is often used in connection with the new paradigm. A holistic perception means simply that the object or phenomenon under consideration is perceived as an integrated whole, a total gestalt, rather than being reduced to the mere sum of its parts. Such a perception can be applied to anything—a tree, a house, or a bicycle, for example. An ecological approach, by contrast, deals with certain kinds of wholes—with living organisms, or living systems. In an ecological paradigm, therefore, the main emphasis is on life, on the living world of which we are part and on which our lives depend. A holistic approach does not need to go beyond the system under consideration, but it is crucial to an ecological approach to understand how that particular system is embedded in larger systems. Thus, an ecological approach to health will not only treat the human organism—mind and body—as a whole system but will also be concerned with the social and environmental dimensions of health. Similarly, an ecological approach to economics will have to understand how economic activities are embedded in the cyclical processes of nature and in the value system of a particular culture.

The full recognition of these implications of the term "ecological" came several years later and was greatly influenced by my discussions with Gregory Bateson. But during the spring and summer of 1978, as I explored the paradigm shift in three different fields—medicine, psychology, and economics—my appreciation of the ecological perspective increased enormously, and my discussions with Hazel Henderson were a crucial part of that process.

Visit to Princeton

In November 1978 I gave a series of lectures on the East Coast and took this opportunity to follow up Henderson's kind invitation and visit her in Princeton. I arrived there by train from New York on a crisp, cold morning, and I remember greatly enjoying the tour of Princeton Henderson gave me on the way to her home. The town was very pretty on this clear, sunny, winter morning, as we drove past its stately mansions and Gothic halls, their beauty accentuated by fresh-fallen snow. I had never been to Princeton but had always known of it as a very special place of learning. It was the home of Albert Einstein and of the prestigious Institute for Advanced Study, at which many ground-breaking ideas in theoretical physics had been generated.

On that November morning, however, I was about to visit a very different kind of institute, which I found even more exciting—Hazel Henderson's Princeton Center for Alternative Futures. When I asked Henderson to describe her institute, she told me that it was a deliberately small, private think tank for exploring alternative futures in a planetary context. She had founded it several years earlier together with her husband, Carter Henderson, who had dropped out of IBM in the meantime to join forces with Hazel. The Center was located in their home, she explained, and was run by herself and her husband with occasional help from volunteers. "We call it our 'mom-and-pop think tank,' " she added with a laugh.

I was surprised when we arrived at Henderson's home. It was large and elegantly furnished and, somehow, did not seem to correspond to the simple, self-sufficient life-style she promoted in her book. But I soon found out that this first impression was very wrong. Henderson told me that they had bought a rambling old house six years earlier and had transformed it by buying their furniture in local junk shops and refinishing it themselves. As she showed me around the house she explained very proudly that they had set themselves a limit of $250 for decorating each room and were able to stay under that limit by making ample use of their own artistic creativity and manual labor. Henderson was so pleased with the result that she was playing with the idea of starting a furniture refinishing business as a sideline to her theoretical and activist work. She also told me that they baked their own bread, had a vegetable garden and compost heap in their backyard, and were recycling all their paper and glass. I was deeply impressed by this demonstration of the many ingenious ways in which Henderson had integrated the alternative value system and life-style she wrote and lectured about into her daily life. I could see with my own eyes how she "walked her talk," as she had put it in our first conversation, and I resolved that I would adopt some of her practices in my own life.

When we arrived at Hazel's home her husband Carter greeted me warmly. During the two days I was their guest he was always very friendly but discreetly stayed in the background, graciously giving Hazel and me all the space we needed for our discussions. The first of these began right after lunch and went on through the entire afternoon and into the evening. It was initiated by my question as to whether the basic thesis of my book—that the natural sciences, as well as the humanities and social sciences, had all modeled themselves after Newtonian physics—was also true for economics.

"I think you could find quite a bit of evidence for your thesis in the history of economics," Henderson replied after some thought. She pointed out that the origins of modern economics coincide with those of Newtonian science. "Until the sixteenth century the notion of purely economic phenomena, isolated from the fabric of life, did not exist," she explained. "Nor was there a national system of markets. That, too, is a relatively recent phenomenon which originated in seventeenth-century England."

"But markets must have existed earlier than that," I interjected.

"Of course. They have existed since the Stone Age, but they were based on barter, not cash, and so they were bound to be local." The motive of individual gain from economic activities was generally absent, Henderson pointed out. The very idea of profit, let alone interest, was either inconceivable or banned.

"Private property is another good example," Henderson continued. "The word 'private' comes from the Latin *privare*—'to deprive'—which shows you the widespread ancient view that property was first and foremost communal." It was only with the rise of individualism in the Renaissance, Henderson explained, that people no longer thought of private property as those goods that individuals deprived the group from using. "Today we have completely inverted the meaning of the term," she concluded. "We believe that property should be private in the first place, and that society should not deprive the individual without due process of law."

"So when did modern economics begin?"

"It emerged during the Scientific Revolution and the Enlightenment," Henderson replied. At that time, she reminded me, critical reasoning, empiricism, and individualism became the dominant values, together with a secular and materialistic orientation that led to the production of worldly goods and luxuries, and to the manipulative mentality of the Industrial Age. The new customs and activities resulted in the creation of new social and political institutions, Henderson explained, and gave rise to a new academic pursuit: the theorizing about a set of specific *economic* activities. "Now these economic activities—production, distribution, moneylending, and so on—suddenly stood out in sharp relief, you see. They required not only description and explanation but also rationalization."

I was impressed by Henderson's description. I could see clearly how the change of world view and values in the seventeenth century created the very context for economic thought. "So what about physics?" I pressed on. "Do you see any direct influence of Newtonian physics on economic thinking?"

"Well, let's see," Henderson reflected. "Modern economics, strictly speaking, was founded in the seventeenth century by Sir William Petty, a contemporary of Isaac Newton who actually frequented the same London circles as Newton, I believe. I guess you could say that Petty's *Political Arithmetick* owed much to Newton and Descartes."

Henderson explained that Petty's method consisted of replacing words and arguments by numbers, weights, and measures. He put forth a whole set of ideas, she said, that became indispensable ingredients of the theories of Adam Smith and later economists. For example, Petty discussed the "Newtonian" notions of the quantity of money and its velocity in circulation, which are still debated by the monetarist school today. "In fact," Henderson observed with a smile, "today's economic policies, as they are debated in Washington, London, or Tokyo, would not be any surprise to Petty, except for the fact that they have changed so little."

Another cornerstone of modern economics, Henderson continued, was laid by John Locke, the outstanding philosopher of the Enlightenment. Locke came up with the idea that prices were determined objectively by supply and demand. This law of supply and demand, Henderson observed, was elevated to equal status with Newton's laws of mechanics, where it stands even today in most economic analyses. She pointed out that this was a perfect illustration of the Newtonian flavor of economics. The interpretation of the curves of supply and demand, featured in all introductory economics textbooks, is based on the assumption that the participants in a market will "gravitate" automatically and without any "friction" to the "equilibrium" price given by the point of intersection of the two curves. The close correspondence to Newtonian physics was obvious to me.

"The law of supply and demand also fit perfectly with Newton's new mathematics, the differential calculus," Henderson continued. Economics, she explained, was perceived as dealing with continuous variations of very small quantities which could be described most efficiently by this mathematical technique. This notion became the basis of subsequent efforts to turn economics into an exact mathematical science. "The problem was and is," Henderson declared, "that the variables used in these mathematical models cannot be rigorously quantified but are defined on the basis of assumptions that often make the models quite unrealistic."

The question of the basic assumptions underlying economic theories brought Henderson to Adam Smith, the most influential of all economists. She gave me a vivid description of the intellectual climate of Smith's time—the influences of David Hume, Thomas Jefferson, Benjamin Franklin, and James Watt—and of the powerful impact of the beginning Industrial Revolution, which he embraced enthusiastically.

Adam Smith accepted the idea that prices would be determined in "free" markets by the balancing effects of supply and demand, Henderson explained. He based his economic theory on the Newtonian notions of equilibrium, laws of motion, and scientific objectivity. He imagined that the balancing mechanisms of the market would operate almost instantaneously and without any friction. Small producers and consumers would meet in the marketplace with equal power and information. The "Invisible Hand" of the market would guide individual self-interests for the harmonious betterment of all, "betterment" being equated with the production of material wealth.

"This idealistic picture is still widely used by economists today," Henderson told me. "Perfect and free information for all participants in a market transaction, complete and instant mobility of displaced workers, natural resources, and machinery—all these conditions are violated in the vast majority of today's markets. Yet most economists continue to use them as the basis of their theories."

"The whole notion of free markets seems problematic today," I interjected.

"Of course it is," Henderson agreed emphatically. "In most industrial societies giant corporate institutions control the supply of goods, create artificial demands through advertising, and have a decisive influence on national policies. The economic and political power of these corporate giants permeates every facet of public life. Free markets, balanced by supply and demand, have long disappeared." She added with a laugh, "Today, free markets exist only in the head of Milton Friedman."

From the origins of economics and its connections with Cartesian-Newtonian science our conversation then moved on to the further unfolding of economic thought in the eighteenth and nineteenth centuries. I was fascinated by Henderson's lively and perceptive way of telling me that long story—the rise of capitalism; the early ecological views of the French Physiocrats; the systematic attempts by Petty, Smith, Ricardo, and other classical economists to cast the new discipline into the form of a science; the well-meaning but unrealistic efforts by welfare economists, Utopians, and other reformers; and, finally, the powerful critique of classical economics by Karl Marx. She portrayed each stage in that evolution of economic thought within its broader cultural context and related each new idea to her critique of current economic practice.

We spent a long time discussing the thought of Karl Marx and its relation to the science of his time. Henderson pointed out that Marx, like most nineteenth-century thinkers, was very concerned about being scientific and often attempted to formulate his theories in Cartesian language. And yet, she maintained, his broad view of social phenomena allowed him to transcend the Cartesian framework in significant ways. He did not adopt the classical stance of the objective observer but fervently emphasized his role as participator by asserting that his social analysis was inseparable from social critique. Henderson also remarked that, although Marx often argued for technological determinism, which made his theory more acceptable as a science, he also had profound insights into the interrelatedness of all phenomena, seeing society as an organic whole in which ideology and technology were equally important.

On the other hand, she added, Marx's thought was quite abstract and rather detached from the humble realities of local production. Thus he shared the views of the intellectual elite of his time on the virtues of industrialization and the modernization of what he called "the idiocy of rural life."

"What about ecology?" I asked. "Did Marx have any kind of ecological awareness?"

"Absolutely," Henderson responded without hesitation. "His view of the role of nature in the process of production was part of his organic perception of reality. Marx emphasized the importance of nature in the social and economic fabric throughout his writings.

"We must realize, of course, that ecology was not a central issue in his time," Henderson cautioned. "The destruction of the natural environment was not a burning problem, so we can't expect Marx to emphasize it strongly. But he was certainly aware of the ecological impact of capitalist economics. Let's see whether I can find some quotations for you."

With these words Henderson went to her extensive bookshelves and pulled out a copy of *The Marx-Engels Reader*. After leafing through it for a few minutes she quoted from Marx's *Economic and Philosophic Manuscripts:*

> The worker can create nothing without nature, without the sensuous, external world. It is the material on which his labor is manifested, in which it is active, from which and by means of which it produces.

After some more searching she read from *Das Kapital:*

> All progress in capitalist agriculture is progress in the art, not only of robbing the laborer but of robbing the soil.

It was obvious to me that these words are even more relevant today than they were when Marx wrote them. Henderson agreed, and she observed that, although Marx did not strongly emphasize ecological concerns, his approach *could* have been used to predict the ecological exploitation that capitalism produced. "Of course"—she smiled—"if Marxists were to face the ecological evidence honestly, they would be forced to conclude that socialist societies have not done much better. Their environmental impact is diminished only by their lower consumption, which in any case they are trying to increase."

At this point we engaged in a lively discussion about the differences between environmental and social activism. "Ecological knowledge is subtle and difficult to use as a basis for a mass movement," Henderson observed. "Redwoods or whales do not provide revolutionary energies to change human institutions." She conjectured that this may be the reason why Marxists have ignored the "ecological Marx" for so long. "The subtleties in Marx's organic thinking are inconvenient for most social activists who prefer to organize around simpler issues," she concluded, and after a few moments of silence she added pensively: "Maybe this is why Marx declared at the end of his life, 'I am not a Marxist.' "

Hazel and I were both tired from this long and rich conversation, and since it was close to dinnertime we went out for a stroll in the fresh air, ending up in a local health food restaurant. Neither of us was in the mood to talk much, but after we had returned to Henderson's home and had settled down in her living room with a cup of tea, our conversation returned once more to economics.

Thinking back to the basic concepts of classical economics—scientific objectivity, the automatic balancing effects of supply and demand, Adam Smith's metaphor of the Invisible Hand, etc.—I wondered how these could be compatible with the active intervention of our government economists into the national economy.

"They are not," Henderson was quick to assert. "The ideal of the objective observer was thrown overboard after the Great Depression by John Maynard Keynes, who was undoubtedly the most important economist of our century." She explained that Keynes bent the so-called value-free methods of neoclassical economists to allow for purposeful government interventions. He argued that economic equilibrium states were special cases, exceptions rather than the rule in the real world. Fluctuating business cycles are the most striking characteristic of national economies, according to Keynes.

"This must have been a very radical step," I conjectured.

"It was indeed," Henderson affirmed, "and Keynesian economic theory had the most decisive influence on contemporary economic thought." To determine the nature of government interventions, she explained, Keynes shifted his focus from the micro level to the macro level—to economic variables like the national income, the total volume of employment, and so on. By establishing simplified relations between these variables he was able to show that they were susceptible to short-term changes that could be influenced by appropriate policies.

"And this is what government economists try to do?"

"Yes. The Keynesian model has become thoroughly assimilated into the mainstream of economic thought. Most economists today attempt to 'fine-tune' the economy by applying the Keynesian remedies of printing money, raising or lowering interest rates, cutting or increasing taxes, and so on."

"So the classical economic theory has been abandoned?"

"No, it hasn't. You see, that's the funny thing. Economic thinking is highly schizophrenic today. The classical theory has almost been turned on its head. Economists themselves, of whatever persuasion, *create* business cycles by their policies and forecasts, consumers are forced to become involuntary investors, and the market is managed by corporate and government actions, while neoclassical theorists still invoke the Invisible Hand."

I found all that quite confusing, and it seemed to me that economists themselves were very confused. Their Keynesian methods did not seem to work very well.

"No, they don't," Henderson asserted, "because these methods ignore the detailed structure of the economy and the qualitative nature of its problems. The Keynesian model has become inappropriate because it ignores so many factors that are crucial to understanding the economic situation."

When I asked Henderson to be more specific, she explained that the Keynesian model concentrates on the domestic economy, dissociating it from the global economic network and disregarding international agreements. It neglects the overwhelming political power of multinational corporations, pays no attention to political conditions, and ignores the social and environmental costs of economic activities. "At best, the Keynesian approach can provide a set of possible scenarios but cannot make specific predictions," she concluded. "Like most Cartesian economic thought, it has outlived its usefulness."

When I went to bed that evening, my mind was buzzing with new information and ideas. I was so excited that I could not sleep for a long time, and I was awake again early in the morning, reviewing my understanding of Henderson's thoughts. By the time Hazel and I sat down for another discussion after breakfast I had prepared a long list of questions, which kept us busy during the entire morning. Again I admired Henderson's clear perception of economic problems within a broad ecological framework and her ability to explain the current economic situation lucidly and succinctly.

I remember being particularly impressed by a long discussion of inflation, which was the most perplexing economic issue at that time. The rate of inflation in the United States had risen dramatically, while unemployment, too, remained at high levels. Neither economists nor politicians seemed to have any idea of what was going on, let alone what to do about it.

"What is inflation, Hazel, and why has it been so high?"

Without any hesitation, Henderson answered with one of her brilliant, sarcastic aphorisms: "Inflation is just the sum of all the variables economists leave out of their models." She gleefully savored the effect of her startling definition, and after a pause added in a serious tone: "All those social, psychological, and ecological variables are now coming back to haunt us."

When I asked her to elaborate her point, Henderson contended that there is no single cause of inflation, but that several major sources can be identified, all of which involve variables that have been excluded from current economic models. The first source, she pointed out, has to do with the fact—still ignored by most economists—that wealth is based on natural resources and energy. As the resource base declines, raw materials and energy must be extracted from ever more degraded and inaccessible reservoirs, and thus more and more capital is needed for the extraction process. Consequently, the inevitable decline of natural resources is accompanied by an unremitting climb of the price of resources and energy, which becomes one of the main driving forces of inflation.

"The excessive energy and resource dependence of our economy is apparent from the fact that it is capital intensive rather than labor intensive," Henderson continued. "Capital represents a potential for work, extracted from past exploitation of natural resources. As these resources diminish, capital itself is becoming a scarce resource." In spite of this, she observed, there is a strong tendency today to substitute capital for labor throughout our economy. With its narrow notions of productivity, the business community lobbies constantly for tax credits for capital investments, many of which reduce employment through automation. "Both capital and labor produce wealth," Henderson explained, "but a capital-intensive economy is also resource and energy intensive, and therefore highly inflationary."

"What you are saying, then, Hazel, is that a capital-intensive economy will generate inflation *and* unemployment."

"That's right. You see, conventional economic wisdom holds that, in a free market, inflation and unemployment are temporary aberrations from the equilibrium state, and that one is the trade-off of the other. But equilibrium models of that kind are no longer valid today. The presumed trade-off between inflation and unemployment is an utterly unrealistic concept. We are now in the Stagflation Seventies. Inflation *and* unemployment have become a standard feature of all industrial societies."

"And that is because of our insistence on capital-intensive economies?"

"Yes, that's one of the reasons. Excessive dependence on energy and natural resources, and excessive investment in capital rather than labor, are inflationary *and* bring massive unemployment. It's pathetic, you know, that unemployment has become such an intrinsic feature of our economy that government economists now speak of 'full employment' when more than five percent of the labor force is out of work."

"The excessive dependence on capital, energy, and natural resources would belong to the ecological variables of inflation," I continued. "Now, what about the social variables?"

Henderson asserted that the ever-increasing social costs generated by unlimited growth are the second major cause of inflation. "In their attempts to maximize their profits," she elaborated, "individuals, companies, and institutions try to 'externalize' all social and environmental costs."

"What does that mean?"

"It means that they exclude these costs from their own balance sheets and push them onto each other, passing them around the system, to the environment, and to future generations." Henderson went on to illustrate her point with numerous examples, citing the costs of litigation, crime control, bureaucratic coordination, federal regulation, consumer protection, health care, and so on. "Notice that none of these activities adds anything to real production," she pointed out. "Therefore, they all contribute to inflation."

Another reason for the rapid increase in social costs, Henderson continued, is the increasing complexity of our industrial and technological systems. As these systems become more and more complex, they become more and more difficult to model. "But any system that cannot be modeled cannot be managed," she argued, "and this unmanageable complexity is now generating a bewildering increase in unanticipated social costs."

When I asked Henderson to give me some examples, she needed no time to reflect: "The costs of cleaning up the mess," she argued emphatically, "the costs of caring for the human casualties of all that unplanned technology—the dropouts, the unskilled, the addicts, all those who cannot cope with the maze of urban life." She also reminded me of all the breakdowns and accidents that now occur with increasing frequency, generating even more unanticipated social costs. "If you take all that together," Henderson concluded, "you will see that more time is spent on maintaining and regulating the system than on providing useful goods and services. All these enterprises, therefore, are highly inflationary.

"You know," she added, summarizing her point, "I have often said that we will encounter the social, psychological, and conceptual limits to growth long before we collide with the physical limits."

I was deeply impressed by Henderson's insightful and passionate critique. She had made it obvious to me that inflation is much more than an economic problem, that it has to be seen as an economic symptom of social and technological crisis.

"So none of the ecological and social variables you mentioned shows up in economic models?" I asked, to bring our conversation back to economics.

"No, they don't. Instead, economists apply the traditional Keynesian tools to inflate or deflate the economy and create short-term oscillations that obscure the ecological and social realities." The traditional Keynesian methods can no longer solve any of our economic problems, Henderson affirmed. They will merely shift the problems around in the network of social and ecological relations. "You may be able to lower inflation with these methods," she argued, "or even inflation *and* unemployment. But you may have a large budget deficit as a result, or a large foreign trade deficit, or skyrocketing interest rates. You see, today nobody can control all these economic indicators simultaneously. There are too many vicious circles and feedback loops which make it impossible to fine-tune the economy."

"So what is the solution to the problem of high inflation?"

"The only real solution," Henderson replied, picking up once more her central theme, "is to change the system itself, to restructure our economy by decentralizing it, by developing soft technologies, and by running the economy with a leaner mix of capital, energy, and materials and a richer mix of labor and human resources. Such a resource-conserving, full-employment economy will also be non-inflationary and ecologically sound."

As I think back to this conversation eight years later, in the fall of 1986, I am amazed at how much Henderson's predictions have been borne out by subsequent economic developments and at how little our government economists have listened to her advice. The Reagan administration brought down inflation by engineering a severe recession and then tried in vain to stimulate the economy with massive tax cuts. These interventions caused tremendous hardships among large sectors of the population, primarily among low- and middle-income groups, by keeping unemployment rates above 7 percent and by eliminating or drastically cutting back a wide range of social programs. All this was advertised as strong medicine that would eventually cure our sick economy, but the opposite has happened. As a consequence of "Reaganomics" the American economy is now suffering from a threefold cancer—a gigantic budget deficit, a steadily worsening foreign trade deficit, and a huge foreign debt that has made the United States the world's biggest debtor. In response to this threefold crisis, government economists continue to stare hypnotically at flickering economic indicators and desperately try to apply the outdated Keynesian concepts and methods.

During our discussion of inflation I often noticed that Henderson used the language of systems theory. For example, she would point out the "interconnectedness of economic and ecological systems," or speak of "passing the social costs around the system." Later on that day I addressed the subject of systems theory directly and asked her whether she had found that framework useful.

"Oh, yes," she was quick to respond. "I think the systems approach is essential for understanding our economic problems. It's the only approach that makes it possible to bring some order into the present conceptual chaos." I was delighted by this remark, as I had recently come to see the framework of systems theory as the ideal language for the scientific formulation of the ecological paradigm, and so we embarked on a long and highly stimulating discussion. I vividly remember our great excitement as we explored the potential of systems thinking in the social and ecological sciences, stimulating each other with sudden insights, generating new ideas together, and discovering many delightful similarities in our ways of thinking.

Henderson began by introducing the idea of the economy as a living system composed of human beings and social organizations in continual interaction with the surrounding ecosystems. "A lot can be learned about economic situations by studying ecosystems," she pointed out. "For example, you can see that everything travels around the system in cycles. Linear cause-and-effect relationships exist only very rarely in these ecosystems, and linear models are therefore not very useful to describe the embedded economic systems either."

My conversations with Gregory Bateson during the previous summer had made me acutely aware of the importance of recognizing the nonlinearity of all living systems, and I mentioned to Hazel that Bateson had called this recognition "systemic wisdom." "Basically," I suggested, "systemic wisdom tells you that, if you do something that is good, more of the same will not necessarily be better."

"Exactly," Henderson responded excitedly. "I have often expressed the very same idea by saying that nothing fails like success." I had to laugh at her witty aphorism. In typical Henderson fashion she hit the nail on the head with her terse formulation of systemic wisdom—that strategies which are successful at one stage may become totally inappropriate at another.

The nonlinear dynamics of living systems brought the importance of recycling to my mind. I observed that today it is no longer permissible to throw away our worn-out goods or dump industrial waste somewhere else, because in our globally interconnected biosphere there is no such place as "somewhere else."

Henderson fully agreed. "For the same reason," she said, "there is no such thing as a 'windfall profit' unless it's taken out of somebody else's pocket, or gained at the expense of the environment or of future generations.

"Another consequence of nonlinearity is the question of scale, which Fritz Schumacher brought to everybody's attention," Henderson went on. "There is an optimal size for every structure, every organization, every institution, and maximizing any single variable will inevitably destroy the larger system."

"This is what is called 'stress' in the health field," I interjected. "Maximizing a single variable in a fluctuating, living organism will make the entire system more rigid, and prolonged stress of this kind will generally lead to illness."

Henderson smiled: "The same is true for an economy. Maximizing profit, efficiency, or the GNP will make the economy more rigid and induce social and environmental stress." We both derived great pleasure from these leaps between systems levels and from picking up on each other's insights.

"So the view of a living system as consisting of multiple,

interdependent fluctuations also applies to the economy?" I asked.

"Absolutely. In addition to the short-term business cycles studied by Keynes, an economy goes through several longer cycles that are influenced very little by those Keynesian manipulations." Henderson told me that Jay Forrester and his Systems Dynamics Group have mapped out many of these economic fluctuations, and she pointed out that yet another kind of fluctuation is the cycle of growth and decay that is characteristic of all life.

"This is what corporate executives find so difficult to get into their heads," she added with a sigh of frustration. "They simply cannot understand that in all living systems decline and death is the precondition for rebirth. When I go down to Washington and talk to the people who run the big corporations, I see that they are all terrified. They all know that hard times are coming. But I tell them: look, it may be a decline for some, but whenever something is declining you know something else is growing. There is always cyclical movement, and you just have to watch which wave you are going to catch."

"So what do you say to the leaders of a declining corporation?"

Henderson answered with one of her broad, radiant smiles: "I tell them that some corporations *have* to be allowed to die. It's *all right*, as long as people have the opportunity to move from the dying ones to the ones that are growing. The world is not breaking down, I tell my corporate friends. Only *some* things are breaking down, and I show them the many scenarios of cultural rebirth."

The longer I spoke with Hazel, the more I realized that her insights are grounded in the kind of ecological awareness I had come to recognize as being spiritual in its deepest essence. Informed by profound wisdom, her spirituality is lighthearted and action oriented, planetary in its scope, and irresistibly dynamic in its optimism.

Again we talked into the evening, and when we both got too hungry to go on we moved into Hazel's kitchen and continued our conversation there while I helped her prepare dinner. I remember that it was in the kitchen, while I was chopping vegetables and she was frying onions and cooking rice, that we hit on one of our most interesting joint discoveries.

It began with Henderson's observation that there is an interesting hierarchy in our culture, as far as the status of different kinds of work is concerned. Work with the lowest status, she pointed out, tends to be cyclical work—work that has to be done over and over again without leaving a lasting impact. "I call this 'entropic' work," she said, "because the tangible evidence of the effort is easily destroyed and entropy, or disorder, increases again.

"This is the work we are doing right now," Hazel continued, "cooking a meal which is immediately eaten. Similar work would be sweeping floors which will soon be dirty again, or cutting hedges and lawns which will grow again. Notice that in our society, as in all industrial societies, jobs that involve highly entropic work are generally delegated to women and to minority groups. They are given the lowest value and receive the lowest pay."

"In spite of the fact that they are essential to our daily existence and our health," I finished her thought.

"And now let's look at jobs with the highest status," Henderson went on. "These involve work that creates something lasting—skyscrapers, supersonic planes, space rockets, nuclear warheads, and all our high-tech gadgetry."

"What about marketing, finance, business administration, the work of corporate executives?"

"That, too, is granted high status because it is connected with high-tech enterprises. It derives its reputation from high technology, however dull the actual work may be."

I observed that the tragedy of our society is that the lasting impact of high-status work is so often negative—destructive to the environment, to the social fabric, and to our mental and physical health. Henderson agreed, and she added that there is a tremendous need today for simple skills involving cyclical work, like repair and maintenance jobs, which have been socially devalued and severely neglected although they are as vital as ever.

As I reflected on the differences between cyclical work and work that creates a lasting impact, I suddenly remembered all those Zen stories about a disciple asking the master for spiritual instruction and the master sending him off to wash his rice bowl, sweep the yard, or trim the hedge. "Isn't it curious," I remarked, "that cyclical work is precisely the kind of work emphasized in the Buddhist tradition? In fact, it is considered an integral part of the spiritual training."

Hazel's eyes lit up: "Yeah, that's right; and it isn't just the Buddhist tradition. Think of the traditional work of Christian monks and nuns—agriculture, nursing, and many other services."

"And I can tell you why cyclical work is considered so important in spiritual traditions," I went on excitedly. "Doing work that needs to be done over and over again helps us recognize the natural order of growth and decay, of birth and death. It helps us become aware of how we are embedded in those cycles, in the dynamic order of the cosmos."

Henderson confirmed the importance of this insight, which showed us once again the deep connection between ecology and spirituality. "And also the connection with female thinking," she added, "which is naturally attuned to those biological cycles." During the subsequent years, as Hazel and I became good friends and explored a variety of ideas together, we would often come back to that essential link between ecology, female thinking, and spirituality.

We had covered a lot of ground in those two days of intensive discussions, and so we spent the last evening in more relaxed conversations, exchanging impressions of people we both knew and of countries we had visited. As Hazel entertained me with lively stories about her experiences in Africa, Japan, and many other parts of the world I realized with amazement the truly global scale of her activism. She maintains close contacts with politicians, economists, business people, ecologists, feminists, and numerous social activists around the world, with whom she shares her enthusiasm and tries to realize her many visions of alternative futures.

When Hazel drove me back to the train station the next morning, the fresh winter air enhanced my feeling of aliveness and excitement. During the preceding forty-eight hours I had made tremendous progress in my understanding of the social and economic dimensions of our shifting paradigm, and even though I knew that I would come back with many new questions and puzzles, I left Princeton with a great sense of completion. I felt that my conversations with Hazel Henderson had rounded out the picture, and for the first time I felt ready to write my book.

7

The Big Sur Dialogues

By THE END of 1978 I had completed the bulk of my research on the paradigm shift in various fields. I had gathered voluminous notes from dozens of books and papers and from my discussions with numerous scholars and practitioners in the many disciplines I had been investigating. I had structured this mass of notes according to the planned structure of my book and had assembled an impressive group of advisers—Stan Grof for the fields of psychology and psychotherapy; Hazel Henderson for economics, technology, and politics; Margaret Lock and Carl Simonton for medicine and health care. In addition to this core group I maintained close contacts with several outstanding scholars—including Gregory Bateson, Geoffrey Chew, Erich Jantsch, and R. D. Laing—whom I could consult whenever I needed further advice.

My last step before I began to write *The Turning Point*

was to organize a meeting that turned into quite an extraordinary event. In February 1979 I assembled my core group of advisers for a three-day symposium during which we reviewed and discussed the entire conceptual structure of the book. Since one of my main aims was to show how similar changes in concepts and ideas are now occurring in various fields, I was eager to see my advisers, with whom I had interacted individually, also interact with each other and to hear in an intensive multi-disciplinary symposium how their ideas and experiences interrelated. I chose health in its multiple dimensions and aspects as the focus and integrating theme for these dialogues, and to complete and round off the group I also invited surgeon Leonard Shlain and family therapist Antonio Dimalanta, who had both decisively influenced my thinking during the previous two years.

As the location for our gathering I chose a beautiful secluded estate on the Big Sur coast near Esalen, the former family home of an acquaintance of mine, John Staude, who uses it now to host small seminars and workshops. Thanks to a generous advance from my publishers, I was able to fly my advisers in from various parts of the country and to rent Staude's estate for three days.

When I picked up Hazel Henderson, Tony Dimalanta, Margaret Lock, and Carl Simonton at the San Francisco airport I could sense the rising excitement in our little group as one after the other arrived. No two of these people had met before but all knew about one another's work. By the time everyone had arrived we were all in very high spirits and were looking forward to the gathering with great expectations. Leonard Shlain joined our group at my home, and as soon as we set out on our journey to Big Sur in a large station wagon the first spontaneous discussions began in a convivial and joyful mood. When we arrived at John Staude's home—well hidden from the road by massive old eucalyptus and cedar trees, perched on the cliffs of the Pacific Ocean, and surrounded by a lush garden—our joyous mood increased even more. We were joined there by Stan Grof and a small group of observers, so that our entire group numbered about a dozen people.

When all of us were finally gathered together on the first evening I felt that a dream I had nurtured for many years had now come true. Once again I was at Big Sur, the place of my inspiring conversations with Gregory Bateson and Stan Grof, where I had spent many weeks in contemplation and concentrated work, a place that held memories of deep insights and moving experiences. The long preparations for my extensive writing project were now completed, and the key people to inspire me and help me with my huge task were all assembled in one room. I was ecstatic.

For the next three days we gathered in that room—a large enclosure designed in the typical Big Sur style with lots of redwood and an expansive glass front overlooking the ocean. As our dialogues unfolded in that magnificent space, we were fascinated again and again to discover how our ideas interconnected, how our different perspectives stimulated and challenged one another's thoughts. This intellectual adventure reached its high point when Gregory Bateson joined the group for the last day of the symposium. Although Bateson spoke only rarely during that day, merely throwing occasional remarks into the discussion, all of us felt that his towering presence was highly stimulating and challenging.

At each session the entire discussion was recorded on tape, and in addition to these taped sessions countless dialogues among smaller groups took place during mealtimes and evenings, many of which lasted until late into the night. It is impossible to reproduce all these interchanges; I can merely convey the quality and diversity of ideas in the following collection of excerpts from the symposium. I have not interrupted these dialogues by any editorial comments but rather chose to let the voices of this extraordinary group of people speak for themselves.

DRAMATIS PERSONAE: Gregory Bateson
                     Fritjof Capra
                     Antonio Dimalanta
                     Stanislav Grof
                     Hazel Henderson
                     Margaret Lock
                     Leonard Shlain
                     Carl Simonton

CAPRA: I would like to begin our discussion of the multiple dimensions of health by simply asking the question "What is health?" From many discussions with all of you I have learned that we may begin to address this question by saying that health is an experience of well-being that arises when our organism functions in a certain way. The problem is how to describe this healthy functioning of the organism objectively. Can it be done at all, and is it necessary to know the answer in order to have an effective system of health care?

LOCK: I think that a huge amount of health care happens at an intuitive level where you can't classify but have to deal with each individual person in terms of their own past experience and individual presentation of complaints. No therapist can go by a set of rules that is laid out. He has to be flexible.

SIMONTON: I agree with that and, in addition, I think that it is important to state that we don't know, that those answers are not available. To me, one of the biggest things I have come up against in medicine is that in the standard textbooks it is not stated that answers to major questions are not known.

SHLAIN: There are three words for which you don't know the definitions. One is "life," the other is "death," and the third is "health." If you look in a standard textbook of biology, in chapter one where they ask what is life, you see that they can't define it. If you listen to an argument between doctors and lawyers about when is somebody dead, you will see that they don't know what death is. Is it when the heart stops beating or when the brain stops working? When does that moment come? Similarly, we can't define health. Everybody knows what it is, just as everybody knows what life is and what death is, but nobody can define it. It is beyond the ken of language for anybody to attempt to define those three states.

SIMONTON: However, if we assume that all definitions are approximate anyway, then to me it is important to approximate a definition as closely as we reasonably can.

CAPRA: I have tentatively adopted the idea that health results from a dynamic balance between the physical, psychological, and social aspects of the organism. Illness, in this view, would be a manifestation of imbalance and disharmony.

SHLAIN: I am uncomfortable with the view of illness as a manifestation of disharmony within the organism. This totally ignores genetic and environmental factors. For example, if a guy worked in an asbestos factory during World War II when nobody knew that asbestos would cause lung cancer twenty years later, and if he then gets lung cancer, can you say that this came from a disharmony within that person?

CAPRA: Not just within the person, but also within the

society and the ecosystem. If you widen your view, then that's almost always the case. However, I agree that we have to take into account genetic factors.

SIMONTON: Let us put the genetic and environmental factors in a proper context. If you look at the number of people who are exposed to asbestos and ask how many of them will develop mesothelioma of the lungs, which is really the disease we are talking about, you find that the incidence is something like one in a thousand. Why does that one person develop the disease? There are many other factors to look at, but the way people talk about it is as if exposure to the carcinogens produced the cancer. We have to be very careful when we say this causes that and this causes that, because we tend to overlook many very important factors. Genetic factors, too, do not have overriding importance. We tend to treat genetics as if it were some sort of magic.

HENDERSON: We also need to recognize that there are a whole lot of nesting systems in which the individual is embedded. If we come up with a definition of health, it will have to incorporate positional logic. You cannot define health, or a manageable amount of stress, in an abstract way. You must always link it to the position. I have this vision of stress as a ball being pushed around the system. Everyone is trying to unload the stress to somebody else's system. For example, take the economy. One way to minister to the sick economy would be to create another percentage point of unemployment. That pushes the stress back onto the individual. We know that one percentage point of unemployment creates about seven billion dollars' worth of measurable human stress in terms of morbidity, mortality, suicide, and so on. What we are seeing here is how different levels in the system manage stress by shoving it somewhere else. Another way of doing this is that the society can shove the stress onto the ecosystem, and then it comes back fifty years later, as in the case of Love Canal. Is this part of this discussion?

SIMONTON: Yes, this is the beautiful part. To me, the most exciting aspect of this discussion is to go back and forth between systems, so that we don't get stuck in looking at one level.

CAPRA: It seems that at the very basis of our health problems lies a profound cultural imbalance, the overemphasis on *yang*, or masculine, values and attitudes. I have found this cultural imbalance to form a consistent background to all problems of individual, social, and ecological health. Whenever I explore a health problem in depth and try to get to the roots of things I find myself coming back to this imbalance in our value system. But then the question arises: When we talk about imbalance, can we go back to a balanced state, or can we discern in human evolution the swinging of a pendulum? And how is this related to the rise and fall of cultures?

HENDERSON: I would like to respond to this by using again the specific example of the economy. One of the basic problems of economics is that it doesn't capture evolutionary growth. Biologists understand perfectly well that growth creates structure, and we are now on a point of the evolutionary curve where nothing is failing like success. Our economy, in this country, has grown to the point where it is creating all of these social disservices and disamenities. The structure has got so set in concrete, rather like a dinosaur, that it can't hear the signals from the ecosystem. It is blocking those signals, and it is blocking the social feedback. What I am going to work out is a set of criteria for social health to replace the GNP.

Now let me say a few words about this cultural imbalance. Current technology, which I call "machismo technology," or "big-bang technology," certainly has to do with the rewarding of competitive activities and the disincentives to cooperative activities. All my models are ecological models, and I know that in every ecosystem competition and cooperation are always in dynamic balance. Where the Social Darwinists went wrong is that they looked at nature with a very gross eye and saw only the redness in tooth and claw. They only saw the competition. They did not see the molecular level of cooperation because it was simply too subtle.

SHLAIN: What do you mean by cooperation at the molecular level?

HENDERSON: The cooperation that exists, for example, in the nitrogen cycle, in the water cycle, the carbon cycle, and so on. All those are examples of cooperation that you could not have expected the Social Darwinists to notice, because they just did not have the appropriate science. They did not see all those cyclical patterns that are characteristic of biological as well as of social and cultural systems.

SIMONTON: In order to understand cyclical patterns in cultural evolution it is helpful to understand one's own developmental cycles. If I understand my own cycles, I am going to have much more tolerance and flexibility, which I think has applications socially and culturally.

CAPRA: I think that feminism will further that, because women naturally are more aware of biological cycles. We men are much more rigid and don't usually think of our bodies as living in cycles, but that awareness will be very healthy and will facilitate the recognition of cultural cycles.

DIMALANTA: A crucial phenomenon in the evolution of systems seems to be what has been called deviation amplification. There is an initial kick, such as a new invention, which initiates change. Then this change is amplified and everybody forgets about the consequences. When the system takes over and continues to amplify the initial deviation, it is capable of destroying itself, and so the curve of cultural evolution goes down. Then there may be a new initiative that is amplified and the whole process may repeat itself. I think this process has not been studied sufficiently. There are many examples of it in the universe. In family therapy, all you have to do sometimes is to destabilize the system in order to introduce change, and one of the most effective mechanisms is to build up a deviation-amplification process. But then you cannot go on to amplify it, you have to use negative feedback. Socially, that is where our consciousness would come in.

CAPRA: When we talk about the cultural imbalance, we should probably first ask: What is balance? Is there such a thing as a balanced state? This problem occurs both in the context of individual health and in the culture as a whole.

SHLAIN: You also have to talk about the rate of change. There has never been a time where so many things happened simultaneously which are introducing new variables. There are rapid changes at the technological, scientific, industrial level, and so on. This is the fastest rate of change in human history, and it is difficult for me to extrapolate anything that has happened in human history to this day and age, and in this way to learn from the past. It is very difficult to know at what stage we are in our cultural evolution, because everything is speeding up so much.

LOCK: Yes, and one of the results of this is that the two

aspects of us, man as a cultural being and man as a biological being, are more widely separated than they have ever been before. We have modified our environment to such an extent that we are really out of sync with our biological base, more than any other culture and any other group of people in the past. Perhaps this is directly related to the problem of competitive attitudes. They certainly seem to have furthered biological adaptability at the hunter-gatherer level. If you are going to survive in that kind of situation, you need aggression, you need competitiveness. But that seems to be the last thing we need in a densely populated environment with huge cultural control. So we have this hangover from our biological heritage, and we are broadening the split with every new cultural innovation.

CAPRA: Why don't we evolve accordingly through adaptation?

SHLAIN: The way animals adapt is through mutation, and that takes several generations, but we are seeing changes of such remarkable speed in a single lifetime that the question is, can we adapt?

CAPRA: Of course, as humans, we have consciousness, and we could adapt consciously by shifting our values.

HENDERSON: That is exactly the evolutionary role that I see for us. The next evolutionary leap *has* to be cultural, if it happens at all, and I think that is what all this introspection and testing of our own capabilities is about. It is going to be a Herculean effort to get us out of what otherwise would be an evolutionary cul-de-sac. So many other species before us have not made it, but we have got an awful lot of equipment to make it with.

CAPRA: Let me now focus the discussion on the concrete question: Are we healthy? It does not seem to make sense to compare health patterns over a long period of time because of their dependence on environmental changes. But over the last twenty years, where the environment has not changed that much, a comparison of health patterns should be possible. Now, if disease is seen as merely one consequence of ill health, a comparison of disease patterns is not enough. Mental illness and social pathologies must also be included. If they are, what is the answer to the question, are we healthy? Are there statistics representing this wider point of view?

LOCK: No, there is no statistic that you could use because the definition of social pathology is something people cannot agree on.

HENDERSON: It always depends on the systems level you are looking at. The moment you decide to focus on a set of criteria to talk about progress in one area, then, in order to get that accuracy, you lose everything else—just like in physics.

SHLAIN: You know its position, but you can't know its velocity.

CAPRA: Nevertheless, it would be helpful, wouldn't it, to be able to take these things into account, because if we eliminate certain diseases and as a result there is more mental illness and more criminality, then we have not done much about health. As Hazel said, we are just shifting around the ball. It would be interesting to measure that and to express it in some reliable way.

SIMONTON: Just the question "Are we healthy?" to me creates a real problem. I have a problem just addressing that issue. That question reflects a very static viewpoint. What comes to my mind is the question "Are we moving in a healthy direction?"

LOCK: I think we have to be clear about the level we are dealing with. Are we talking about individuals, populations, or other levels when we are asking that question?

SIMONTON: That is why it is important to integrate those levels when addressing the question. We have to formulate the answer both in the context of the individual and of the society.

HENDERSON: I encounter very similar problems when I work with a study group in Washington, called the Office of Technology Assessment. We run into these problems all the time, and the only way that I have found to do some useful work is to describe the system we are looking at very carefully, together with all its nested systems. You have to specify at the outset what exactly you are looking at. What you find then is that, if something is technologically efficient, it may be socially inefficient. If it is healthy for the economy, it may be ecologically unhealthy. You get into these terrible problems when you bring people together from several different disciplines to do these technology assessments. You can never integrate all the different viewpoints and interests. All you can do is be honest at the outset, and it's the honesty that is so painful.

CAPRA: It seems to me that you will never succeed if you insist on being static and want everything at the optimal level. But if you have a dynamic way of living, where sometimes, say, you opt for social ill health and have a trade-off in other fields, and at other times you do it the other way around, then you may be able to keep the whole thing in a dynamic balance.

SHLAIN: Why is the death rate now falling if we are doing so many things wrong with our diet, our life-styles, the way we create stress, and so on? I sense that the focus of this discussion is going to be that we live in a technologically advanced society which is pretty unhealthy. If this is so, how come each year we are living longer? In the last ten years we have increased the life span by four years. Now, I am not talking about the quality of life, but if we live in a pretty unhealthy society, then how do we account for this parameter?

SIMONTON: To me the length of the life span is not the only thing to look at. If we look at cancer, for example, we see that the incidence of cancer is now reaching epidemic proportions, according to our definition of epidemic. If we look at the economy, we see that inflation is reaching epidemic proportions. So it all depends on what you want to look at. The total picture seems to tell us that change will be necessary if we want to survive as a culture. There are many positive aspects to the increase of life span, such as the decrease of heart disease, but to take the length of the life span as an absolute, for me, is to stick my head into the sand.

SHLAIN: Nevertheless, it is a meaningful statistical parameter, and I think that it must be related to the general change of awareness that we observe in our culture. There is a whole change in people's perceptions about their diets, there is an emphasis on physical fitness—just look at all the joggers—and there are a lot of other positive changes going on.

CAPRA: I think when we talk about "our culture" we have to distinguish between the majority culture, which is declining, and a minority culture that is on the rise. Joggers and health food stores, the human potential movement, the environmental movement, the feminist movement, all these are part of the rising culture. The whole social and cultural system is complex and multidimensional, and there is no way you can use a single variable, whatever variable it may be, to reflect the system in its entirety. So it may well be that this particular combination of the rising and the declining cultures has helped us to increase life expectancy, but at the same time there are still a lot of unhealthy attitudes around.

CAPRA: This brings me to the related question: Is medicine successful? Opinions about the progress in medicine are often diametrically opposed and thus quite confusing. Some experts talk about the fantastic progress medicine has made in recent decades, while others state that in most instances doctors are relatively ineffective in preventing disease or preserving health by medical intervention.

SIMONTON: An important aspect of this question is, what does the average person think of medicine? We can get some indication about this from things like lawsuits, the prestige of physicians, and so on. When I look at how society is viewing medicine, I see that this view has deteriorated dramatically in the last thirty years or so. When I look at medicine from inside, I see that the direction in which it goes is unhealthy. There are many indicators that show that medicine is moving in an unhealthy direction—unhealthy for itself and, because it is not filling the needs of society, unhealthy also for society.

SHLAIN: Let's keep things in perspective, though. There can be no question that medicine made a tremendous sweep with its cure of infectious diseases and its understanding of some of the basic disease processes of other illnesses. There is certainly no doubt that within a time frame of one hundred years the advances have been astonishing. Before, diseases like smallpox and the bubonic plague were a constant threat to one's existence. Every family anticipated losing one out of three children. You did not expect a family to grow up without losing children or the mother in childbirth.

SIMONTON: Certainly, the shift has been astonishing. I would be reluctant to call it advancement categorically.

SHLAIN: Because of the discovery of the causes and the treatments for many killers that routinely threatened the population, those diseases are just not around anymore.

SIMONTON: That's right, but neither is leprosy, and that was not eradicated through medical management. If you go back historically, you find the same thing happening. It is almost an evolutionary process, and not due to some form of intervention. I am not saying that what has happened is *not* because of medicine, but to say that it is because of medicine is to deny history.

SHLAIN: I agree that you cannot isolate medicine and disease from the social fabric in which they exist, and certainly every advance that we make in sanitation and hygiene and standard of living improves the situation. There is definite improvement in the number of women that are dying when their babies are born, the number of children that grow up to adulthood, the number of people that live to be older. Of course, that gets into the problem of what you use to measure the quality of life. The fact that people are living longer does not necessarily mean improved health. Nevertheless, there is no doubt in my mind that the human species, as a species, is in the midst of a breeding storm. We are expanding our numbers absolutely, and the length of life has increased. Life expectancy is still climbing in the United States. In ten years it has gone up from sixty-nine to seventy-three.

LOCK: That is because of the problems related to poverty and the fact that many people in various parts of the United States are still just beginning to get proper nutrition, and so on. At the same time, the life expectancy of American Indians is only forty-five.

SIMONTON: That's what I'm saying. We can say that there have been certain changes, but to say who is responsible for those changes or to give a single cause, that is a real trap.

LOCK: Absolutely. I absolutely agree.

SHLAIN: Now, wait a moment. I take care of a lot of old people, and I know that the way I can take care of them now is different from the way I could take care of them ten years ago. There has been improvement. Some things are not improving, but a lot of them are. The chances of my taking on somebody who is critically ill and having them walk out of the hospital are greater today than ten years ago.

And then there is something else. If somebody comes to me, for example, with recurrent attacks of gallstones, I can search into their family history, cultural background, dietary habits, and so on, but they've still got gallstones. Now, if I take their gallbladder out, the pain goes away. You can say that I have keyed in on the one piece in the clock that is not working and have removed that, and now the clock is working again. And you can say that that is a bad model, but it works.

SIMONTON: Everything that works is not good for the system. The fact that an intervention alleviates pain and suffering does not necessarily mean that this approach should be continued. I think it is important to state that everything that alleviates suffering temporarily is not necessarily good. Surgical intervention is an example of that. If you do that to the exclusion of looking at other things, then in the long run this approach can be unhealthy for the overall system.

CAPRA: I think what Carl is saying is based on the view of illness as a way out of a personal problem or a social problem. If I have this problem and develop a certain disease in my gallbladder, and if you then take out my gallbladder, you still haven't solved my problem. The problem will continue and may lead to some other disease—to mental illness, or to some antisocial behavior, or whatever. In this wider view of illness surgery becomes like treating a symptom.

SIMONTON: If you look at the history of health and health care in the United States over the past one hundred years, to me, there is no real doubt that very dramatic changes have occurred in many aspects of daily life and health. One of the problems I have is that many people try to take all the credit for these changes, rather than integrate things. What I have been told in my education was that these changes were due to advances in medicine, and to me there is significant truth in that. I can see how medicine has changed and how that has affected our lives. However, the reason why medicine has changed has to do with other changes that have occurred in society, and all these aspects become so interdependent that it is impossible to separate them out. Whenever people want to take all the credit for a good thing, this reflects a very possessive attitude, and it becomes an excuse for funneling more money into certain enterprises or activities, and that to me is the really unhealthy aspect.

LOCK: We see a good example of that in the introduction of Western medicine to developing countries. For example in, say, Tanzania, there are the elite doctors who have been trained in the West or Russia and want a lot of technology. There is the local government, which in this case is a left-wing government and wants medicine in the rural areas. Then there is the World Health Organization with various inputs from various power sources; and, finally, there are the local people in Tanzania. Now, if you lay out the interests of these various groups and try to be honest about why they are involved in the things they are doing, you will find that few people really care about whether a person in Tanzania gets penicillin or not. Nepal is an even better example. In Nepal, there are over thirty-five projects sponsored by developmental agencies from around the world, all present in Katmandu, all trying to introduce health to the Nepalese. One of the main reasons, obviously, is that everybody wants to be in Katmandu enjoying the Himalayas, and the whole health process is a cover-up for why they are there. I think it is awfully important to expose the real motives behind all these developments.

CAPRA: The emphasis on symptoms, rather than underlying causes, is exemplified by the drug approach of current medical therapy. I would like to discuss the basic philosophy behind giving drugs. There seem to be two views. One holds that the physical symptoms of illness are caused by bacteria, and in order to get rid of the symptoms you have to kill the bacteria. The other view says that bacteria are symptomatic factors that are present in disease but are not the cause of disease. Therefore, you should not bother so much about the bacteria but try to get to the underlying causes. What is the present status of these two views?

SHLAIN: If you take someone who is under great stress and introduce him to the tuberculous organism, then he is likely to get tuberculosis. Whereas, if you introduce it to a healthy person, he will not necessarily develop the disease. However, once the disease develops, the bacteria will destroy the organism, unless you do something about them.

CAPRA: Why can't you strengthen the organism so that it will get rid of the bacteria by itself?

SHLAIN: That was the treatment before they came up with a drug treatment for tuberculosis. They put the patients up in the Swiss Alps, they gave them clean air, good nutrition, a life without stress, special nurses, all kinds of therapies, and it did not work. But when somebody developed the appropriate drug, that was the end of that disease, which was the world's largest killer.

LOCK: Thomas McKeown is a British epidemiologist who has looked at all the drops in death rates over the end of the last century in England and Sweden. He showed that, for all the major infectious diseases, the death rates had plummeted before the development of vaccines and of drugs for any of them.

SHLAIN: That had to do with hygiene and sanitation.

LOCK: Exactly. And it did produce a profound effect long before the drugs were developed.

SHLAIN: Nevertheless, when I see a patient today who happens to be so unfortunate as to have tuberculosis, and if I treat him with drugs, he gets better. Whereas, if I send him to a sanitarium and give him the right diet and clean air and the whole number, the chances are that that is not going to make him better.

DIMALANTA: I think the problem we have here is that we are looking at all or nothing. If there are bacteria and we have an antibiotic, we should use it. But at the same time we should look into the system to find out what made that individual susceptible to that disease.

SHLAIN: I won't argue with that.

SIMONTON: But there are reasons not to do that. Because it takes so much time. And besides, people don't want to have their life-style examined and to be confronted with their own unhealthy behavior. As a society we don't *want* good medical care, and when you try to push good medical care on a society that does not want it, you got problems.

CAPRA: The drug approach of medical therapy is encouraged and perpetuated by the pharmaceutical industry, which exerts a tremendous influence on doctors and patients. You can see it every night on TV in all those drug commercials.

LOCK: Advertising on television is not just a problem for drugs; it is problematic for detergents and cleaning agents also.

SIMONTON: Drug commercials, however, say that they are different.

HENDERSON: The only thing that is different in drug advertising is that contraindications are mentioned. This is not true for the rest of advertising. For example, they do not tell you that certain detergents will give you sparkling dishes but that you have to give up the sparkling rivers and lakes. Or, to mention just one other example, the advertising of presweetened cereals to infants on Sunday morning television shows does have serious contraindications. So, it is less common in consumer advertising to make clear the contraindications of the products that are advertised than it is in advertising of drugs to doctors.

SIMONTON: That is why I felt there was something different in the advertising by the pharmaceutical industry. There is a tone of piety, of nobility, the notion that they would not deceive you, that they had your best interest in mind—but that's not true. They are out for monetary gain, and the more they cover this with a cloud of nobility, the more dishonest it becomes.

LOCK: What I would like to know is why the major journals put out among medical professionals are financed by pharmaceutical companies. The medical profession is the only profession which allows that. In other professions people pay to produce their own journals. But the medical profession allows the pharmaceutical companies to do that.

SIMONTON: They also allow pharmaceutical companies to throw big parties.

LOCK: Right. That happens more than in any other profession. I would feel a lot better about the medical profession if I saw a move to bring back integrity.

SHLAIN: Is the general conclusion that the pharmaceutical industry is a bad thing that produces no good? I can think of an old lady who has heart problems. Her pump is not working well. It just is not strong enough to get that blood around, so fluid builds up in her ankles, and she has trouble walking, she has trouble breathing at night. And I give her one pill, or two pills, that cause that water to get out of her system. That pill that I give her today is an infinite improvement on the pill you had to give her ten years ago, or fifteen years ago. Because they have been refining it and refining it, and it has been getting better and better with fewer and fewer side effects. Now this woman can sleep through the night, and she can live a little bit longer and more comfortably with a better quality of life. That came about through this monster that we are talking about, the pharmaceutical industry.

HENDERSON: We are talking about trade-offs here.

SHLAIN: I understand that, but it is important to add a little balance. We should keep in mind that it isn't this ogre that is eating us alive by pushing drugs on us that have serious side effects and don't work. We have got some incredible drugs now that do work. We have got people with rheumatoid arthritis and with degenerative diseases who, ten years ago, would have been a lot more miserable—and would still be if it were not for some of the newer drugs on the market.

HENDERSON: There is another aspect to this. Whenever I see a lot of order and structure in a system, I tend to look for disorder somewhere else. Remember what happened with Parke-Davis and chloramphenicol, an antibiotic which they produced. The drug was banned in this country for all but very restricted uses, but the company sold it in Japan over the counter for headaches and as a cold remedy. It has been documented that the incidence of plastic anemia increased in direct proportion to the sales of this antibiotic. I have been in other countries where I have noticed the same pattern. The moment a drug gets banned in advanced industrial countries, multinational drug companies just sell it in some other parts of their market. That is part of my image of stress getting pushed around the system.

LOCK: The Children's Hospital in Montreal encourages all their staff to limit themselves to about forty drugs. With those forty drugs they think they can deal with every single problem—and that includes aspirin and penicillin, and so on.

SHLAIN: By contrast, the *Physicians' Desk Reference* has been growing enormously year after year. Part of the reason is that for each drug the list of complications gets longer, as well as the addition of new drugs. However, I think that most doctors stay within reasonable limits. I don't think that I ever use more than forty drugs. When they come to me and say, "Use this, this is new," I say, "No, leave it on the market for ten years, and then maybe I'll think about it."

CAPRA: But what does that mean, "leave it on the market"? Somebody must prescribe the drug if they leave it on the market.

SIMONTON: Of course. There are these detail men, and they come in and bring you these gifts. Those guys make their living on how many drugs they push. They start you off when you are in medical school. They bring you a new stethoscope. They give you bags. They invite you to parties. The whole business really has some unhealthy aspects to it. My brother-in-law is a general practitioner out in southwest Oklahoma, and you should see what all the detail men bring to him. He is always using new drugs.

SHLAIN: There is another side to it, too. Every time a detail man walks into my office, he leaves a sample of drugs with me. These samples are usually very valuable, expensive drugs, which I can then give to people who cannot afford to pay for them.

SIMONTON: But that is not why they are doing it. And if everybody did that, they would stop doing it. This is not the way the game is played.

LOCK: That's right. The organization of the drug companies is such that the promotion is done in a subtle way so as to induce doctors to prescribe ever more drugs. That starts in medical school and goes on from there.

SHLAIN: Well, doctors are members of the community and of the culture. If the culture is an entrepreneurial culture, doctors will be somewhat affected by that.

LOCK: I agree. I am willing to accept that most doctors are dedicated and are not in it just to make money out of prescribing more drugs. You have to deal with the wider context and recognize how they are manipulated, like we all are.

SHLAIN: One thing that impresses me about the whole drug business is that the competition between the drug companies is so fierce that, after a while, the best drug wins out. When the tranquilizers first came out, there was a great number of them, and many of them are still around, but after a while doctors began to realize which of these produced too many side effects. When you introduce something new it takes time for the balance to be struck. It sounds as if doctors were incredibly naive and would use everything they were given by the drug companies, but it does not work that way.

CAPRA: When we talk about medicine and health, it might also be interesting to examine the health of physicians themselves.

SIMONTON: I think it is a question that is central. Historically, healers were considered to be healthy people. They had often been through a serious illness, but they were expected to be healthy. As you expected your religious leaders to be in tune with God, you expected your healers to be in tune with healthful practices and to be healthy people. That's no longer true today.

CAPRA: Maybe this is just part of the general pattern in our society. Our priests are not very spiritual, our lawyers are not beyond reproach as far as breaking the law is concerned, and our physicians are not very healthy.

SIMONTON: You are right. And it is generally not appreciated just how bad the health of physicians is. In the United States, the life expectancy of physicians is ten to fifteen years less than that of the average population.

LOCK: And physicians not only have a higher rate of physical disease, they also have high rates of suicide, divorce, and other social pathologies.

CAPRA: So, what is it that makes being a physician so unhealthy?

SHLAIN: It begins in medical school. If you look at medical school, you will see that it is very competitive.

CAPRA: More so than other parts of the educational system?

SHLAIN: Yes. Competitiveness and aggressiveness in medical school are extreme.

SIMONTON: In addition, we have to remember the high responsibilities of physicians and the tremendous anguish associated with them. You know, you don't sleep because you are concerned that the nurse won't carry out the order for a critical patient. So you call up the hospital at four o'clock in the morning to make sure that it is being done. There is all this compulsive behavior because of a feeling of tremendous responsibility. Also, you are not taught to deal with death, and then there is guilt and blame when patients die. Then there is the tendency of taking care of yourself last, after you have taken care of everybody else. For example, it is not uncommon for physicians to work for a full year without any vacation. So there are many reasons why physicians are so unhealthy.

SHLAIN: The essence of medical training is inculcating the notion that the patient's concerns come first and that your well-being is secondary. That is thought to be necessary to produce commitment and responsibility. So the medical training consists of extremely long hours with very few breaks.

LOCK: An awareness of the problems inherent in medical education is something that really has to be developed. Doctors are forced into a role that many of them don't want to play.

SIMONTON: Yes, the pressure of conforming with that role is extremely high. In medical practice, when a physician starts to take care of himself, peer pressure is phenomenal. It's "Oh, you are going off skiing again," and all these remarks from your colleagues that are really painful.

HENDERSON: I think the bad health of physicians is part of a phenomenon that we can observe throughout our society: "Do what I say, not what I do." It is a consequence of the Cartesian split, the exhaustion of the logic of patriarchy, specialization, and of many other things. We can observe the dictum "Do what I say, not what I do" in education, in technology, and everywhere else.

A similar problem existed in the environmental movement. At a certain stage of the movement, people began to realize that in order to be serious environmentalists, it was not good enough to belong to the Sierra Club and to pay your dues if you did not also try to separate your garbage, turn off the lights, and practice voluntary simplicity. There has been a whole evolution of consciousness in the environmental movement. The people on the leading edge of the movement are now those who embrace right living and voluntary simplicity. Narrowing the distance between what you say and what you do has almost become the *sine qua non* of the environmental movement. It is becoming a moral imperative that once you begin to make all these connections, you can no longer speak with forked tongues. You can no longer go around describing what everybody should do without being a model yourself. So you end up not pointing the way but being the way, and if you can't be the way, you just have to get out of the ballgame because you become such a charlatan.

DIMALANTA: In psychiatry there is tremendous pressure to be a missionary—that is, to save everybody but to forget about yourself. That is one of the reasons why the suicide rate is so high among psychiatrists. What happens is that the patients transfer their problems to the psychiatrist, and if psychiatrists cannot take care of themselves they reach the point where they become desperate and commit suicide. Therefore, when I do family therapy, I make the family understand that part of my role is to take care not only of the family, but also of myself. If I have needs, I make them understand that this is part of the whole system that we are dealing with. When there is conflict between my needs and the needs of the family, then to hell with the family. Usually people cannot understand that.

SIMONTON: Right. They think that this is not acceptable.

DIMALANTA: But how can I tell them to take care of themselves, and then they see me not taking care of myself? The problem is when to stop and recognize that you have reached your limit. You have to recognize that your own needs are part of the system you are dealing with as a therapist.

SHLAIN: Who has the wisdom to know that?

SIMONTON: Only by practice will we ever approximate that wisdom.

DIMALANTA: I think that through our intuitive capacities as therapists we can know that, but only when we have given up the delusion of our omnipotence. For me, that is a very painful process. But, at the same time, this is where psychotherapy begins to be really exciting, and I think that it is not limited to psychiatry but applies to all of medicine.

SHLAIN: In the course of my day, the people I see come into my life at a moment that is the most frightening moment in their lives. When I get involved with them, they are in a state of high anxiety, so that I'm constantly dealing with people who are very anxious. For them our interaction is the single most important thing that is happening to them, whereas for me it is my daily work. It is very hard for me to be cavalier about this. I need to be constantly in their intensity, which is very draining, very tiring, and very exhausting. But it's very hard not to be that way because, if you are going to be part of making them well, if you are in the role of the healer, you have to be with them.

HENDERSON: I think we all accept the idea that the doctor should be dedicated. Now, if as a result of this dedication the interaction with the patient is draining, then this just means that you have to see fewer patients, and that clashes head-on with the economics of medicine.

CAPRA: Also, the way the physician or therapist deals with his own health, as compared to the health of his patients, will depend very much on the kind of work he is doing. The work of a surgeon is very different from the work of a family therapist. I can understand very well that, when somebody comes to the surgeon in a moment of her life's crisis, this is very different from dealing with a complex family situation.

SHLAIN: Not only that. If I operate on a patient and something goes sour, I cannot turn to somebody else and say, would you do me a favor and take this thing over. It is my responsibility. I am locked in a dance with that patient right to the end. That is the unwritten contract that you make with them. If some doctor calls me and says, "I have an alcoholic whom I found in a doorway on Third and Mission and he is vomiting blood. Will you see him?" and I say "Yes"—at that instant we are locked. Many times I don't even know the guy. He comes in half unconscious and I have to take care of him. I cannot walk away from him.

GROF: Many things you see happening in the medical profession are coming from psychological motives. In one of my workshops on death and dying there was an internist from San Francisco who had a very strong emotional reaction during the workshop. He realized that he had this terrible problem of the fear of death, and the way it manifested in his everyday practice was that he was the one who stepped in when everybody else around him had given up. He would stay there over the hours with Adrenalin and oxygen, and so on. And now he realized that he wanted to prove to himself that he had control over death. So he was really using his patients to deal with his own psychological problem.

SHLAIN: One of the reasons why a lot of people go into medicine is that they are intrigued about death, about the mystery of birth, and so on. It was one of the motivations why I wanted to be a doctor. I wanted to be as close to those mysteries as I possibly could, because I really wanted to know more about them.

CAPRA: When we discuss the Simonton cancer therapy, we should keep in mind that the Simontons see their work as a pilot study. They select their patients very carefully, and they want to see how far they can go in the ideal case with highly motivated patients to understand the dynamics underlying cancer.

SIMONTON: That is true. This year I will not see more than fifty new patients. I am very committed to that because we deal intimately with our patients and we are very committed to them. Our commitment to our patients is to follow them forever—until they die or until we die. Because of that long-term commitment we cannot afford to see large numbers of patients. This also means that my main income does not come from treating patients. It comes from writing and lecturing.

One of the problems that we have is how to determine the motivation of our patients. We assume that we are dealing with highly motivated patients, but in fact there is a wide spectrum.

GROF: I think that you will not be able to measure the degree of motivation as a single variable. This is a complex dynamic with quite a variety of psychodynamic constellations. They will go all the way to extremes, which I have seen a number of times in psychiatric patients. For example, people with a very strong competitive pattern may tell you: "I am not going to get well to become a number in your statistics of successes." It goes that far. The idea that they would somehow enhance your professional image becomes an important factor for them.

DIMALANTA: I agree. Resistance is one of the most crucial problems we encounter in psychotherapy. Patients will test your strength and they often have great difficulty in trusting another person.

SIMONTON: Yes, because they don't trust themselves.

DIMALANTA: Right. In the family and the social environment where they grow, denial is one of the most effective mechanisms of survival.

CAPRA: Carl, can you tell us about some of your most extreme experiences of personal involvement in the therapeutic process?

SIMONTON: The most extreme thing that we ever did was to bring in some of our sickest patients and live with them for one month to try and test the limits of our approach. We brought in six or seven patients. Two died in the retreat during that month; the rest of them died within a year, except for one. The one who lived is a woman who just ran a marathon in Hawaii. It was an intriguing experience and so difficult for us physically that I would never do it again. I have been around death; that is part of my regular work as an oncologist. But to live with those people so closely is quite different. I slept with one patient the night he died—it was incredible.

LOCK: So you got a real feeling for what the close family members are going through?

SIMONTON: Yes, because we were in essence a family. The real education for me was to experience how conscious the dying was. The guy who died was a twenty-five-year-old leukemic. He said that morning that he was going to die that day. When we walked down to breakfast, he told one of the other patients, "I am going to die today," and he died at about seven o'clock that evening.

SHLAIN: I have to say, Carl, that in the medical profession there are only a few who can do what you are doing. It is the closest to sainthood that one can come. I feel that what you are doing about providing caring and love to dying patients is something that is invaluable. I am sitting here realizing that I disagree with a lot of what you said, and I am reluctant to disagree with it because of what you are doing, but I feel that we are here mixing up two different things. We are looking at what is going on with you as a healer, and we are trying to make it scientific. I am uncomfortable with that, and I will say why.

By and large, most of your patients are from out of state. That tells me that none of them wanted to die. The fact that they are flying to Fort Worth to see you puts them in a separate category of cancer patients. I also bet that your patients are fifteen to twenty years younger than the overall statistics of cancer of breast, colon, and lungs. They are in a much higher socioeconomic group, which means they are usually much more motivated, because that is how they got into their socioeconomic group.

These patients come to you, and you have outlined what you do with them, but I am convinced that you as a physician are the healer. There are several cancer specialists who get results that nobody can duplicate because they are healers. The patient who comes to see you because of who you are will live that much longer statistically. You are comparing your statistics to the national average, which includes many patients who are elderly and really don't want to live, for whom the cancer is a blessing because it is the end of their lives. If you had a control group with the same age distribution, the results would look very different, because people who are forty-eight really don't want to die.

SIMONTON: Nonsense!

SHLAIN: Okay, I understand that there is a certain amount of wanting to die in cancer but, relatively speaking, it is much harder to get somebody who is eighty-four and has advanced colon cancer to put up a fight than somebody who is forty-five and has a family.

SIMONTON: I agree, but when you say that the forty-five-year-old patient does not want to die, that is something that we as a society project onto people. Let us put it this way: The problem of a forty-five-year-old tends to be different from the problem of an eighty-four-year-old.

SHLAIN: Okay, that's all I'm saying. I am not going to go in and give an eighty-four-year-old man a pep talk on why he should really fight that thing. I would see that as unnatural. But if I had a thirty-five-year-old woman with breast cancer— my God, I would do just everything I could to keep her going.

CAPRA: What you are saying, Leonard, is that Simonton's results are not characteristic of the broad population of cancer patients. As far as I understand, he is very conscious of that. He wants to select, very consciously, the best possible cases in order to examine their underlying dynamics.

SHLAIN: What I am saying is that I am not sure that by isolating this select group and being the caring person he is, in the atmosphere he is working in, he can conclude that his patients survive longer because of his insight into the dynamics of the disease and his techniques of treatment.

I am concerned about the presentation of Carl's results to other doctors who put all their faith in statistics. They don't believe that who he is and who the patients are is a significant element. They will look at the statistics and see that Carl is getting twice as long survivals using a certain technique, not weighing the fact that part of it is him and part of it is the patient. They will just look at the technique and say: "Here is this interesting model. We should apply that nationwide." That's what I'm concerned about.

CAPRA: To me, it is clear from Carl's model that, in order to apply it, you have to be a certain type of personality. Anybody can do the visualization technique, but not the psychotherapy. The psychotherapy, however, is an integral part of the Simonton model, and it involves a very intimate contact between therapist and patient.

SHLAIN: You see, I am constantly evaluating different cancer therapies, for many different reasons. For example, there was a man in Cleveland whose name was Turnbull, a superb surgeon who developed the "no-touch technique" of colon cancer. He said that when you operate on colon cancer, you must not touch the tumor. So for several years this was the teaching: You have to operate around the thing without touching it, which is, of course, almost impossible.

I read his article very carefully, and then I talked to one of the residents in the clinic. What I heard was that Turnbull took care of his patients in an incredible manner. He gave them his home telephone number, they could call him anytime, and so on. Now, Turnbull publishes statistics in scientific journals which show that this no-touch technique is better in terms of survival rate than if you touch the tumor. That is nonsense. It's Turnbull! It probably makes little difference whether you touch the tumor or not. No matter what technique you use, if the patient loves the doctor and the doctor loves the patient, then that patient is going to do better.

GROF: I think that the statement that motivation has such a strong influence on the development of cancer implies a very different view of cancer in the first place. When you say, Leonard, that Carl's patients are doing so much better because of their motivation and also because he is a healer, none of those things could be interpreted within the old understanding of what cancer is about.

LOCK: Right. In the standard biomedical model it really doesn't matter whether the man is a doctor or a healer.

CAPRA: But now medical science has developed to a point where this sharp distinction between things material and things spiritual is being overcome. Therefore, to say that this is because somebody is a healer does not put it in a black box any longer. We can ask: What does that mean? Let us investigate the dynamics of what a healer does.

LOCK: Still, I share a little bit of Leonard's concern. I am a little concerned, Carl, whether you are not forcing the scientific model a little too much to present the data; whether, in having to constantly confront the medical world, you are not pushed into using statistics too much, trying to quantify the quality of life. Are you not seduced a little bit into playing the game to survive?

SIMONTON: I want to be able to quantify things for me, so that I can feel comfortable about my own observations. What matters to me is the ability to make systematic observations and to report these observations so that we can learn something from them. That is important to my basic nature.

LOCK: I feel that if we are going to break out of this linear thinking and reductionistic framework, we have to not be afraid of using our subjective and emotional responses to events, and to express them in situations where we are dealing with people who only work within the scientific framework. We have to beat them with the idea that there are other ways of expressing things. Even systematic observation is not the only technique one can use. Purely subjective experience is valid information that should be used and worked on.

SIMONTON: I agree that with an in-depth look at one case history a whole system can be elaborated, but that requires really careful observation from a broad perspective.

HENDERSON: I am very sympathetic to this problem. I have the same problem when I try to communicate with the representatives of this culture. I am constantly dealing with the incredible problems of people trying to create social indicators of the quality of life—how much value to put on a human life, and so on. It's the same problem: how to communicate with this super-reductionist culture.

SIMONTON: My problem is not so much one of communication. I am attempting to measure and quantify for me. I want to be comfortable about the direction in which I am going in my work. It is very easy for me to delude myself if I don't have sound measures of my progress. That, to me, is what is important. These numbers are mostly for me.

HENDERSON: But you have to take the cultural reference point.

SIMONTON: I have to take what makes sense to me.

CAPRA: But, Carl, this depends on your value system, and your value system is that of the culture. You are a child of your time, and if we could change the value system of the culture so that things that are not quantified would also make sense to you, then you would not be forced to insist on quantification.

SIMONTON: That, of course, would be the ideal, but I don't deal with ideals, I deal with practicalities.

LOCK: I agree. Under the circumstances, and given that you are a child of your culture, you are doing exactly the right thing. But for the future it would be nice if we could revert to leaning a little bit less on quantitative data. This would mean more acceptance of the value of intuitive understanding and of the spiritual side of life.

SHLAIN: In one of your lectures, Fritjof, you talked about the problem of trying to use the scientific model to measure the paranormal. You said it was like Heisenberg's uncertainty principle. The more scientific you get, the less you will see of the phenomenon you want to study. My concern is that here you are setting up a scientific model to measure something that probably cannot be measured.

CAPRA (after a long pause): For the first time this weekend I was feeling uneasy. I felt that, somehow, things were slipping way from me. Especially, having my own lecture thrown at me made me somewhat uncomfortable [laughter]. But now I have had a few minutes to reflect, and I think I have found the answer.

What is happening here is that we are mixing up levels. There are several levels at which you can talk about health and health care. Leonard was talking about the level where the scientific approach may not be applicable. You can call it the paranormal, or spiritual, level where psychic healing takes place. This level is probably very significant in Carl's work, but there is another level just below that where we try to integrate the physical, psychological, and social aspects of illness. What Carl is trying to do is get people to the level where you see the physical, psychological, and social dimensions of the human condition as a unity, and where therapy treats them as a unity. He is exploring the interdependence of psychological and physical patterns.

Now, it will be difficult to separate this exploration from the level of psychic healing, because typically the people who are introducing these new unifying approaches are also spiritual people. Therefore, it will be difficult in studying their work to separate the spiritual aspect from the other level. Nevertheless, I think it is worthwhile doing that. You can achieve a lot at the level of integrating physical, psychological, and social approaches. And I think there you can also be scientific—not in the sense of reductionist science but in the general systems sense of science.

DIMALANTA: In my practice, I am very aware of the limitations of language. The only way I can communicate something beyond rational thought is when I use metaphor, sometimes even what I call metaphoric absurdity. Now, when I communicate with a family, the clearer I become, the better they understand me, the less it helps. This is because I am then describing a reality which is an abstraction.

LOCK: I agree with that, and I think that in the healing process the most important part of communication takes place at the metaphoric level. Therefore, you have to have shared metaphors. A healer-patient situation will only work if there is some shared knowledge. This is what healers in traditional cultures have always been able to do, and what doctors working within the so-called scientific idiom have lost. The knowledge is not shared adequately anymore between patients and doctors. I also think that this kind of shared knowledge cannot be quantified.

CAPRA: When the Simontons do their visualization process, they work with metaphors, and they experiment with metaphors to find out which ones are the most useful. But those metaphors don't show up in their statistics, and they don't have to.

LOCK: That's right, and that is what I really like about Carl's approach, the flexibility that he obviously has in his whole system. That is very exciting.

CAPRA: One of the most puzzling and intriguing questions in the entire medical field, to me, is the question: What is mental illness?

GROF: Many people get diagnosed as psychotics, not on the basis of their behavior or maladjustment, but on the basis of the content of their experiences. Somebody who is really able to handle everyday reality but has very unusual experiences of a transpersonal, or mystical, kind may get electroshocks, which is absolutely unnecessary. Many of those experiences are really in the direction of a model that is now coming out of modern physics. What is fascinating to me is that even cultures that have shamanism do not condone just any type of behavior. They know what is a shamanic way of transformation and what is being crazy.

LOCK: Yes, absolutely. There are crazy people in shamanic cultures.

GROF: You see, in contemporary anthropology there is a strong trend to equate the so-called "shamanic illness" with schizophrenia, epilepsy, or hysteria. Those primitive non-scientific cultures, it is often said, don't have psychiatry, and so any kind of bizarre incomprehensible thoughts or behavior patterns will be interpreted as supernatural and sacred. That simply is not true. Genuine shamans have to go into non-ordinary realms of experience and then come back and integrate them with everyday reality. They have to show adequate, if not superior, functioning in both realms. A good shaman knows everything that is happening in the tribe, has great interpersonal skills, and is often a creative artist.

LOCK: Yes, they have to use society's symbols. You can't

use idiosyncratic symbolism because it has to fit with what the society needs from you as a shaman. People who can only symbolize idiosyncratically are the ones who are going to get labeled as mentally ill in any culture. I really think that there is something that is mental illness. In any culture, there are certain people who are unable to communicate even their rudimentary needs successfully.

CAPRA: So the social context is crucial to the idea of mental illness?

LOCK: Yes, absolutely.

CAPRA: If you took a mentally ill person out of his society and put him in the wilderness, then he would be all right?

LOCK: That's right.

GROF: You can also put a person from one culture into another. Somebody who is crazy here might not be considered crazy in another culture, and vice versa.

DIMALANTA: The question is not whether you can go into psychosis, but whether you can go in and out of psychosis. You see, all of us can go a little bit crazy once in a while. That gives us a different perspective on our linear thinking, and that's a very exciting thing. It makes us very creative.

LOCK: And that is the criterion for a good shaman, too. Somebody who can control the experience of altered states of consciousness.

CAPRA: So, you can say that part of mental illness is the failure to use the correct symbols in society. You can't just say that it is society's fault. There is something the individual cannot handle.

DIMALANTA: Sure.

LOCK: Definitely.

DIMALANTA: I agree with Carl Whitaker, who distinguishes three kinds of craziness. One is to be driven crazy, for example in a family. The other is acting crazy, which all of us can do some of the time and which is very exciting if you can turn it on and off. The third is being crazy, when you have no control over it.

SHLAIN: I am having trouble with the word "crazy." To me, being crazy, or schizophrenic, means that you are out of contact with reality, with this reality right at this moment. When you are driven crazy, you respond in an inappropriate fashion, but you are not in another world. I think we should be very strict about how we define schizophrenia and severe mental illness, because otherwise we have to talk about what is an appropriate response and what is an inappropriate response, and it becomes so vague that we are not going to be able to focus on anything.

CAPRA: That's why Tony distinguishes between being driven crazy and being crazy.

SHLAIN: Yes, but he says that you can go crazy and come back without any problem at all. Do you mean that you just act crazy in the colloquial sense of the word, or that you are really out of contact with reality?

DIMALANTA: What I mean by acting crazy is the ability to go beyond social norms. There are many socially accepted ways of acting crazy. You can do it in dreams, by getting drunk, and in many other ways.

SIMONTON: When you say, Leonard, that being crazy means being out of touch with reality, you seem to imply that it means being out of touch with all aspects of reality, which is not true.

HENDERSON: One of the things that I am doing when I go into other states of reality is to get inside the heads of people in the Defense Department and see the world the way they do, and then I try to bring that back and communicate it in a different way. When you do that, you get a sense of that definition of craziness. For example, we had a debate in Washington last week with members of the Department of Defense about the response to a nuclear attack. They are talking about the strategy of Mutually Assured Destruction, also known as MAD! It was very interesting to me to see how the reductionists were talking about this. So-and-so many million deaths if the wind speed is zero, so-and-so many million with a downwind drift of radiation, and so on. They were dealing with questions like, how many people would die weeks after the attack, how many years after the attack, and so on. To see how they were talking about these things, for me, was really an altered state of reality, and to enter the reality of those people in the Defense Department was indeed some form of temporary craziness.

SIMONTON: That is really a social corollary to mental illness in the individual.

HENDERSON: That's what it is, isn't it? I make speeches about what I call psychotic technology, about the fact that technology moves into a psychotic range. For example, there is an optimum amount of daily consumption of energy. Beyond that, it becomes pathological. I am trying to take those sorts of concepts and force people to listen to them at the policy level.

DIMALANTA: It seems that what you are describing is a much more destructive kind of psychosis.

HENDERSON: Oh, it is unbelievably destructive.

CAPRA: I am very uncomfortable with the term "schizophrenia." It seems that psychiatrists call everything they can't understand schizophrenia. That seems to be sort of a blanket term for a wide variety of things.

DIMALANTA: It is really a label that is put on somebody whose behavior you cannot understand with your logical thinking. I believe in the biological aspects of schizophrenia, but most schizophrenics we see are usually social deviants. It is a family problem and, to me, it is an index of pathology of the system. We tend to label somebody schizophrenic, or crazy, and so on, until he internalizes that behavior.

SHLAIN: That really puts a tremendous responsibility on the other members of the family. I don't really think that when you have an autistic child, for example, you can say that it's the mother's or the father's fault. If you talk about family systems, and you say that one member of the system is diseased because of something going on in the system, that completely obviates the possibility that, maybe, there is something wrong with the kid's wiring.

SIMONTON: When you say "fault," that implies intent, motivation, and so on, all kinds of things that are inappropriate.

DIMALANTA: There is a big chunk of literature about how a social deviant becomes mentally ill and is labeled by institutions to be schizophrenic.

CAPRA: Do you think that the labeling itself drives the person into a pronounced state of psychosis?

DIMALANTA: Yes.

HENDERSON: I would like to draw an analogy to another systems level. If psychiatrists label a certain syndrome they don't understand "schizophrenia," that's precisely how the term "inflation" is used by economists. From a broader systemic viewpoint, inflation is simply all the variables they left out of their models. There is a lot of mystification going on right now in the discussion about inflation. It has to do with where you push the stress around the system. If you hypothesize that the inflation is all coming from one place, that is a form of laying the blame, and that creates a set of remedies. So it's all in the diagnosis, you see?

DIMALANTA: Diagnosis in psychiatry is a key part of the ritual, and it defines boundaries of behavior. I have to act in a certain way, otherwise I am labeled as crazy.

SIMONTON: One of the problems is the rigidity, and the sense that once you are labeled, then that is you, and you are that forever. Language and labeling, of course, are necessary, but they do have problems.

DIMALANTA: In families where one member is labeled as schizophrenic, if you ask the family "Is your son crazy?" or "Is your mother crazy?" they will often say: "No, that's just the way he is." They completely distort the reality because it serves a function in the family.

LOCK: I think, again, that there are different levels of this. There really is something that is schizophrenia. It is not all due to society.

SIMONTON: Just like there is physical illness.

LOCK: Exactly. There is the other end of the spectrum. There are certain illnesses, including some cases of mental illnesses, where the biological aspects are dominant and the psychological and social components are minimal. There are some schizophrenic problems that are mainly due to social influences, whereas in others the genetic component is dominant. For example, if you study the evolution of schizophrenia in children, it is clear that those genetic components are there.

DIMALANTA: The lesson to learn from this is that some of the diseases are diseases of the system. When the system is in control of the individual, it produces tremendous stress on the individual, and that produces what is labeled mental illness. Now, there are some biological diseases with genetic components which will arise in whatever environment the individual is placed. In other cases there may be a complementary interaction between the biological and the environmental component, so that the symptoms will appear if there is a genetic predisposition and if the individual finds himself in a certain type of environment.

CAPRA: Stan, would you tell us about some of the new trends in psychotherapy you have been observing?

GROF: The old psychotherapies were based, by and large, on the Freudian model, which held that everything that was happening in the psyche was biographically determined. There was tremendous emphasis on verbal exchange, and therapists operated just with psychological factors and left out body processes.

The new psychotherapies represent a more holistic approach. Most people now feel that verbal interaction is somehow secondary. I would say that, as long as you are using verbal therapy only, which means sitting or lying down and talking, you will not really do anything dramatic to the psychosomatic system. In the new therapies there is tremendous emphasis on firsthand experience. There is also a lot of emphasis on the interplay between mind and body. Neo-Reichian approaches, for example, attempt to remove psychological blocks through physical manipulation.

CAPRA: One almost finds it difficult to call these techniques psychotherapy. It seems that we have to transcend the distinction between physical therapy and psychotherapy.

GROF: Another aspect is that the old therapies were really intraorganismic or intrapsychic, that is, therapy was done with the organism in isolation. A psychoanalyst did not even want to see the patient's mother or talk to her on the phone. By contrast, the new therapies emphasize interpersonal relations. There is couple therapy, family therapy, group therapy, and so on. Also, there is now a tendency to pay attention to social factors.

CAPRA: Can you say something about the idea of bringing the organism into a special state where the healing process is initiated? When you do therapy with LSD, obviously, you are doing something like that in a very drastic way. Do you see this as part of all therapy?

GROF: This is my personal credo, that psychotherapy will be going in this direction. Ultimately, you will not come with any concept of what you want to achieve, or what you want to explore. You will, somehow, energize the organism. This is based on the idea that emotional or psychosomatic symptoms are condensed experiences. Behind the symptom is an experience which is trying to complete itself. This is called an incomplete gestalt in gestalt therapy. By energizing the organism, you unblock this process. The person will then have experiences, which you support whether or not they fit your theoretical framework.

CAPRA: What ways are there to energize the organism?

GROF: Psychedelics are the most obvious example, but there are many other methods, most of which have been used in various aboriginal cultures for millennia—sensory isolation or sensory overload, trance dancing, hyperventilation, and so on. Music and dancing, especially, can be very powerful catalysts.

DIMALANTA: Therapists can also act as catalysts. For example, when I introduce myself into the family, I can become a catalyst for certain special modes of behavior which break the usual pattern.

GROF: Being a catalyst, the therapist tends to be merely a facilitator. There is much more emphasis on patient responsibility in the new therapies. It is *your* process that is being studied. You are the expert. You are the only one who can figure out what is wrong with you. As the therapist, I can offer techniques and share the process as an adventure with you, but I am not going to tell you what you should do, or where you should end.

DIMALANTA: It seems to me that communication is crucial. In family therapy, you first have to know how to enter their house. I usually enter through the back door instead of the front door. In other words, you have to learn their way of thinking so that you can make an entry point. Some will accept you to their bedroom right away, others you will have to approach through the kitchen. Most of the time humor is the most important tool.

CAPRA: How do you use humor?

DIMALANTA: I use humor when there is a discrepancy between what they say and how they behave. Language is often used to deny the behavior, and I use humor to point out the inconsistency. Sometimes I amplify the behavior to the point where it becomes absurd, and then there is no way to deny it.

GROF: When you offer some kind of activating technique, you don't let your own conceptual thinking interfere with that process. In fact, you actually try to eliminate the intellect of the patient, because his concepts, which are also limited, will be getting in the way of the experience. The intellectualization comes afterwards and, in my opinion, is really irrelevant in terms of the therapeutic outcome.

CAPRA: It seems that we have been talking about two different approaches here. Tony is working with the network of interpersonal relationships within a family, whereas Stan is working by energizing the mind/body system of a single individual.

DIMALANTA: In my view, there is no contradiction between what I am doing and what Stan is doing. I am not working exclusively with families. The identified patient within a family, and there can be more than just one patient, will eventually need individual therapy. While I am working with the family, I am trying to improve the interaction between the individual family members and to make the whole system more flexible. When that has happened, I can go on and work with the identified patient individually and get involved with more intense therapy. For me, family therapy is not a technique. It is a way of looking at problems, of seeing how problems are interconnected.

GROF: When I was doing LSD therapy with individual patients, the primary emphasis was on the work with that individual, but most of the time I could not leave out the family, especially when dealing with younger patients. In the beginning, I was expecting great appreciation from the family when the patient made tremendous progress, but often that was not at all the case. For example, the mother would say, "What have you done to my son? He is now talking back." If that attitude continues you should, ideally, expand the therapy to include the whole family. On the other hand, I don't believe in working only at the interpersonal level without including some in-depth individual work.

DIMALANTA: I agree with you. Sometimes I even see the identified patient first before seeing the whole family.

HENDERSON: Are there any studies that see social activism as self-therapy? Having been involved with public interest groups and environmental groups for many years, I have become terribly aware of what people are working out. This does not mean that their work is not sometimes very good and very much in phase with social change, but there is this self-therapeutic aspect. You know, five million people are involved in environmental activism. They are a very interesting group of people. Are they doing it because of their altruism, or are they doing some self-therapy?

LOCK: So your question is really: Are they conscious of the self-therapeutic aspects?

HENDERSON: I know that I have been conscious of it for years and enjoying it tremendously.

GROF: There is a lot of literature that gives psychodynamic interpretations to social activity, to revolutions, etc., but it does not deal with conscious self-therapy through social activity.

HENDERSON: I just think I can't be the only one. Many people must do this kind of self-therapy consciously.

BATESON: But do they give it up when they are cured?

HENDERSON: That would be an interesting question to pursue. Some of them do. I just wonder whether anybody has studied them as a population.

BATESON: Shakespeare.

[laughter]

8

A Special Quality of Wisdom

FOUR MONTHS after the Big Sur Dialogues, in June 1978, I finally sat down and began to write *The Turning Point*. For the next two and a half years I followed a rigorous discipline of rising early in the morning and writing during regular hours every day. I began with four hours a day, gradually increased my writing time as I got deeper into the text, and at the very end, in the final editing phase, spent eight to ten hours a day with the manuscript.

The publication of *The Turning Point* at the beginning of 1982 marked a closure of a long intellectual and personal journey that had begun fifteen years earlier during the heydays of the sixties. My explorations of conceptual and social change had been filled with personal risks and struggles, with beautiful encounters and friendships, with great intellectual excitement, deep insights, and moving experiences. At the end I was extremely gratified. Building on the inspiration, help, and advice of many remarkable women and men, I had been able to present in one volume a historical review of the old paradigm in science and society, a comprehensive critique of its conceptual limitations, and a synthesis of the emerging new vision of reality.

A journey to India

While the book was being published in New York I spent six weeks in India to celebrate this closure of my work and gain a different perspective on my life. My journey to India came in response to three invitations I had received independently during the previous year: one from the University of Bombay for a set of three lectures known as the Sri Aurobindo Memorial Lectures, one from the India International Centre in New Delhi to deliver the Ghosh Memorial Lecture, and the third from my friend Stan Grof to participate in the annual conference of the International Transpersonal Association, which Grof organized in Bombay around the theme "Ancient Wisdom and Modern Science."

A few days before my departure I received the first advance copy of *The Turning Point* from Simon and Schuster, and as I leafed through the book during my flight to Bombay I reflected on the curious fact that, although Indian culture had exerted such a powerful influence on my work and my life, I had never been to India or to any other part of the Far East. In fact, I mused, the easternmost point in my life, so far, had been Vienna, where I was born, and it was by going west—to Paris and to California—that I made my first contacts with Eastern culture. And now, for the first time, I was actually on my way to the Far East—again by flying west to Tokyo and Bombay, following the sun across the Pacific.

My stay in Bombay began with a good omen. The university had booked me into the Nataraj, a traditional Indian hotel bearing the name of Shiva Nataraja, the Lord of Dancers. Every time I entered the hotel I was greeted by a giant statue of a dancing Shiva, the Indian image that had been most familiar to me during the past fifteen years and had such a decisive influence on my work.

From the first moments in India I was overwhelmed by its masses of people and by the multitude of archetypal images I saw all around me. Within the period of a short walk in Bombay I saw tiny old women in their saris sitting on the pavement selling bananas, small stalls along a wall where barbers were shaving men of all ages, another row of men squatting along a wall having their ears pierced, a group of women beggars with babies huddling in the shade, a girl and a boy sitting in the dust playing an ancient board game with shells as dice, a sacred cow ambling by unmolested, a man gracefully balancing a load of long wooden poles on his head as he made his way through the crowd. . . . I felt I had been thrown into an entirely different world, and that feeling never left me during my entire stay in India.

At other times I would walk along a park or across a bridge thinking that I was near some special event, because there were hundreds of people in the streets, all walking in the same direction. But I soon discovered that they were there every day—a constant stream of humanity. Standing in this human stream or walking against it was an unforgettable experience. I saw a never-ending variety of faces, expressions, skin tones, clothes, color marks on people's faces—I felt that I was encountering all of India.

Traffic in Bombay was always very dense, composed not only of automobiles but also of bicycles, rickshaws, cows and other animals, and people carrying enormous loads on their heads or pushing overloaded carts. Taxi rides were nerve-racking experiences; every few minutes it seemed to me that we escaped an accident by a hair's breadth. However, the most astonishing observation was that the taxi drivers—mostly bearded Sikhs in colorful turbans—were not tense at all. Most of the time they had only one hand on the steering wheel and were completely calm while missing other cars, pedestrians, and animals by fractions of an inch. Each taxi ride reminded me of Shiva's wild dance—arms and legs flailing, hair flying, but the face in the center relaxed and calm.

Indian society is often associated with great poverty, and indeed I saw a lot of poverty in Bombay. But, somehow, it did not depress me as much as I had feared. The poverty was there right in the open in all the streets. It was never denied and seemed to be integrated into the city's life. In fact, as I walked through the streets and rode around in taxis for several days, I had a very strange experience. One word came to my mind again and again, which seemed to describe life in Bombay better than any other—"rich." Bombay, I reflected, is not a city. It is a human ecosystem in which the variety of life is incredibly rich.

Indian culture is extremely sensuous. Daily life is full of intense colors, sounds, and smells; food is strongly spiced; customs and rituals are rich in expressive details. Yet, with all its sensuousness it is a gentle culture. I spent many hours in the lobby of the Nataraj watching people come and go. Virtually all of them wore the traditional soft and flowing clothes which, I soon discovered, are the most appropriate garments for the hot Indian climate. People moved gracefully, smiled a lot, and never seemed to get angry. During my entire stay in India I did not observe a single instance of the "macho" behavior so common in the West. The whole culture seemed to be more oriented toward the feminine. Or perhaps, I wondered, would it be more accurate to say that Indian culture is just more balanced?

Although the sights and sounds around me were wonderfully exotic, I also had a strong feeling of "coming back to India" during these first days in Bombay. Again and again I rediscovered elements of Indian culture I had studied and experienced over the years—Indian philosophical and religious thought, the sacred texts, the colorful mythology of the popular epics, the writings and teachings of Mahatma Gandhi, the magnificent temple sculptures, the spiritual music and dance. At various times during the previous fifteen years all of these elements had played significant roles in my life, and now they all came together, for the first time, in one fabulous experience.

Conversation with Vimla Patil

My feeling of "coming back to India" was further enhanced by the warm and enthusiastic reception I was given by countless Indian men and women. For the first time in my life I was treated as a celebrity. I saw my picture on the front page of the *Times of India*; I was received by high-level representatives of public and academic life; I was besieged by crowds of people who asked me for autographs, brought presents, and wanted to discuss their ideas with me. Naturally, I was very startled by this tremendous, totally unexpected response to my work, and it took me several weeks to understand it. By exploring the parallels between modern physics and Eastern mysticism I had addressed myself to scientists and people interested in modern science, as well as to those practicing or studying Eastern spiritual traditions. In India, I found that the scientific community was not too different from that in the West, but the attitude toward spirituality was totally different. Whereas Eastern mysticism interests only a fringe of society in the West, it is the cultural mainstream in India. The representatives of the Indian Establishment—members of parliament, university professors, corporate presidents—had already accepted those parts of my argument that were viewed with suspicion by Western critics, and since many of them were keenly interested in modern science they embraced my book wholeheartedly. *The Tao of Physics* was not better known in India than in the West, but it had been accepted and promoted by the Establishment, and that, of course, made all the difference.

Among the many conversations and discussions I had in Bombay, one that stands out especially in my memory is a long exchange of ideas with Vimla Patil, a very remarkable woman who is the editor of *Femina*, a large women's magazine. Our conversation began as an interview but soon turned into a long and animated discussion during which I learned a lot about Indian society, politics, history, music, and spirituality. The longer I spoke with her, the more I liked Vimla Patil, a worldly wise, warm, and motherly woman.

I was especially interested in learning more about the role of women in Indian society, which I found quite puzzling. I had always been very impressed by the powerful images of Indian goddesses. I knew that female deities exist in great numbers in Hindu mythology, representing the many aspects of the archetypal goddess, the female principle of the universe. I also knew that Hinduism does not despise the sensuous side of human nature, traditionally associated with the female. Accordingly, its goddesses are not shown as holy virgins but are often pictured in sensual embraces of stunning beauty. On the other hand, many of the Indian customs around marital and family relationships seemed very patriarchal and oppressive of women.

Vimla Patil told me that the gentle and spiritual Indian

character, which has had a fairly balanced view about men and women since ancient times, was strongly influenced by the Muslim oppression and then by the British colonialization. From the wide spectrum of Indian philosophy, she explained, the British implemented those parts that corresponded to their Victorian views and fashioned them into an oppressive legal system. Nevertheless, Patil continued, respect for women is still an integral part of Indian culture. She gave me two examples. A woman traveling alone in India will be safer than in many Western countries, and women are now emerging more and more in India's political life at all levels.

INDIRA GANDHI

With these remarks our conversation naturally turned to Indira Gandhi, the woman who held India's highest political office. "The fact that we have had a woman as prime minister for so long has had a tremendous influence on public and political life," Patil began. "There is now a whole generation in India who has never known a male national leader. Just imagine what a strong effect this must have on the Indian psyche."

Yes, but what kind of woman was Indira Gandhi? In the West she was usually portrayed as tough and ruthless, autocratic, and obsessed with power. Was that the image Indians had of her?

"Maybe some Indians," Patil conceded, "but certainly not the majority. Mrs. Gandhi is very popular in India, you know; not so much with intellectuals but with the simple people whom she understands extremely well." When she traveled in different parts of the country, Patil explained, Indira Gandhi would wear her saris in the styles of those regions; she would participate in the festivities of tribal and rural communities, hold hands with the women, join in the local folk dances. "She has a very direct rapport with simple people. That's why she is so popular."

Patil went on to explain that Indira Gandhi's autocratic tendencies must be understood in the context of her family background. As an aristocratic Brahmin, daughter of Jawaharlal Nehru, India's first prime minister, and closely associ-

ated from early childhood with Mahatma Gandhi, her obsession was not so much with power as with a sense of destiny.
She felt that it was her destiny to lead India, that there was a
mission she had to fulfill.

"It is true that Mrs. Gandhi is a very strong-willed woman,"
Patil continued with a smile. "She can get very furious and
is associated by most Indian men, at least subconsciously, with
Kali" (the fierce and violent manifestation of the Mother Goddess).

"What about the time when Mrs. Gandhi proclaimed a
state of emergency, imposed strict press censorship, and im-
prisoned the entire leadership of the opposition party?"

"There is no doubt that she made mistakes, but she has
grown from her mistakes and has become a very spiritual
person."

As Vimla Patil continued to answer my questions with
perceptive observations and reflections, I realized more and
more that I would have to revise my image of Indira Gandhi
considerably, that her personality was much more complex
than the one portrayed in the Western press.

"What about Mrs. Gandhi's attitude toward women?" I
finally asked, returning to the initial subject of our conversation. "Does she support women's causes?"

"Oh, yes, definitely," Patil replied. "In her own life, she
has broken with several conventions oppressive of women. She
married a Parsi, a man of different religion and social class,
and she rejected the role of a traditional Indian wife by en-
tering national politics."

"And how does she support women's causes as India's
leader?"

"In many subtle ways," Patil said, smiling. "She rules the
country in such a manner that the men think she works for
them, but at the same time she quietly supports women's rights
and women's causes. She lets various movements concerned
with women's causes grow and creates a favorable environment
through noninterference. As a consequence, women are now
very visible in the Civil Service, even in high positions."

Patil then told me of an incident in which Indira Gandhi
did in fact interfere in support of a woman's cause. Some time
ago, Air India refused to grant a pilot's license to a woman,
whereupon Mrs. Gandhi "banged her fist on the table" and

forced Air India to grant the license. "These isolated actions get a lot of publicity," Patil explained. "They have helped women enormously. Today every Indian woman knows that no position is closed to her. There is tremendous pride and self-confidence among young women in India."

"So, Mrs. Gandhi must be even more popular with Indian women than with men?"

Patil smiled again: "Oh, yes. Indian women see in her not only a leader of great courage, wisdom, and perseverance, but also a symbol of women's emancipation. This is one of her great political strengths. She has a guaranteed fifty percent of the vote—that of the women."

At the end of our conversation Vimla Patil urged me to try by all means to meet Mrs. Gandhi when I was in Delhi. I found that suggestion rather extravagant and just nodded politely, never imagining that I was indeed to meet Indira Gandhi very soon and would have a long, unforgettable exchange of ideas with her.

Indian art and spirituality

In my conversation with Vimla Patil we also talked a lot about art and spirituality, two inseparable aspects of Indian culture. From the beginning I had tried to approach the Eastern spiritual traditions not only cognitively but also experientially, and in the case of Hinduism my experiential approach had been mainly through Indian art. Accordingly, I had decided that I would not seek out any gurus in India, or spend time in any ashrams or other meditation centers, but rather spend as much time as I could experiencing Indian spirituality through its traditional art forms.

One of my first excursions in Bombay was to the famous Elephanta caves, a magnificent ancient temple dedicated to Shiva with huge stone sculptures representing the god in his many manifestations. I stood in awe in front of these powerful sculptures whose reproductions I had known and loved for many years: the triple image of Shiva Mahesvara, the Great Lord, radiating serene tranquility and peace; Shiva Ardhanari, the stunning unification of male and female forms in the rhythmic, swaying movement of the deity's androgynous body and in the serene detachment of his/her face; and Shiva Nataraja, the celebrated four-armed Cosmic Dancer whose superbly balanced gestures express the dynamic unity of all life.

My experience of Elephanta foreshadowed an even more powerful experience of Shiva sculptures in the secluded cave temples of Ellora, a day's journey from Bombay. Since I had only one day available for this trip I took an early morning flight to Aurangabad, which is close to Ellora. In Aurangabad there was a tourist bus to the temples leaving from a platform clearly marked in English, but I eschewed it in favor of the regular local bus, which was harder to find but promised much more of an adventure. The bus station itself was impressive. On white walls the platforms were identified by red symbols on orange disks, which I took to be numbers, surrounded by black inscriptions, evidently listing the destinations of the buses. These inscriptions, in the classical Indian script with heavy horizontal bars joining the letters in each word, were so beautifully composed and delicately balanced against the red and orange of the numbers that they looked to me like verses from the Vedas.

The station was crowded with country folk whose calm dignity and strong sense of esthetics impressed me deeply. The women's clothes were much more colorful than the ones I had seen in Bombay—cotton saris in lapis blue and emerald green, lavishly interwoven with gold, the jewel-like colors accentuated by heavy silver necklaces and bracelets. Women and men alike displayed great elegance and serenity.

The bus to Ellora was packed and made countless long stops during which people loaded and unloaded large bundles, baskets with chickens and other animals, and even a live sheep, all stored on the roof of the bus. Thus the fifteen miles to Ellora took almost two hours. I was the only non-Indian on this bus, but I was dressed in the traditional *khadi* (cotton), wearing *chappals* (sandals) and a simple jute shoulder bag. Nobody bothered to take much notice of me, so that I could observe the flow of life all around me without any interference. Like everybody else I constantly had to lean against men, women, and children in the overcrowded bus, and again I noticed that people were extremely gentle and friendly.

The villages we passed were clean and peaceful. Many of the scenes and activities I observed were known to me only from fairy tales and dim childhood memories—the well where the womenfolk gather to draw water and chat, the market where men and women squat on the ground surrounded by fruits and vegetables, the blacksmith on the edge of the village. The technologies I noticed—for example, those used for irrigation, spinning, and weaving—were simple but often ingenious and elegant, reflecting the exquisite esthetic sensitivity characteristic of India.

As the bus made its way past cotton fields and into rolling hills, I was overwhelmed by the beauty of the countryside and of the people living in it—the bleached gray and golden yellow of the giant teak trees that lined the road; old men dressed in white with turbans in brilliant pink riding on two-wheeled bullock carts, the bullocks with long, elegantly curved horns; people washing their clothes at the river in the time-honored way of beating them rhythmically against a flat stone and then laying them out to dry in colorful patterns; girls in delicate saris with brass vases on their heads floating through the hilly landscape like dancers—every vista a picture of serenity and beauty.

I was thus in a very special, enchanted mood when I reached the sacred cave temples of Ellora, where ancient artists had spent hundreds of years carving a city of temple halls and sculptures out of solid rock. Of the more than thirty Hindu, Buddhist, and Jain temples, I visited only three of the most beautiful, all of them Hindu. The beauty and power of these sacred caves are beyond words. One of them is a Shiva temple built into the mountainside. Its main hall is filled with heavy rectangular columns, broken only by a central passage that connects the sanctuary at the innermost and darkest part of the temple with the light-filled arcades overlooking the surrounding landscape. The dark recess of the sanctuary contains a cylindrical block of stone representing Shiva's *lingam*, the ancient phallic symbol. At the outer end the central passage is blocked by a life-size sculpture of a reclining bull. Relaxed and calm, he gazes meditatively toward the sacred phallus. On the walls around the hall sculptured panels show Shiva's divine figure in a variety of traditional dance poses.

I spent over an hour in meditation in this temple, most of the time completely alone. Walking slowly from the sanctuary toward the outer arcades I was spellbound by the calm and powerful silhouette of the bull in front of the serene Indian countryside. Turning back and looking toward the *lingam*, past the bull and the massive columns, I felt the tremendous tension created by the static power of these male symbols. But with a few glances at the sensuous, feminine movements of Shiva's exuberant dance in the panels around the hall the tension was resolved. The resulting feeling of intense maleness without any trace of machismo was one of my deepest experiences in India.

After many contemplative hours at Ellora I returned to Aurangabad as the sun was almost setting. I could not get a flight back to Bombay that evening and had to return by overnight coach. The morning flight to Aurangabad had taken twenty minutes. The ride back in the "super express" coach, on country roads crowded with people, carts, and animals, took eleven hours.

To my great fortune a major festival of Indian music and dance took place in Bombay during the two weeks I stayed there. I went to two performances, both of them extraordinary, one of music and one of dance. The first was a concert by Bismillah Khan, India's illustrious master of the shehnai. One of the classical instruments of Indian music, the shehnai, a double-reeded wind instrument similar to the oboe, requires great breath control to produce a strong, continuous tone. Vimla Patil very kindly invited me to attend the concert with her and her family. I greatly enjoyed this opportunity of going there with Indian friends, who explained and translated many things for me which I would not have understood on my own. As we stood around chatting and sipping tea during the intermission, I was introduced to friends and acquaintances of the Patils, several of whom complimented me on my clothes—the traditional long and flowing silk *kurta* (shirt), cotton trousers, sandals, and a long woolen shawl for the cool breeze in the open-air concert hall. By that time I had become very comfortable wearing Indian clothes and this was evidently appreciated.

As in all Indian concerts, the performance went on for many hours and gave me one of the most beautiful musical experiences of my life. Although I had heard Bismillah Khan on records, the sound of the shehnai was much less familiar to me than that of the stringed sitar or sarod. At the concert, however, I was immediately enchanted by the master's brilliant performance. According to the changing rhythms and tempos of the classical ragas in his program, he produced the most exquisite variations of melodic patterns evoking shades of mood ranging from lighthearted joy to spiritual serenity. Toward the end of each piece he would raise the tempo and display his great virtuosity and astonishing control of the instrument in an exuberant, emotional finale.

During the long evening, the magical, haunting sounds of Bismillah Khan's shehnai and the wide range of human emotions they triggered affected me very deeply. At the beginning his improvisations often reminded me of those of the great jazz musician John Coltrane, but then my associations shifted to Mozart, and on to the folk songs of my childhood. The longer I listened, the more I realized that Khan's shehnai transcends all musical categories.

The audience responded with great enthusiasm to this enchanting music, and yet there was a certain sadness in their affectionate admiration. It was clear to everyone that Bismillah Khan, at sixty-five, no longer had the breath and stamina of his younger years. Indeed, after playing brilliantly for two hours he bowed to the audience and announced with a sad smile: "In my younger years I could play through the whole night, but now I have to ask you to allow me a short break." Old age, Don Juan's fourth enemy of the man of knowledge, had arrived for Bismillah Khan.

On the very next evening I had another, no less extraordinary experience of Indian art, this time of movement, dance, and ritual. It was a performance of Odissi, one of the classical Indian dance forms. In India, dance has formed an integral part of worship from ancient times and is still one of the purest artistic expressions of spirituality. Every performance of classical dance is a dance drama in which the artist enacts well-known stories from Hindu mythology by communicating a series of emotions through *abhinaya*—an elaborate language of stylized body postures, gestures, and facial expressions. In Odissi dance, the classical poses are the same as those of the deities in the Hindu temples.

I went to the performance with a group of young people whom I had met after one of my lectures, one of them a student of Odissi dance herself. They told me very excitedly that the special attraction of that evening was not only to see Sanjukta

Panigrahi, India's foremost Odissi dancer, but also her celebrated guru, Keluchara Mohaparta, who does not generally
dance in public. This evening, however "Guruji," as everybody
called him, would also dance.

Before the performance, my dancer friend and a fellow
student of hers took me backstage to meet their dance teacher
and, possibly, to see Guruji and Sanjukta prepare themselves
for the performance. When the two young women encountered
their teacher they bowed down and touched with their right
hands first the teacher's feet and then their own foreheads.
They did so with natural, flowing ease; their gestures hardly
interrupted their movements and conversation. After I was introduced we were allowed to peek into an adjoining area where
Sanjukta and Guruji were engaged in an intimate ritual. Fully
dressed for the performance, they faced each other in prayer,
whispering intensely and with closed eyes. It was a scene of
utmost concentration, which ended with Guruji blessing his
student and kissing her on the forehead.

I was amazed by Sanjukta's elaborate dress, makeup, and
jewelry, but I was even more fascinated by Guruji. I saw a
pouchy older man, half bald, with a delicate, strange, and compelling face that transcended conventional notions of male and
female, young and old. He wore very little makeup and was
dressed in some kind of ritualistic garment, which left his torso
naked.

The performance was magnificent. The dancers evoked a
ceaseless stream of emotions through a dazzling display of the
most refined movements and gestures. Sanjukta's poses were
fascinating. It seemed to me as if the ancient stone sculptures,
which were so fresh in my memory, had suddenly come alive.

The most wondrous experience, however, was to see Guruji
perform the initial invocation and offering, which begins every
performance of classical Indian dance. He appeared at the left
of the stage with a plate of burning candles in his hand, which
he carried across the stage as an offering to a deity represented
by a small statue. To see this oddly beautiful old man float
across the stage in swirling, twisting, flowing movements, the
candles flickering all about him, was an unforgettable experience of magic and ritual. I sat there spellbound, staring at
Guruji as if he were some being from another world, a personi-
fication of archetypal movement.

Meeting with Mrs. Gandhi

Shortly after this memorable performance I flew to Delhi for three days to give my lecture at the India International Centre, a research and lecture center for visiting scholars. I was received as enthusiastically in Delhi as I had been in Bombay. Again I had to give many interviews and met high-level representatives of India's academic and political life. To my great surprise I learned immediately after my arrival that the prime minister had agreed to preside at my lecture but would not be able to attend it, after all, because of her extremely busy schedule. Parliament was in session and in addition an important "South-South" conference of Third World countries took place in Delhi that week, which made it impossible for her to honor her promise. However, I was told that she might be able to receive me briefly on the day after my lecture. When my hosts noticed my great surprise they told me that Mrs. Gandhi was familiar with my work and, in fact, had repeatedly used quotations from *The Tao of Physics* in her speeches. Naturally, I was quite startled by all this unexpected honor but also very excited at the prospect of meeting Indira Gandhi.

On the evening of my arrival I was invited to a small but very elegant dinner party in the home of Pupul Jayakar, a renowned authority on traditional hand looms and textiles who is very active in promoting Indian handicraft and ornamental arts throughout the world. When Mrs. Jayakar heard about my interest in Indian art she gave me a tour through her wonderfully decorated villa. Her art collection included several magnificent antique statues, as well as a fabulous variety of printed textiles, her expertise and passion. The dinner was a traditional Indian banquet, which began very late and lasted for many hours. I remember that everybody around the table was splendidly dressed; I felt as if I were among princes and princesses. The evening's conversation revolved mainly around Indian philosophy and spirituality. In particular, we spoke quite a lot about Krishnamurti, whom Mrs. Jayakar knew very well.

Naturally, I was also eager to hear more about Indira Gandhi. I discovered to my great joy that one of the guests, Nirmala Deshpande, was an old friend and confidante of Mrs. Gandhi. She was a quiet, diminutive, gentle woman who led an ascetic life in the ashram of Vinoba Bhave, the activist-sage and close associate of Mahatma Gandhi. Nirmala Deshpande told me that this ashram was run by women and that Mrs. Gandhi was a frequent visitor who would always fully submit to the ashram's rules and customs while she stayed there. Once again I heard a description of Indira Gandhi that was totally different from her public image in the West, which increased my bewilderment together with my curiosity and excitement.

Two days later I was notified that the prime minister would indeed receive me, and a few hours after her message reached me I sat in Indira Gandhi's office at Parliament House, waiting to meet the woman whose enigmatic personality had dominated most of my thoughts and conversations during my visit to Delhi. While I waited I glanced around the office and noticed that it was rather austere—a large, bare desk with a writing pad and a jar of pencils, a simple bookcase, a giant map of India on the wall, a small statue of a deity by the window. As I looked around, a host of images of Indira Gandhi flashed through my mind—the dominant figure in India for almost two decades; a woman of commanding presence; a strong-willed, autocratic leader; tough and arrogant; a woman of great courage and wisdom; a spiritual person, in touch with the feelings and aspirations of simple people. Which Indira Gandhi would I meet, I wondered.

My ruminations were interrupted when the door opened and Mrs. Gandhi walked in, accompanied by a small group of men. As she stretched out her hand and welcomed me with a friendly smile, the first impression I had was great surprise at how small and frail she was. In her water green sari she looked very delicate and feminine, as she sat down at her desk and looked at me expectantly without a further word. Her eyes, surrounded by the familiar deep rings, were warm and friendly, and I could easily have forgotten that I was facing the commanding leader of the world's largest democracy, had it not been for the three telephones within easy reach on a small table to her left.

I began the conversation by saying how honored I was to meet her and thanking her for receiving me in spite of her demanding schedule. I then expressed my gratitude, on this first visit to India, to her country as a whole. I told her how deeply Indian culture had affected my work and my life and what a great privilege it was for me to come to India and give a series of lectures. I ended these words of thanks by saying that I hoped I was able to repay some of my debt by communicating some insights I had gained partly from my contacts with Indian culture, and that it was my hope that this would help facilitate the cooperation and exchange of ideas between East and West.

Mrs. Gandhi remained silent, answering my little speech with a warm, encouraging smile, and so I continued. I told her that I had just published a new book, in which I extended the argument of *The Tao of Physics* to include the other sciences, as well as discussing the present conceptual crisis in Western society and the social implications of our current cultural transformation. With these words I took my advance copy out of my bag and presented it, adding that it was a great privilege for me to be able to give this first copy of *The Turning Point* to her.

Mrs. Gandhi acknowledged my present with a gracious gesture, still not saying anything. I had the uncanny feeling that I was facing a vacuum, a person who, contrary to all my expectations and preconceptions, appeared to be quite egoless. At the same time, I felt that her silence was a test. Indira Gandhi had not taken time off from her political duties to engage in small talk with me. She was waiting to enter into a conversation of substance, and it was up to me to provide that substance to the best of my abilities. I was not intimidated by that challenge. On the contrary, I felt stimulated and excited as I launched into a concise summary of my main arguments.

I have discussed these ideas for many years with people from all walks of life and have acquired a good sense of whether people really understand what I am saying or whether they just listen politely. With Mrs. Gandhi it was clear to me right from the start that she really understood the issues I was addressing. I immediately felt that she had examined them herself in great detail and was familiar with most of the ideas I presented to her. As I continued my summary, she began to respond with brief comments and soon involved herself more and more in the conversation. She agreed with my initial assertion that the major problems of today are systemic problems, which means that they are all interconnected. "I believe that life is one and that the world is one," she said. "As you know, in Indian philosophy we are always told that we are part of everything and everything is part of us. So the world's problems, necessarily, are all interlinked."

She was also very receptive to my emphasis on ecological awareness as the basis of the new vision of reality. "I have always been very close to nature," she told me. "I was fortunate to grow up with a strong sense of kinship with the whole of living nature. Its plants and animals, its stones and its trees were all my companions." She then added that India had an ancient tradition of environmental protection. India's great emperor Ashoka, who reigned for forty years during the third century B.C., considered it his duty not only to protect his citizens but also to preserve the forests and wildlife. "Throughout India," Mrs. Gandhi told me, "we can still see edicts carved on rocks and stone pillars twenty-two centuries ago, which foreshadow today's environmental concerns."

To conclude my brief synopsis, I mentioned the implications of the emerging ecological paradigm for economics and technology. In particular, I spoke of the so-called soft technologies that incorporate ecological principles and are consistent with a new set of values.

After I had finished, Mrs. Gandhi paused for a few moments and then spoke in a serious tone and very direct manner: "My problem is, how can I introduce new technologies into India without destroying the existing culture? We want to learn as much as we can from Western countries, but we want to keep our Indian roots." She went on to illustrate this problem—which, of course, is the same throughout the Third World—with many examples. She spoke of the "warm relationship" people had with their crafts in the past, which has largely disappeared today. She mentioned the great beauty and durability of the old costumes, the wood carvings, the pottery. "Today it seems much easier and cheaper to buy plastic than to spend time with these crafts," she said with a sad smile. "What a pity!"

As she continued, Mrs. Gandhi became especially lively when she spoke of the tribal folk dances: "When I watch these women dance, I see such tremendous gaiety, such spontaneity, and then I am afraid that they will lose their spirit when they achieve material progress." She told me that folk dances were part of the annual Republic Day parade in Delhi, and that in previous years tribal people would travel to Delhi from distant villages and then dance throughout the day and night. "You simply could not stop them," she said animatedly. "When you told them they had to stop, they would just go off to some park and continue to dance. But now they want to be paid, and their performances get shorter and shorter."

As I listened to Indira Gandhi, I realized how deeply she had thought about these problems. More than that, I was impressed that this world leader, who had introduced her country to space-age technology, placed so much value on keeping the beauty and wisdom of the old culture alive. "The people of India," she said, "no matter how poor they are, have a special quality of wisdom, an inner strength which comes from our spiritual tradition. I would like them to keep this quality, this special presence, while ridding themselves of poverty."

I pointed out that the soft technologies I was advocating were in fact very appropriate for preserving traditional customs and values. They tend to be very much of the kind promoted so vigorously by Mahatma Gandhi—small scale and decentralized, responsive to local conditions, and designed to increase self-sufficiency. I then focused on solar energy production as a soft technology par excellence.

"I know." Mrs. Gandhi smiled. "I spoke about all this a long time ago. You see, I live in a solar-heated house myself." And after a pensive moment she added: "If I could start from zero, I would do things quite differently. But I have to be realistic. There is a large technological base in India which I can't throw away."

During our conversation Mrs. Gandhi was not in the least bit authoritarian. On the contrary, her demeanor was very natural and unassuming. Our conversation was simply a serious exchange of ideas between two people who shared a concern about certain problems and were trying to find solutions. Continuing her comments about technology and culture, Mrs. Gandhi mentioned how easily people in India, as everywhere else, were seduced by the glitter of modern technological gadgets that are not of much value and are destructive to the old culture. What was the best way to select the really valuable and appropriate technology, she wondered, and to conclude her remarks she looked at me and said very simply: "You see, this is the main problem I am facing. What shall I do? Do you have any ideas?"

I was astounded by this frank and totally unpretentious question. I suggested to Mrs. Gandhi that she should create an office of technology assessment, consisting of a multidisciplinary team that would advise her on the ecological, social, and cultural impact of new technologies. I told her that such an office existed in Washington and that its Advisory Council included my friend Hazel Henderson. "If you had such an institution," I ventured, "with a view toward long-term solutions, with an ecological vision, and with a strong sense of traditional culture, it would help you enormously to assess your options and your risks."

Again I was amazed by Indira Gandhi's reaction. As I was speaking, she simply reached for the writing pad on her desk, picked up a pencil, and began to take notes. She wrote down all the details I mentioned, including Hazel Henderson's name, without any further comment.

Changing the subject, I asked Mrs. Gandhi what she thought about feminism.

"Well, I am not a feminist," she replied, and then added quickly, "but my mother was.

"You see," Mrs. Gandhi continued, "as a child I could always do what I liked. I never felt that it made any difference whether I was a boy or a girl. I whistled, I ran and climbed trees like boys. So the idea of women's liberation did not occur to me."

She went on to explain that India, throughout its history, has had not only numerous women who distinguished themselves in public activities, but also enlightened men who supported the emancipation of women. "Gandhiji was one of them," she said, "and so was my father. They recognized that a nonviolent movement such as ours would not succeed unless it could count on the sympathy and active interest of our women. So they consciously and deliberately drew women into the national movement, and this greatly accelerated the emancipation of Indian women.

"And what do *you* think about feminism?" Mrs. Gandhi returned my question. I spoke about the natural kinship between the ecology movement, the peace movement, and the feminist movement, and expressed my belief that the women's movement was likely to play a pivotal role in the current change of paradigms. Indira Gandhi agreed:

"I have often said that women today may have a special role to play. The world's rhythm is changing, and women can influence it and give it the right beat."

A full fifty minutes had gone by as our conversation drew to a natural close and Mrs. Gandhi indicated with a friendly gesture that she had to leave and attend to other matters. I thanked her again for receiving me, and as I said good-bye I mentioned that I would be extremely interested in any comments she might have on *The Turning Point* and very honored if she wrote to me about them.

"Oh, yes," she said cheerfully, "let's keep in touch."

Three years later I remembered these words with tears in my eyes when I learned about Indira Gandhi's tragic, violent death. Her assassination, an eerie reminder of that of Mahatma Gandhi, her namesake and mentor, forced me to put my experience of the gentle and graceful nature of the Indian people into a different perspective. At the same time, my conversation with her etched itself even deeper into my memory.

Indira Gandhi was certainly the most remarkable woman I had ever met. Before I went to India my image of her had been one of a commanding world leader, shrewd and rather cold, arrogant and autocratic. I don't know to what extent this image was correct. What I do know is that it was vastly one-sided. The Indira Gandhi I met was warm and charming, compassionate and wise. As I left her office and walked out of Parliament House, through anterooms and corridors, past cabinet secretaries and security guards, R. D. Laing's phrase came to my mind as the perfect description of what I had just experienced: an authentic meeting between human beings.

Bibliography

NOTE: *The bibliography is restricted to works mentioned in the text.*

BATESON, GREGORY. 1972. *Steps to an Ecology of Mind.* New York: Ballantine.

———. 1979. *Mind and Nature.* New York: Dutton.

CAPRA, FRITJOF. 1972. "The Dance of Shiva," *Main Currents,* Sept./ Oct.

———. 1974. "Bootstrap and Buddhism," *American Journal of Physics,* Jan.

———. 1982. *The Turning Point.* New York: Simon and Schuster.

——— and CHARLENE SPRETNAK. 1984. *Green Politics.* New York: Dutton.

———. 1985. "Bootstrap Physics: A Conversation with Geoffrey Chew," in Carleton De Tar, J. Finkelstein, and Chung-I Tan, eds., *A Passion for Physics.* Singapore: World Scientific.

CARLSON, RICK J. 1975. *The End of Medicine.* New York: Wiley.

CASTANEDA, CARLOS. 1968. *The Teachings of Don Juan.* New York: Ballantine.

CLEAVER, ELDRIDGE. 1968. *Soul on Ice.* New York: Dell.

COREA, GENA. 1977. *The Hidden Malpractice.* New York: Morrow.

DUBOS, RENÉ. 1968. *Man, Medicine and Environment.* New York: Praeger.

EHRENREICH, BARBARA, and DEIRDRE ENGLISH. 1978. *For Her Own Good.* New York: Doubleday.

EINSTEIN, ALBERT. 1951. "Autobiographical Notes," in Paul Arthur Schilpp, ed., *Albert Einstein: Philosopher-Scientist.* New York: Tudor.

Friedan, Betty. 1963. *The Feminine Mystique.* New York: Dell.

FUCHS, VICTOR R. 1974. *Who Shall Live?* New York: Basic Books.

GREER, GERMAINE. 1971. *The Female Eunuch.* New York: McGraw-Hill.

GROF, STANISLAV. 1976. *Realms of the Human Unconscious.* New York: Dutton.

HEISENBERG, WERNER. 1962. *Physics and Philosophy.* New York: Harper & Row.

HENDERSON, HAZEL. 1978. *Creating Alternative Futures.* New York: Putnam.

———. 1981. *The Politics of the Solar Age.* New York: Anchor/Doubleday.

HESSE, HERMANN. 1929. *Steppenwolf.* New York: Random House.

HUXLEY, ALDOUS. 1954. *The Doors of Perception.* New York: Harper & Row.

ILLICH, IVAN. 1976. *Medical Nemesis.* New York: Pantheon.

JANTSCH, ERICH. 1980. *The Self-Organizing Universe.* New York: Pergamon.

JUNG, CARL GUSTAV. 1928. "On Psychic Energy," in Herbert Read, Michael Fordham, and Gerhard Adler, eds., *The Collected Works of Carl G. Jung,* Vol. 8. Princeton: Princeton University Press.

KRISHNAMURTI, J. 1969. *Freedom from the Known.* New York: Harper & Row.

KÜBLER-ROSS, ELISABETH. 1969. *On Death and Dying.* New York: Macmillan.

KUHN, THOMAS S. 1970. *The Structure of Scientific Revolutions.* Chicago: University of Chicago Press.

LAING, R. D. 1962. *The Divided Self.* New York: Pantheon.

———. 1968. *The Politics of Experience.* New York: Ballantine.

———. 1982. *The Voice of Experience.* New York: Pantheon.

LOCK, MARGARET M. 1980. *East Asian Medicine in Urban Japan.* Berkeley: University of California Press.

MARX, KARL. 1844. *Economic and Philosophic Manuscripts*, in Robert C. Tucker, ed., *The Marx-Engels Reader*. New York: Norton, 1972.

————. 1891. Capital, in Tucker, *supra*.

McKEOWN, THOMAS. 1976. *The Role of Medicine: Mirage or Nemesis?* London: Nuffield Provincial Hospital Trust.

MERCHANT, CAROLYN. 1980. *The Death of Nature*. New York: Harper & Row.

MONOD, JACQUES. 1971. *Chance and Necessity*. New York: Knopf.

NAVARRO, VICENTE. 1977. *Medicine Under Capitalism*. New York: Prodist.

NEEDHAM, JOSEPH. 1962. *Science and Civilisation in China*, Vol. 2. Cambridge, England: Cambridge University Press.

REICH, WILHELM. 1979. *Selected Writings*. New York: Farrar, Straus & Giroux.

RICH, ADRIENNE. 1977. *Of Woman Born*. New York: Norton.

SCHUMACHER, E. F. 1975. *Small Is Beautiful*. New York: Harper & Row.

————. 1977. *A Guide for the Perplexed*. New York: Harper & Row.

SIMONTON, O. CARL, STEPHANIE MATTHEWS-SIMONTON, and JAMES CREIGHTON. 1978. *Getting Well Again*. Los Angeles: Tarcher.

SINGER, JUNE. 1976. *Androgyny*. New York: Doubleday.

SOBEL, DAVID, ed. 1979. *Ways of Health*. New York: Harcourt Brace Jovanovich.

SPRETNAK, CHARLENE. 1981. *Lost Goddesses of Early Greece*. Boston: Beacon Press.

————, ed. 1981. *The Politics of Women's Spirituality*. New York: Anchor/Doubleday.

THOMAS, LEWIS. 1975. *The Lives of a Cell*. New York: Bantam.

WATTS, ALAN. 1957. *The Way of Zen*. New York: Vintage.

————. 1962. *The Joyous Cosmology*. New York: Random House.

————. 1966. *The Book*. New York: Random House.

WILBER, KEN. 1975. "Psychologia Perennis: The Spectrum of Consciousness," *Journal of Transpersonal Psychology*, No. 2.

————. 1977. *The Spectrum of Consciousness*. Wheaton, Ill.: Theosophical Publishing House.

Index

About the Author

Fritjof Capra received his Ph.D. from the University of Vienna and has done research in high-energy physics at several European and American universities. In addition to his many technical research papers, Dr. Capra has written and lectured extensively about the philosophical implications of modern science. He is the author of *The Turning Point* and *The Tao of Physics*, an international best-seller that has sold over half a million copies and has been translated into a dozen foreign languages.